RECENT APPROACHES TO THE
SOCIAL SCIENCES

Edited by H. K. Betz

RECENT APPROACHES TO THE SOCIAL SCIENCES

FACULTY OF SOCIAL SCIENCES
PAPERS OF THE SECOND SYMPOSIUM

H
22
.F3
1978 / 58,342

The Social Sciences Symposium Series, Volume Two.
Volume One in this series is A. W. Rasporich, ed.
The Social Sciences and Public Policy in Canada
ISBN No. 0-88953-000-9

Publications may be ordered from the Faculty of Social Sciences,
The University of Calgary, Calgary, Alberta, Canada
2500 University Drive, Calgary, Alberta T2N 1N4.

Table of Contents

List of Participants

Kenneth J. Arrow, Noble Laureate and Joan Kenney Professor of Economics, Stanford University, formerly James Bryant Conant University Professor, Harvard University.

Kenneth E. Boulding, Distinguished Professor of Economics, University of Colorado.

John M. Broughton, Associate Professor of Psychology and Education, Teachers College, Columbia University.

Michael Chandler, Associate Professor of Psychology, The University of British Columbia.

Barry Cooper, Associate Professor of Political Science, York University.

Adrienne Harris, Associate Professor of Psychology, Rutger's University, Newark, formerly of York University.

E.K. Hunt, Professor of Economics, University of Utah.

I.C. Jarvie, Professor of Philosophy, York University.

Kai Nielsen, Professor of Philosophy, The University of Calgary.

J.M. Porter, Professor of Political Science, University of Saskatchewan.

Ken Reshaur, Associate Professor of Political Studies, The University of Manitoba.

Edmund V. Sullivan, Professor of Psychology, The Ontario Institute for Studies in Education.

Introduction

On April 1, 1976, the then Faculty of Arts and Science at The
University of Calgary was divided into a University College
(mainly for first-year students) and the three disciplinary faculties
of Humanities, Science and Social Sciences. Among a number of
other distinct advantages, this newly created administrative
arrangement provided the disciplinary faculties with a unique
opportunity to replace a relatively vague and perhaps even
anonymous existence within the Arts and Science Faculty con-
glomerate, with a more distinct, visible and cohesive identity.
This was a particularly significant prospect for the new Faculty of
Social Sciences which was to represent by far the most heterogeneous array of disciplines and departments (Anthropology,
Archaeology, Economics, Geography, History, Linguistics, Political Science, Psychology, Sociology). At the respective ends of
their spectrum, the disciplines merge into the humanities and
natural sciences; in addition, the new faculty represented a good
traditional balance between "pure" and "applied" scholarship.
Concomitantly, it is well suited not only to pursue the traditional
role of critic and conscience of society, but also as its advisor by
means of contributions to public policy development.

One proposal made upon the inauguration of the new faculty
was to initiate a series of annual or biannual national and
international symposia to enhance the particular identity, visi-
bility and "relevance" of the social sciences generally. This has
been considered all the more appropriate since there still prevails
among the general public a rather marked lack of appreciation of
the basic subject matter, procedures and methods of inquiry and
analysis in the social sciences. In contrast to the natural sciences,
whose techniques are more generally agreed upon, whose results
are more straightforward and obvious and whose solutions are—
or appear to be—more plausible and, at times, even spectacular,
the applied social scientist, in particular, is often frustrated by
society's lack of definition regarding the nature of its problems
not to mention the "political" obstacles which any suggested
solutions will encounter.

The distinguished economist Fritz Machlup more than once
addressed himself to the question of the "inferiority" of the social
to the natural sciences as alleged by both scientists and laymen
and contracted in the form of an "inferiority complex" by many
social scientists. In the course of an interesting methodological
exercise, he compared the social sciences and natural sciences in

terms of, among others: invariability of observations, objectivity of observations and explanations, verifiability of hypotheses, exactness of findings, measurability of phenomena, constancy of numerical relationships, and predictability of future events. While the social sciences were found to be "inferior" in terms of "invariance," "verifiability," and "numerical constants" these are not "defects to be remedied but fundamental properties to be grasped, accepted and taken into account." He concludes by saying that, "The social sciences are 'really inferior' regarding the place they are accorded by society and the priorities with which financial and human resources are allocated. This inferiority is curable."[1]

This brings me back to our symposia; hopefully they can become part of the cure which is so badly needed. The Inaugural Symposium of the Faculty of Social Sciences took place in February of 1977 under the theme "The Social Sciences in Canada." It brought together distinguished academics, leading politicians and prominent figures of public life from across Canada to discuss and debate social issues of importance to contemporary Canada with special reference to the public policy involvement of social scientists. Both the calibre of the participants and the particular problem-orientation made the event an outstanding success.[2]

In October of 1978, the Second Symposium took place. Its theme was "Recent Approaches to the Social Sciences" with the proceedings contained in this volume. The chosen focus was on methodology at this conference because of its indispensable bridge between the pure and applied aspects of the various social sciences. Methodology in this context is to be taken in its more traditional meaning as referring to the philosophy of knowledge which is appropriate, in our case, to the human and social sciences.

During the four sessions of the Symposium the participants addressed themselves to such topics as value judgments, hermeneutics, science of man, structuralism and methodology and the "real world."

Before introducing the various contributions, I would like, however, to make a few overall observations regarding the conference. First, it brought together social scientists from a number of disciplines and philosophers who engaged in dialogue with one another. Of course, man, his mind and his actions, are the common concern of all (albeit from different perspectives), nevertheless we all know that such dialogues are all too infrequent given the apparently higher rewards for greatly specialized and compartmentalized research within each of the constituent social sciences.

Second, there is an increasing concern among social scientists to grapple with, as part of their scientific endeavours such, at least traditionally, methodological vexing and controversial concerns as values, value judgments and interpretation. Third, the discussion among and dialogue between all conference participants was distinguished by the complete absence of the above-mentioned "inferiority complex," no doubt a tribute to the outstanding calibre of the scholars represented.

The first session was entitled "Value Judgments and Hermeneutics" and featured contributions by Professor Kenneth J. Arrow, Nobel Laureate, and Professor Barry Cooper of York University. Professor Arrow's Keynote address on "Rational Discourse and Conflicts in Value and Judgment" analyzes the problems and possibilities of rational analysis of policy alternatives in situations characterized by underlying value conflicts and/or differences of opinion.

Cooper, in his presentation on hermeneutics—as it has emerged from historicism—discusses, analyzes and demonstrates the limits as well as complementarity of its two approaches: interpretation by way of phenomenology that leads to a symbolic participation in reality experienced as truth and interpretation by way of demythologization leading to a vision of heretofore hidden reality considered now to be necessary and articulated by social, political, or philosophical science.

The discussion of the contributions by the social sciences to a science of man marked undoubtedly the greatest degree of controversy. Much of it was induced by the extensive reference to Marxian values, beliefs, concepts and interpretations. Additional sparks were generated by the role of philosophy in all of this: "misunderstood" and "confused" by Hunt, the economist (according to Nielsen, the philosopher) and demonstrating by way of Nielsen's argument a "self-proclaimed poverty" (according to Hunt). Much of the controversy centres on Hunt's attempt to show that "rational" and "self-caused" behaviour is as amenable to human understanding as is passive, causally determined behaviour.

There also exists disagreement, though considerably more subdued, between Jarvie and Reshaur on the reasons for the requirement to dismantle the entrenched distinctions between the natural and the social sciences. It is Jarvie's contention in "The Notion of a Human Science" that science is no more than a specification of the general rational method and, for this reason, is continuous with our body of practical experience; that no part of our world can be unproblematically demarcated, and that the problem of human science has therefore to be reformulated.

The third session was devoted to a critical analysis of structuralism in a psychological and historical context. Broughton, in "Developmental Structuralism: Without Self, Without History" addresses not only the nominalist, functionalist, humanist and positivist arguments on structuralism, but also presents a detailed critique of Piaget's work and concludes by pointing out the possibilities "to transform and deepen the traditional structuralist approach simultaneously at the empirical and theoretical levels." Towards this endeavour he calls upon the continued efforts of intellectual historians, philosophers, sociologists and ideology-critics.

Sullivan in "Structuralism in a Psychological Context" presents us with an overview of the "structural" conceptions of Piaget, Kohlberg and Chomsky with a specific critique of some of the shortcomings of these structural theories in an attempt to formulate alternative future outlooks.

Originally, the last session on social science methodologies and the "real world" was to be introduced by Professor Boulding's presentation followed by a general summing up on the symposium as a whole. However, the extensive and enthusiastic nature of the response to and discussion of Boulding's paper on the "Appropriate Methodology" simply did not permit this. Nevertheless, his analysis of the relation between the methodology of science and the nature of the field (with special reference to the inappropriate use of mechanistic natural-science methods to the relatively unstable realm of human behaviour) represented a fitting climax to and summing up of what, in retrospect, may be considered a highly successful happening for the social sciences.

Last, but certainly not least, I would like to give special thanks to those whose dedication and co-operation in the planning of the Symposium have contributed to its success, in particular the members of the faculty committee: Professors A. Buss, Psychology, S. Drury, Political Science, A. Frank, Sociology, and A. Parel, Political Science. On behalf of the Faculty of Social Sciences, I also wish to express my gratitude for the substantial financial assistance rendered by the Social Sciences and Humanities Research Council of Canada as well as the Special Projects Fund of The University of Calgary.

H.K. Betz,
Dean
Faculty of Social Sciences
The University of Calgary

Notes

[1]Fritz Machlup, "Are the Social Sciences really inferior?" in Fritz Machlup, *Methodology of Economics and Other Social Sciences* (New York: Academic Press, 1978), p. 367.

[2]See also A. W. Rasporich (ed.), *The Social Sciences and Public Policy in Canada*, vol. 1, (The University of Calgary, 1979).

Session One

Value Judgments
and Hermeneutics

Rational Discourse and Conflicts in Value & Judgment
Kenneth J. Arrow, Harvard University
"Superstition ain't the way," Stevie Wonder

I

For a group of social scientists from diverse fields, I should make clear immediately that in this talk, at least, I am using the term "rationality" as an economist's word. I refer to a precise fitting of means to ends, a self-conscious and frequently rather formal analysis of conditions and constraints and the choices made under them and evaluated with respect to some more or less explicit criterion. Further I will emphasize rather the applications or attempted applications of rational analysis in social policy than the more programmatic formulations and purely theoretical analyses.

The idea of a rational process of social decision-making has been immanent in the literature of economics since the classical period and reasonably explicit in the marginal "revolution" of the late nineteenth century. The fundamental theorem of welfare economics states that under certain ideal circumstances a competitive system yields an efficient allocation of resources. It can be turned around to say that the equations which describe the competitive equilibrium can be solved by a planner to yield a rational solution. Once the economic problem was clearly perceived as one of optimization under constraints, the way was opened for explicit optimization as a basis for social policy.

It was Vilfredo Pareto who set forth most clearly the role and limitations of rational analysis in the resolution of social issues. Pareto's active career covered about thirty years from the late 1880's to the middle of World War I. He had been originally trained as an engineer but made himself over into an economist and then subsequently broadened his interests into sociology and indeed into general scientific method. He became an apostle of the new methods of analysis in economics, particularly in their more mathematical manifestations as developed by the French economist, Léon Walras, and was Walras's chosen successor in his chair at the University of Lausanne. Though himself a laissez-faire liberal, Pareto retained a lively interest in socialist systems.

At the grand level of the economy as a whole the economics of socialism offered an interesting field for rational planning.

Walras identified himself as a socialist and had made a rather cloudy identification of the notions of competitive equilibrium and of an optimum. It remained for Pareto to clarify the concepts involved and to state more dramatically the meaning of the choice between the unregulated market and the planned economy. On the conceptual side, Pareto was the first to make clear the sense in which a competitive equilibrium can be regarded as achieving optimality. He introduced the definition of what is now called Pareto optimality or Pareto efficiency; an allocation of resources is Pareto efficient if there is no other allocation among uses and among individuals which will make everyone better off (more precisely make everyone at least as well off and one person better off). There are of course a great many allocations which are Pareto efficient, and some of these correspond to very unequal distributions of welfare; indeed an allocation which is entirely devoted to maximizing the welfare of one individual would be Pareto efficient according to this definition. In order to achieve optimality in any more restricted sense, a criterion of justice in allocation has to be added to the criterion of efficiency. In a later and little noted paper, Pareto in fact introduced a formalism for expressing interpersonal comparisons of utility which could define optimal allocations according to some prescribed welfare criterion; the concept was reinvented many years later by Abram Bergson (1938) and termed by him a "social welfare function."

Pareto also noted that the competitive equilibrium is characterized by a very large number of equations, somewhat more, in fact, than the product of the number of individuals in society and the number of commodities. He noted that in principle one could think of solving them by numerical methods but that the market in fact constituted a kind of analog computer for them. Later one of his students, Enrico Barone (1908), spelled out the implications of Pareto's theory for a socialist economy; one could devise a set of operating rules, based on trial and error considerations, which could solve the system of equations describing competitive equilibrium and thereby enable a socialist economy to achieve an optimum. Essentially his was an attempt at embodying an iterative process for achieving a constrained maximum in an institutional plan.

Pareto and Barone in many ways set the terms of the debate over the economics of socialism which subsequently attracted some of the best minds in economics. But I am mainly concerned with the possibility of explicit calculation, even though these authors felt it had to be replaced or supplemented by institutional processes, either the market or a planning agency. Clearly for a calculation to be possible the scale of the problem had to be much smaller, particularly at a time when computational technology was so much more limited.

The possibility of explicit rational analysis for smaller scale problems had in fact been brilliantly exemplified as early as the 1830's by a French civil servant, Jules Dupuit, of modest fame among economists and, I am sure, virtually unknown elsewhere. For good or evil, he single-handedly created the discipline of benefit-cost analysis, understood its logical structure and the proper definitions of benefits and costs, and was deeply concerned with empirical implementation. He was an Inspector of Bridges and Highways. In the true spirit of Descartes, he sought an intellectual foundation for his daily problems. When should a bridge be built? Clearly bridges are designed to serve a purpose. They also represent a drain on the resources of the community. When is it worthwhile? Reasoning like a modern economist, he postulated that a bridge should be constructed if and only if the users in the aggregate valued the services of the bridge at more than the cost. He understood further that this comparison did *not* imply that the users should necessarily be charged the costs, that an attempt to do so might lead the bridge to be under-utilized compared with the socially efficient outcome. This is not the place for an elaboration of the technical details of Dupuit's work, though I must candidly say that it is precisely in those details that his true mastery appears. His work apparently had actually some influence on French practice, particularly in the pricing of the services of the French national railroads.

Parenthetically, it is curious that French economics has been largely a development of the highly able civil servants, whose best work has frequently been theoretical reflections on practical problems. This generalization remains true to the present day.

II

So much for ancient history, which, in our current ahistoric era, ends about 1940. The possibility of systematic rational calculation was given a strong push by certain aspects of the conduct of World War II. Surprisingly, it was the British, despite their long lasting cult of the amateur, who brought in scientists to think about rational improvement of procedures. They came to understand that there could be innovations not only in technology but in systems in which technology was used; indeed new technologies can only be exploited successfully if appropriate changes in systems were instituted. The analytic model for "operational research," as the British call it, or "operations research," in the American language, was an explicit means-end formulation, albeit frequently on a small scale. A particular mission, e.g., antisubmarine warfare, was described as well as could be by a simple set of analytic relations. Limited resources were specified and an objective function formulated. Sometimes the problem was explicitly optimized, sometimes solutions were merely tested for satisfactory performance. There were, needless to say, many errors made in the process, particularly in formulation of objective functions. The descriptive modelling, too, had its problems; there was the eternal question of simplification to strike a suitable compromise between detailing so excessive as to be analytically unmanageable and suppression of crucial aspects.

The study of a variety of optimization problems led to the significant development of new analytic techniques. The most important of all was undoubtedly linear programming, developed by George Dantzig, Marshall Wood, and others at the United States Army Air Forces. A complex strategic plan, such as the Normandy invasion, gave rise to a whole host of interrelated activities; thus, the output of the training activity was an input of personnel into the active forces. The description of each activity might be relatively simple, but there were so many, with such complex interrelations, that it seemed hopeless to understand the system as a whole by intuitive study or simple calculations.

Interestingly enough, the same set of problems had already been noticed in industrial production in the Soviet Union by the mathematician L. V. Kantorovitch, who had suggested the same formulation. In both cases, both the activities and the objective function to be maximized were given linear representations. Criteria for solutions were developed independently by Kantorovitch and by the Americans. It was only in 1947 that a systematic procedure for solving linear programming problems, the so-called simplex method, was developed by Dantzig, and it has proved to be crucial in practical application. For the first time, problems involving many, even hundreds of variables, could be solved in routine fashion.

This development depends, however, for its practical significance on a remarkable development in computers. The mathematical problem that has to be solved in each step of a linear programming solution is known as a matrix inversion; the same problem occurs in finding estimates of statistical relations by the method of least squares, and those of us who are old enough to remember working hand computers will speak feelingly of the enormous change that had taken place. What would take a skilled operator a whole day is now a matter of seconds. The applications of both linear programming and statistical analysis on a large scale have been made possible and even perhaps too easy.

Work both during and after World War II and in both military

and in non-military contexts continued the impetus. New techniques were developed with great rapidity. Especially interesting
were contributions to the handling of uncertainty, the theory of
queues, the control of inventories and water reserves behind dams,
and the loosely related variety of techniques subsumed under the
general heading of "dynamic programming." These technical
developments were of the greatest importance in connecting the
formulation of an optimization problem with its solution by
calculation. They were necessary intermediate steps in which the
maximization is reduced to a reasonably well-defined and limited
set of procedures.

Of course not all problems are tractable even with modern
computers. It is still perfectly easy to formulate optimization
problems, especially those involving discrete choices, which
cannot yet be solved practically. When enough progress had been
made, enough more could be hoped for that one could plausibly
entertain the view that previous failures to use systematic rational
analysis were merely due to analytic and technological shortcomings. It appeared that problems of much vaster scale than
those previously understood and of much greater significance
could seriously be studied.

Even this brief discussion indicates that progress is by no means
confined to the realm of problems previously considered to be
economic. Explicit solutions could be found to replace the vague
injunction to be rational.

One application in the United States has proved to be of great
use both in itself and as a precedent. I refer to benefit-cost analysis
of water resource projects. Economists have long seen the
irrigation and flood control projects in the Western part of the
United States as very likely to be a waste of resources by any
rational criterion. About 1950 an inter-agency committee recom-
mended that every water resource project be accompanied by a
cataloguing of social benefits and social costs, as well as of
financial benefits and costs. Although there is no legal requirement that a project have a benefit-cost ratio greater than one to be
accepted, the calculations clearly have some significance for
policy. It is no longer possible to accept absurdly uneconomic
projects. Among other things, this requirement stimulated a great
deal of research to determine what social benefits and social costs
were, and the arguments have become quite refined over the years.
Further, although there is no single legal arbiter of correctness,
the consensus of the relevant scientific comunity has become a
powerful force. Egregious types of double counting of benefits
that were common to begin with have been purged. The
discussion of government policy has been forced into relevant

channels, such as opposing views of the social rate of discount and other real issues, and the discussion has been clarified thereby.

A body of analysis and conceptual clarity was built up which has been extended to other realms of government policy, though on the whole with relatively little success. Systems analysis has become an integral part of decision-making in the defense area, though it has not prevented major errors of judgment, and of course it is never used for really large decisions. In the Johnson administration a premature attempt was made to extend benefit-cost analysis to all the operations of the government, but neither the data nor the analytic capability nor the political will was sufficient to sustain the effort. Nevertheless, evaluation of social programs has become a fixity of at least the American political scene, and in a recent conference I found there was a quite extensive Canadian commitment to this area.

I must also pay tribute to the remarkable work done by some branches of the French civil services, continuing in the great tradition of Dupuit. Perhaps the best work of all has been in the nationalized electricity industry, Electricité de France.

III

It is clear that the high hopes of at least some of us that explicit rational analysis would have a profoundly liberating effect on social policy, even at the highest level, were bitterly disappointed. The accomplishment fell far short of our aspirations. Even at much less global levels, even in advice to individual business firms, much is now made of the "intangible factors" that are omitted in simple rational analyses. For a time at least, a variety of voices proclaimed the narrow limits of rational behavior. There has always been a strong and in recent years, stronger conserva-tive movement, which has stressed that human nature is complex beyond human understanding, that the social and cultural institutions which exist embody rich layers of instinctive wisdom better not brought up to the light of day. On the left we have the extreme wing of the revolt of young intellectuals in the 1960's; one of their slogans was, "I am a human being; do not bend, mutilate, or spindle." The emotional force on both sides is greatly and perhaps sadly diminished, to be replaced more by a pragmatic conformism than a genuine belief in the possibility of rational discourse.

The currently and perhaps temporarily dominant neo-con-servative viewpoint rather uses the weapons of rational analysis against itself. The very evaluations of social programs that rationalism called for have been used to call the products into question.

Let me return to the more interesting problems raised by the conservatives and radicals a few years ago about the possibilities of rational analysis. They might be summed up by saying that values are not adequately reflected in the analyses and particularly that the world is full of conflict which a social engineer will necessarily ignore.

The elements of a typical rational analysis are a maximization under constraint, with a set of values embodied in a total ordering of alternatives and a set of constraints governing the actions possible. For the moment, assume that the constraints are well defined. There are still two problems with the formulation of values. (1) Even for an individual it is hard to articulate his or her values in a space of many dimensions, so there is a strong tendency to substitute some simplification of unknown validity. (2) If there are many people involved, as in social policy, or even in a firm considered as a multi-person organization, then their values will differ. They may differ for objective reasons; clearly concern over the local environment may depend on your position and interests. They may also differ for subjective reasons; even similarly situated people may differ on their relative priorities. In any case, values may differ simply because different individuals are competing for pieces of the same pie.

Whatever may be said about the possibility of resolving or at least compromising value conflicts, the process will surely require communication of values. This fact raises a question of their articulation. Is it really possible for an individual to express his or her values sufficiently clearly? Since it is difficult to articulate one's own values to oneself, this is not a trivial requirement. Further, ideally, the process should be such that everyone should be heard. But the communication process is itself costly; if nothing else, it requires time for participation of all. Asking for universal participation or universal representation is in itself inefficient and uneconomic, not to say simply impossible.

The communication of values thus represents a fundamental set of issues which can never be fully resolved. Whatever language or communication mechanism is used for discourse can therefore never fully express the values of all the participants or even all the values of any one of them.

The emphasis on communication and its intrinsic limits has another implication. There can never be a definite resolution of any issue. Instead, the process is intrinsically open. Whatever decision is made and whatever state of communication of values has been achieved, there is always room for improvement. Hence, there is a strong argument for always keeping social policy in a tentative state, one always open to further improvement through the articulation of additional values and points of view. This openness has of course a price. Precluding irrevocable decisions means foregoing a certain set of alternatives which may, under certain conditions, be efficient.

IV

I speak therefore of *rational discourse*, rather than rational decision-making, to emphasize the open nature of the process. So far I have emphasized the difficulties in the communication of values but it is also true that the communication of the constraints on action is necessary, problematic, and costly.

All actions are future-oriented to a greater or lesser extent and many indeed to a great extent. The consequences of any action in the future are always somewhat uncertain. Hence, the constraints that we speak of are not hard facts, as we usually think, but judgments about the future uncertainties. Now when there are uncertainties, clearly individuals can have different perceptions of them.

While there is more than one formalism for expressing uncertainty, it seems to be true that the most convenient remains the calculus of probabilities. In these terms it is customary to say that each individual has subjective probabilities for these events that can occur in the future.

All probabilities are conditional upon observed events, and indeed a good part of the theory of probability concerns the relation between probability beliefs held prior to and those held posterior to an observation. If there has been a common experience for a number of individuals, then their posterior probabilities will usually be somewhat more alike than they were prior to the observation. But in a world of continually new possibilities, where past experiences are not decisive, probability beliefs may continue to differ.

Let me report on one point of view, associated with the names of John Harsanyi and Robert Aumann, which argues that beliefs of different individuals may nevertheless tend to converge, at least with sufficient communication. First, it is argued that the true prior probabilities, those which the individual has before any experiences, should be the same for all. Then, if everyone had the same experiences, the posterior probabilities would also be the same. If they had different experiences, but communicated them fully to each other, then again they would have the same posterior probabilities.

Aumann pushes the argument one step further. Supposing individuals have had different experiences. Instead of communicating experiences, individuals communicate only their conditional probabilities based on their own experiences. These probabilities supply information to other individuals, since they limit the range of observations the first individual might have had. This, in turn, causes a revision of the probabilities of other individuals and a new communication. Aumann has shown that the equilibrium of such a process can only be a situation in which every individual assigns the same probabilities to all events to which probabilities can be assigned at all.

This kind of result is at least hopeful in understanding the possibility of agreement on the beliefs about the relations between actions and consequences. The argument is of course vulnerable on several counts. The assumption of agreed prior probabilities in some (perhaps mythical) initial state is dubious and possibly meaningless. Genetic and cultural factors may cause irreducible divergences in belief. Further, if we pass over this point, the communication of complete probability systems is clearly a non-trivial requirement. It is in fact of the same order of difficulty as the full communication of values.

Nevertheless this paradigm is interesting, for it shows at least the possibility of convergence of beliefs.

V

If there is some encouragement to the idea of agreement on beliefs, is there an analogous possibility for convergence of values? Can we assume that somewhere or another individual differences in values can be eliminated with enough communication and by taking a sufficiently universal point of view?

In fact several writers on the theory of value have suggested a position which is analogous to the idea of common prior probabilities. It is what John Rawls has called, "the original position." This is a myth, but one conceptually useful for starting an analysis of values. Similar ideas had been put forward earlier by William Vickrey and by John Harsanyi.

A social value, to have ethical significance, should be something which is universalizable. I may have an interest in more of the good things of life for myself, but in a context of social discourse, I cannot rationally use this as an argument. The argument must be couched in terms that are symmetrical among individuals, however much the arguments may disguise personal interest. A way of thinking about the requirement of universalizability is to assume that there is some original position in which individuals do not know what position they will hold in society. Harsanyi and Vickrey think of this as a situation in which one could with equal probability be anyone in society; Rawls has a somewhat looser viewpoint. In this original position, the individuals may agree to rules which will govern when they do know who they are.

One implication of this position is that at least in some sense differing individuals are able to understand each other. I can know what it would mean to hold values which I do not hold and I might even be able to make statements of the kind, "I, with my values, am better off than you, with your values," or the opposite. It is even possible to compare two different individuals in two different social situations, i.e., statements of the form, "John Adams would be better off if we adopt a more generous welfare policy than Bill Smith would be if we did not adopt such a policy."

Roughly speaking, we may expect every individual to have certain characteristics which define his preferences. We may further imagine, in the original position, that we can have a joint preference ordering over the goods of life and the characteristics by which we enjoy them, and *this* large preference ordering is a human characteristic, the same for all. Everything which differentiates one individual from another has been explicitly listed and included in the definition of the alternative states over which we have preference orderings.

For interpersonal comparisons of a major order, considered possible by mankind, we may cite the inscription allegedly found on a headstone: "Here lies Martin Engelbrodde, / have mercy on my soul, Lord God, / as I would do were I Lord God, / and thou wert Martin Engelbrodde." Perhaps I can also cite Blaise Pascal's argument that the aspects which differentiate people are characteristics which are attached to the person and not intrinsic to him or her: "If we love a woman for her beauty, we do not love her for herself, for the smallpox may destroy her beauty."

Whatever the attempts to supply a foundation, the upshot is some kind of interpersonal comparability of satisfaction or, as we say, of utility. Like the possibility of a consensus on beliefs, these comparisons rest on the idea that in some fundamental sense, people are alike. One classical form the comparison can take is that embodied in the utilitarian ethic. The utility difference between two states to an individual is an interpersonally meaningful construct; that is, utility differences of two individuals can be compared. With some reasonable postulates on what we mean by good social action, it will follow from the acceptability of these comparisons that the sum of the utilities would be a natural maximand.

Alternatively, a different formulation has come up in recent years based on a different postulate of interpersonal comparability. Supposing, following the kinds of statements I made a few paragraphs back, we can compare the level of utilities of different individuals in different social states. Then again, a natural axiomatic approach leads to the conclusion that society ought to maximize the smallest utility of an individual or, alternatively, the largest utility of any individual. That is, in each social state, one considers the individual with the smallest utility (or largest utility) and chooses that state which makes the smallest utility as large as possible (or alternatively, the largest utility as large as possible). This result has been found independently by two young scholars, Peter Hammond, and Steven Strasnick. The maxim in approach itself is reminiscent of Rawls, but the interpretation in terms of utility is somewhat different than his.

We observe then that alternative attempts to study social value, that is to aggregate individual values into a social judgment, lead to different results. We can compare different concepts of social value, and the comparison is not dissimilar to the problem of comparing individual values. There is a core of understanding and of articulation and a large grey area of vagueness and cross purposes.

VI

Philosophical discussions of this kind are really part of the process by which we arrive at social decisions. The fact that they exist reinforces the fundamental theme that social decision-making is actually part of an ongoing discourse, not a once-and-for-all edict.

The actual form in which the discourse takes place receives and needs institutionalization. We do not of course arrive at overall social decisions but only at bits and pieces of them. But since different parts of the social world interrelate, the decision in any one part is dependent upon the decisions of others and in turn, reacts upon them. Hence, there is in a sense a continuing stream of social decisions, subject to continuous modifications in small increments. While formalization of the whole process is impossibly costly, the formalization of small parts of it is in fact a clarification and an improvement. Indeed, formalization is essential to an economy in the communication process. It is from this point of view that I think benefit-cost analysis has been a very important first step. Its value is precisely in creating a language for communication of values and beliefs. Abandonment of benefit-cost analysis in response to its limitations is moving precisely in the wrong direction. What is needed are larger and more complex forms of value analysis into which as much clarity should be built as possible.

The institutional forms and the communication languages

should reflect as accurately as possible the difficulties in arriving at social rationality. One way this can be done is to recognize, for the purposes of process, the multi-dimensionality of values. Obviously it is comforting and useful to attempt to reduce values to a single dimension so that maximization becomes a meaningful procedure. In general, this is not possible, at least if the stakes are at all significant. The conflicts of present against the future, of lives against economic resources, are probably best expressed by discussing the payoffs and the costs in all the terms simultaneously. Perhaps as time goes on, we can recognize tradeoffs of different values and collapse them into one. No doubt also as time goes on, we shall recognize new dimensions that we have not previously foreseen. The environmental considerations that are now so prominent were not included as recently as ten years ago, and I believe we may expect the future to throw up new conflicts as well as resolve old ones.

We cannot even say that the forms in which decisions are presented will remain constant as the nature of the conflicts over value and belief changes.

This kind of process-oriented articulation of social conflicts, whether value or belief, has of course considerable precedent. Its two chief exemplars are the common law and the activity of science. Each is an example of an open process in which the past does not unduly constrain the future. Both permit new values and new evidence to change decisions and beliefs. Yet each has deficiencies which should be transcended. The common law tends to ascribe such high value to fairness that it has become settled into a rigid format and especially into the strict use of adversary procedures. This goes to the point that the communication of new information, which may be important to all in the resolution of social conflicts, is inhibited. No individual is responsible either technically or in terms of values and aspirations for the discovery of truth. It is for this reason that I am concerned with the widespread use in the United States of the courts as a method of adjudicating environmental and social policy disputes. Science offers a better precedent on this side in its openness to new ideas and new information and in its professional pride in valuing improved knowledge over individual interests. But it suffers in another direction. It is not decision-oriented. It is quite proper, and in its own sphere, very desirable, to abstain from opinion when there is insufficient evidence. But a social decision must be made; that is the definition of a decision. The decision may indeed be to postpone further action, but that is also a decision and one which has in many cases, real costs. The scientific mode is, in this dimension, inferior to the legal mode.

Ultimately, in both systems the validation of the outcomes is based on consensus, not on authority. Even though the courts have an authoritarian form, decisions do not stand unless they are widely accepted. The mandating of truth is not and should not be left to particular agencies. A few years ago, in the course of the debates in the United States over an arms agreement with the Soviet Union, one side felt that the other was misusing its data. It appealed to the Council of the Operations Research Society of America, and got a judgment from it that the other side had been guilty of professional misconduct in using its figures. This procedure struck me as being outrageous; the debate was out in the open and both sides had full opportunity to refute each other. To suppose that any particular group of people was in a position to pass an authoritative judgment was reminiscent of the persecution of Galileo. I suppose one needn't really worry about it; the Council had no moral authority, and its decision had no perceptible effect on anybody's belief.

There is, to be sure, room for committees, such as those of the National Academy of Sciences in the United States, of experts to assemble the relevant evidence at the moment and to sum up the state of knowledge, with all its limitations. A proposal has been made for a Science Court to make these same factual judgments in a more systematic way. Provided it is understood that at any moment the judgments arrived at are tentative and valid, at best, for the time at which they are made, there is no great harm in these, and there may be some good. The sheer assembly of evidence from many different fields relevant for a matter of social policy is a non-trivial task and can be socially very useful. However, the Science Court proposed was based on an adversary procedure, and I feel a good deal could be lost there.

VII

This speech has been full of doubts and problems and not much on answers. I will conclude by offering one more difficulty in the formation of social policy. Suppose we have some kind of formalization of information gathering and decision-making for specific problems, with full recognition of their openness and the need for revision. The United States requirement of an environmental impact statement for each major undertaking is an example of such a formalization. The question of quality control arises. Even a single irrigation project will have a large number of detailed consequences, specific to the area at hand. Who is willing to read these statements carefully enough to criticize them? How indeed are the writers going to be motivated to do their best and how are we going to insure that the proper scholarship and ability is brought into play? In science, considered as a social activity, we rely upon the competition for scientific fame and the usual promotion standards of universities and research institutions. Scientific statements of some generality are supposed to be published in scientific publications. The refereeing process and the judgments of one's peers upon publication are important. The legal process relies upon criticisms from adversaries and on the review of experts called judges.

In social policy situations, particularly of a local kind, there are, to be sure, adversaries. But if the knowledge involved is relatively technical, the adversaries may be too poorly informed to do their task properly. The statements that come out are not sufficiently general in nature to be worth publishing and therefore there is no criticism from the larger technical community. I don't doubt that problems of this kind can be solved or at least their solution can be improved upon, but more thought than has been given is needed.

Hermeneutics and Political Science

Barry Cooper, York University

It is inevitably a source of happiness to have one's ideas confirmed by events, so I shall begin somewhat anecdotally. I completed a draft of parts of this paper last spring and spent some months this summer in France. Following the national elections and the defeat of the French left, posters appeared proclaiming their victory because the two leftist parties had together gained 62%, or so, of the popular vote, a clear majority. As Hegel would say, this was moralism. The left in France was, and doubtless yet is, living in a world where they "ought to win." Moralism like this is not confined to France nor, I suppose, to the left. I recall viewing on TV one of our defeated local MP's, at the time of the last election, berating his backward constituents in a suburban Toronto riding for lacking the moral fibre to return him to his rightful place in Ottawa. In any case, the French left knew it ought to win. Now, everyone knows there is a difference between what is and what ought to be.

What, then, was I, a political scientist, to make of such moral phenomena? Shivering in a Paris café, I recalled the argument I had made in this paper and concluded as follows: The French left knew their goals and purposes were honourable, just, and good, and judged events, such as the election, in light of that knowledge. Thus, they won a moral victory because they *ought* to have won the election but *did* not. The French right, I noticed, put up no posters and offered no very prominent justification of their goals at all. Why not? because visibly they *are* political reality and see no need to justify what *is* in terms of a non-existent *ought*. The right, that is, saw the election as a real appearance, the actual, empirical configuration of French society manifesting itself politically; as a real appearance, events, while they did not speak for themselves, at least did not require decipherment by means of clever, moralizing insights. The left, in contrast, saw events as mere show behind which could be found the truth, in this case, their own moral victory.

Here, then, were illustrated the two strategies of interpretation that I would like to speak about: reality is interpreted as real appearance, reality is interpreted as mere show.

Before, like Plato in the *Republic*, I make a second, more arduous beginning, I would make a preliminary remark: mainly I shall be talking theoretically about two theories or strategies of interpretation and not, therefore, about the practice of interpretation, that is, how we decide who is right in an actual argument.[1]

To be scrupulously exact, I shall have something to say about the question of adequacy at the conclusion of the paper.

Reflection on the principles of interpretation, that is, hermeneutics, typically has occurred following the dissolution of familiar ways of understanding things. (There are two exceptions, to which I shall refer shortly.) More recently, as Gadamer has pointed out,[2] the flowering of hermeneutics dates from the romantic era, and most notably in the heartland of romanticism, Germany. The aspect of romanticism of interest here, is the opinion that the contemporary epoch is wholly and totally different, which is simply another way of saying that the past or, if you like, tradition, is strange, foreign, alien. Two things may immediately be noted about modern hermeneutics: first, interpretation is tacitly affirmed to be an historical enterprise, the recovery of a truth that once upon a time was clear but now is hidden; and second, interpretation is chiefly the avoidance of *mis*-understanding, as Schleiermacher said, rather than the art of understanding. We shall argue below that this is both the strength and the limitation of the modern procedure.

So far as the political, social, or human sciences are concerned (what the Germans call *Geisteswissenschaften*), identifying the origins of hermeneutics with the era of romanticism is but a first approximation, sorely in need of precision. Specifically, and regardless of what other qualifications may be added, one must take note of the pragmatic success and accompanying prestige of Newtonian or Baconian natural-scientific knowledge, and its justification in Kant's *Critique of Pure Reason*. Henceforth the problem, which still plagues political science, would be: how to establish an analogous theoretical justification for the knowledge of political science. Initially, debate was essentially epistemological. On the one side were the neo-Kantians, Windelband and Rickert, and the South-West German school, and on the other Dilthey, historicism, and psychologism. Dilthey, no less than the neo-Kantians, was concerned for objectivity, but he could not avoid confronting directly the fact that the knowing subject is a part of the object he studies. That is, he does not confront history, politics, society, etc., as he would confront a thing. He participates in the object of his study; he is part of a larger whole.

This fundamental participation of the scientist in the things he studies lies at the root of the famous hermeneutical circle. Stated most broadly, a text, which includes, analogically, all meaningful action,[3] cannot be understood except by understanding its context. This holds, for example, for a word: the meaning depends on the sentence of which it is a part; the sentence on the paragraph; the paragraph on the chapter; the chapter on the book; the book on the whole of the literary form concerned, and so on. That is, ultimately our understanding of *a* part depends on our understanding of *the* whole. But the whole is not a given that is prior to the individual element—in this example, the word.

Here, then, is the central paradox of interpretation: we must presume the unity of the many so as to designate them by a common name and then use that name to define the unity of the many. First, then, the evidence must persuade us; *it does the* prescribing. And then we use a concept as a norm on the basis of which evidence is to be included as relevant; now *our concept* does the prescribing. Thus, we move from experience or feeling of unity to postulated principle, and back to a critically re-assigned unity.[4] The circularity of the argument will, I trust, have escaped no one. Two things seem to follow from this. First, interpretation in political science involves risk because, eventually, it demands commitment to one thing and not another. But second, the manifold of reality is full of endless shadings, qualifications, and interpenetrations of phenomena so that a simply true or, to speak historically, a final interpretation is impossible. Inevitably there exists in interpretation a mediation or translation of another experience into the present. Whether the meaning of the otherness that is so transmitted is one of historical separation or non-every-dayness is, for the moment, unimportant.

There are two exceptions to this structural demand for commitment within an ambiguous field, both of which antedate post-Kantian hermeneutics. These were (and are) legal hermeneutics and Biblical hermeneutics. The former is a set of rules used to fill in the gaps in codified law so as to assist a magistrate in rendering consistent judgments; the second is a set of rules intended to insure that God's word be consistently understood. In both cases, however, the presumption of dogmatic delimitation—the law is coherent, God does not tell lies, etc.—makes the ambiguity surrounding the interpretation of merely human actions effectively disappear. Both are essentially practical, ancillary aids to judges or priests. But it is precisely here that the dissolution of tradition is believed, by those who live it, not to have occurred. In the human sciences, however, with their requirements of explication and discursive rationality, such confidence in tradition is just what is lacking: hence the circularity of interpretative argument.

Unfortunately, circular arguments are never very satisfying. Consequently, we should not be surprised to see attempts to break out. There are, I believe, two ways that this has been attempted, but neither has been a complete success (or so I will argue) on its own.

The first bursts through the ambiguity of the present by seeing it as a result, the second does so by seeing the present as anticipation of an intentional, non-ambiguous future. The first, to use my earlier language, sees ambiguity as mere show, the second as real appearance. According to the first, then, hermeneutics is genealogy, demystification, the reduction of illusion; in this way ambiguity will be dispelled. According to the second, it is the manifestation and restoration of meaning that is addressed indubitably to me in the manner of a commandment, proclamation, or message—which I may disobey but can in no way ignore or deny its meaning. To quote Ricoeur: "Hermeneutics seems to me to be animated by this double motivation: willingness to suspect, willingness to listen; vow of rigour, vow of obedience."[5] The first he called the school of suspicion; the second, the school of reminiscence.

Before proceeding, let me gather up some of the threads of the argument. Whether we see something as mere show or real appearance, we necessarily are aware of its possible double meaning: it could be either. And this double meaning is what calls for interpretation. A linguistic expression that carries such a double meaning is a symbol. Literally, i.e., etymologically, a symbol is a throwing together, a use of everyday terms to designate non-everyday experiences analogically. The one who speaks in symbols is a narrator; he transmits meanings that are too abundant to control by the lexical sense of his words. But this very density of meaning is what solicits his understanding and moves him to add more words to what are already there. And yet, innocent analogy or unaffected narrative may really be cunning distortion. Hence *the* problem of hermeneutics involves the deciphering of symbols.

Let us consider further Ricoeur's distinction: first, interpretation as recollection or restoration of meaning. There are three stages to the procedure. The first is a phenomenological description of the object and the animating intention that sees things that way. That is, the first step is to believe with the believer in the reality and truth of his words or actions—but without any commitment to the absolute validity of the object of his belief.

But second—and especially with texts in political science that claim to tell a truth about human affairs generally, as distinct from texts that describe particular factual situations—the question of absolute validity must be raised and faced. We do not bother to read a text, a great one, that is, unless we expect to be *addressed* by it. This expectation presupposes a confidence in the language symbols used: we look upon them first of all in terms of being addressed *to* human beings such as oneself and not as spoken *by* human beings and so possibly doubtful or wrong. We have confidence in the truth of symbols, that they fulfil their signifying intention by actually transmitting an intended meaning. For example, Plato's account of the three parts of the soul gains its persuasive force on the basis of a nonarbitrary relationship between the observations we have of others and of ourselves, and Plato's symbolic account of *our* experience. But by talking of persuasive force we have already violated our initial phenomenological neutrality. This is inevitable insofar as the truth of something is addressed to me as a subject and not constituted by me as a scientific analyst. That is, one is made to participate in the meaning of what is said because there is no other way it can be understood. The analogue from sense experience is hearing. We may not like what we hear, we may disregard what we hear, but the meaning of the message is not in doubt for, precisely on the basis of our certainty that we have grasped it, do we respond by dislike or disobedience, by veneration, submission, or whatever.

The third step is reflexive: one commits oneself in the manner described above because one is concerned for the truth. And one *is* so concerned because of the inadequacy—that is, the untruth—of already present but empty signs, formalized language, dogmas, and silence. One could almost say that, by rights, one expects the truth. In this respect, when the truth is not experienced, political science becomes an act of resistance to untruth. Ultimately this resistance demands a rejection of what Leo Strauss called our oblivion of eternity.[6] Such resistance appears to us positively as an act of reminiscence, first of all as an historical recollection, but then, later, to use George Grant's wonderful paraphrase, as a vision of "the beautiful, as the image, in the world, of the good."[7]

The result, finally, is a kind of non-result: there is a progressive synthesis where each meaning is clarified by further images that are seen as more comprehensive. The best example of this I know is the first seven chapters of Hegel's *Phenomenology*.

The second interpretative strategy conceives the task of hermeneutics as demystification. Again we proceed in three steps.

First, the primacy of the object is called into doubt, and with it the ability of the representation to fulfil its meaning by incorporating the subject into its truth. The great danger is illusion, which is not an epistemological category like error but, as Freud said in Chapter 6 of *The Future of an Illusion*, "what is characteristic of illusions is that they are derived from human wishes." Consciousness itself may be false or subverted by emotion, and in any case is dubious. This is a radical or reflexive Cartesianism: Descartes doubted that things are as they appear, but he did not doubt that consciousness is as it appears to itself. Now, however, we do.

Secondly, however, the "school of suspicion" is not simply destructive. Descartes doubted things in order to make way for the indubitable and mathematical truths of consciousness. Likewise his successors follow their doubts about consciousness with an interpretation or deciphering of the expressions of consciousness. If consciousness is not what it thinks it is, the relation between what it is, and what it thinks it is, must be accounted for. Here the fundamental relation, to use Robert Merton's term, is between what is latent and what is manifest. What we must do is replace the untrustworthy consciousness of meaning with a *science* that is irreducible to consciousness and so avoids the untrustworthiness of it. Here, if I may use a rather bizarre image, Karl Marx and David Easton join hands; the two suspicious interpreters confront what they take to be men of guile. They reverse the works of falsification by their own science, their own praxis, of demystification. If the analogy from sense-experience in the first strategy was hearing, in the second one it is sight. There is no response to a call, but rather insight into an object.

Third, even though the illusions of consciousness are suspect, it turns out that consciousness is not totally distrusted. Marx, for example, wished historical necessities to be understood. That is, the purpose of undergoing the hard discipline of reducing appearances to their psychological or sociological causes, of explaining them by an account of their individual or historic genesis, of analyzing their emotional or ideological function— the purpose of this reduction, suspicion, and destruction is to lay bare, and force us to confront, necessary reality. Indeed, to confront necessity is to submit to it, to accept it. If one could argue with necessity or change it, it would not be necessity. To the extent that the demystifying hermeneutic is successful, then, it results in resignation—a reasonable resignation, but resignation nonetheless. The exemplary text is Spinoza's *Ethics*: one finds oneself a slave; one understands one's slavery; one rediscovers one's own freedom within an understood necessity.

Here the result, in Ricoeur's words, is "a clearing of truth-fulness in which the lies and ideals and idols are brought to light and their occult role in the strategy of desire is unmasked."[8] We have reached a threshold of ethics or political science with the destruction of idols. Now what?

It seems to me we are faced with two options: to erect another idol and declare it final, or to become reflexive; that is, our interpretation must incorporate into itself a demystifying analysis of its own analysis. In this case it becomes an archaeology of the subject, a discourse on the origin of one's intellectual acts as much as an analysis of the object. Merleau-Ponty, in his later work, called this a hyperdialectic.

There is, in fact, a third option, which only needs to be mentioned in order to be rejected. This is the position of the enlightened wise guy who criticizes simply to prove a proposition wrong and lets it go at that. The purpose of criticism, one must insist, is not to show off intellectual superiority but to clarify an insight that has been given an inadequate or unsatisfactory formulation.

To return to reflexive demythologizing or archaeology: the first stage is invariably a return to the archaic, to history, but not to the arche, the beginning or ground. On the contrary, genesis is conceived as a sort of quasi-ground, what Eric Voegelin called historiogenesis.[9] There are, however, certain serious difficulties involved. We can see them in a most spectacular way in a famous text of Marx, written in 1844.[10]

Here Marx is concerned with the relationship between creation and dependence and how slavery results from the consciousness that one owes both the continuation of one's life and its source to another. In place of the illusion that God created the world Marx substitutes "the science of geognesy" that is, "the science that portrays the formation of the earth as a process of spontaneous generation." But this is not wholly convincing, as Marx well knew, for he then introduced as a debating partner, Aristotle, who wondered not simply about the generation of an individual from his parents but also about the progression of generations as a whole, "which leads to the point where I [i.e., the Aristotelean questioner] ask: who created the first man and nature as a whole? I can only reply [said Marx], your question is itself a product of abstraction . . . give up your abstraction and at the same time you abandon your question. . . . Do not think, do not ask me any questions, for as soon as you think and ask questions your abstraction from the existence of nature and man becomes mean-ingless." The Aristotelean replies: "I only ask you about the act of the creation of nature, just as I ask the anatomist about the formation of bones." And Marx silences him with the observa-tion: "Since, however, for socialist man, the whole of what is called world history is nothing but the creation of many by human labour, and the emergence of nature for man, he, there-fore, [i.e., socialist man] has the evident and irrefutable proof of his self-creation, of his own origins" so that the questions raised by his imaginary (and rather simple) Aristotelean interlocutor that searched for an arche, "become impossible in practice."

This text is, or should be, an embarrassment to Marxists who pride themselves on the master's lack of dogmatism. What it illustrates, so far as the present discussion is concerned, is the limit of Marx's own demystifying archaeology. A limit, I should add, is not an external boundary, a sort of impenetrable barrier, but is a function of the internal validity of a theory. In the example just given, Marx's theory breaks down and becomes propaganda: for all I know, socialist man does believe he created himself.

However that may be, there is a genuine point at issue between Aristotle and Marx, namely, does the question "who created the first man and nature as a whole?" make sense? Is it, as Marx said, an abstract question—that is, is it nonsense? Let us remove any concern for a "who" who may have done the creating and ask simply what it means to be concerned with the origin of "nature as a whole," which for Marx, certainly included man. In exploring what this question means, we adopt the attitude of hard-nosed, modern, Nietzschean, scientific cosmologists and physicists.

The story, so far as I understand it, goes as follows. Ever since the observation of the Doppler effect in the shift of spectral lines in light from stars as compared to sunlight, it has been possible to calculate stellar velocities. The red shifts of distant galaxies have indicated to those who know about such things that the universe is expanding. Since the discovery in 1964 of the cosmic microwave radiation background—what has been called the radiation left over from the big bang—cosmologists have been able to offer reasonably confident accounts of the early universe. Interestingly enough, however, they have not been able to say anything about its origin, and not for reasons of piety, but for reasons of physics. Steven Weinberg, for example, said it was impossible to begin at time 0 because the temperature at that "time" would be infinite. Nor can he say how big the universe was even at very early times. What he does say is this: "We can make a crude estimate that the temperature of $10^{32°}$ K was reached some 10^{-43} seconds after the beginning, but it is not really clear that this estimate has any meaning. Thus, whatever veils may have been lifted, there is one veil, at a temperature of $10^{32°}$ K, that still obscures our view of the earliest times."[11] Weinberg, in effect, leaves us at a threshold, but of what?

An answer (and I do not say *the* answer) is suggested by Fritjof Capra, a high-energy physicist concerned with the same problems as Weinberg. Capra said that humans are necessary not simply to observe atomic physical properties but are participants in the act of measurement. In other words, for contemporary nuclear physics it would seem that there is no universe "out there."[12] Perhaps most remarkable of all, so far as the limits of analytical hermeneutics is concerned is the "bootstrap" or "nuclear democracy" hypothesis of Geoffrey Chew.[13] He argued that the universe, ultimately, is not an assemblage of fundamental entities, but a web of interrelated events none of which is fundamental and all of which follow from the properties of the other parts. The implication is obvious: in order to explain one event we must explain all other events. Capra has drawn the appropriate conclusion: the bootstrap theory of nature leads beyond itself to a vision of nature "transcending the realms of thought and language, leading out of science and into the world of the *acintya*, the unthinkable" where intellectual distinctions disappear.[14] In other words, if we push analysis and demythologization far enough we end up with something like a myth. A persistent, consistent and, I should say, courageous archeological hermeneutics uncovers an origin over which we have no control, a veil beyond which we cannot pass. Marx could have discovered this in Aristotle had he read him with more sympathy.

Consider, for example, the famous words with which Aristotle opened his book on what he called first philosophy: "All human beings naturally desire knowledge. An indication of this is their esteem for the senses (*agapesis aistheseon*); for even apart from their use, they are esteemed for their own sake, and of all, the sense of sight is esteemed most. . . . The reason (*aiton*) for this is that, of all the senses, sight best helps us know many things, and makes plain many distinctions in things" (*Meta.* 980a 22). Now, Aristotle was not John Locke. He was not talking about eighteenth-century "sense-perception" as the fundamental basis for our understanding of reality. Rather, he was expressing the experience of the instantaneous presence of the cosmos transmitted through light and perceived by sight. On the basis of this experience of visual presence arises the desire to reach after (*orego*) knowledge; later in the *Metaphysics* Aristotle described the experience of questioning: "Whoever is perplexed (*aporon*) and whoever wonders (*thaumazon*) is aware of being ignorant (*agnoein*)" (*Meta.* 982b 18). Ignorance induces anxiety, and from this anxious ignorance one searches and is pulled in one's questioning. The factor that directs the search in the direction of knowledge Aristotle called *nous*; it is a suitably ambiguous term, as it indicated both the human desire and the knowledge gained. At one point he symbolized this process as the participation of *nous* in its own activity of knowing (*Meta.* 1072b 20).[15] This summary remark of Aristotle had been preceded by an argument using mythic symbols that explained the genesis of beings from greater beings of the same name (*Meta.* 993b 20). The result, therefore, is that human noetic searching for knowledge is possible only because of the preceding · or, to use modern language, the ontologically prior, genesis of human *nous* by a greater *nous*, which Aristotle called divine *nous*. Consequently, there was a mutual participation of two *nous*-entities. The symbol participation, *metalepsis*, is therefore a term by which noetic experience interprets itself. And the most immediate awareness of this participation, to return to the opening words of the *Metaphysics*, is found in the experience of visual presence.

One need not make a detour into the technicalities of Aristotelean exegesis to grasp the same point. The experience of an intelligible reality surrounding us, of a cosmos, which is grasped by sight, is not derived from our experience of physical reality. Again to refer (but for nearly the last time) to Aristotle: like any good academic, he surveyed the literature in Chapter One. Among his predecessors one of whom, he said, was very crude and could be completely ignored, was Xenophanes, the teacher of Parmenides. As an example of his crudity Aristotle gave the following example of Xenophanes's wisdom: "gazing up at the whole of heaven (*ton holon ouranon apoblepsas*), he [Xenophanes] said: 'the one (*to hen*) is the god' " (*Meta.* 986b 24). Xenophanes's exclamation, I think, corresponds exactly to the experience many of us have had, especially when we were young and especially here on the prairies: lying on one's back, on a summer night in the foothills one can gaze at the whole of heaven.

Something similarly crude moves astronomers and physicists like Weinberg, Capra, and Chew. Why do they bother to construct models of the universe that they know beforehand cannot be validated empirically? Because these models are demythologized mathematical symbolisms of the cosmos as an intelligible whole. They are equivalent in this respect to other cosmologies that employ symbolism of divine creation, of eternally divine being, and so on.[16] That is, human beings create myths, undertake Aristotelean noetics, build modern cosmological models, because they care about understanding the universe. Particle physics and modern cosmology are, then, demythologized equivalents to cosmogenic myths, myths of nature, and so on. All very interesting, you may say, but what has it to do with political science?

My first purpose in talking about physics was rhetorical. Physics is the hardest of sciences and hard sciences have a grand reputation as models of truth. If physicists end up with the equivalent of myth, there is no reason why we political scientists should avoid myths as assiduously as we do. But that is *merely* rhetorical: very few political scientists want to copy Quételet or Comte and create a *physique sociale*. The more important purpose is to show by looking at the apparently unpromising evidence of physics how archaeology eventually turns into teleology. Eventually, that is, the methodical, reductive search for the arche becomes a reflective questioning. It finds an answer not in a fundamental zero-point but rather in a personal commitment, a wager, a vow. Since this vow is the *basis* of rigorous scientific discourse, it can in no way be explained by science or by any analogous reduction.

Likewise one could argue that a coherent teleological hermeneutic also contains an archaeology. I have already mentioned some Greek symbols of philosophical experience: wondering (*thaumazein*), searching (*zetein*), questioning (*aporein*), being moved (*kinein*) or drawn (*helkein*), there is Plato's image of the cave, where the prisoner is moved by an unnamed force to turn away from the shadows and begin the hard way to the light, and so on. There are, moreover, contemporary equivalent symbolisms. The topic of Ricoeur's book, from which I have lifted several key terms, was the greatest of modern archaeologists of the psyche, Freud, whose purpose, whose telos, was health. Similarly, in the introduction to the English version of *Anamnesis*, Eric Voegelin emphasized the need to clarify the constitution of one's own philosophic consciousness through personal remembrance of significant experiences of reality.[17] But rather than work through the problem from this other side (which, in any case, would take another paper), let me begin to conclude with a thematic summary of what the argument has been. The conflict between a hermeneutic of suspicion and a hermeneutic of reminiscence remains a conflict only so long as it remains abstract and non-reflexive. When however, demystifying analysis incorporates into itself discourse on its own analysis, it turns into an archaeology of the subject. This archaeology, in turn, is but one pole of a dialectic whose other element is teleology, which, in turn, is accompanied by its own phenomenological hermeneutic.

A counterproof of this argument can be seen in the familiar experience of talking past one another. Often, though obviously not exclusively, what is involved is a one-sided and incomplete emphasis of one strategy of interpretation and a forgetfulness of its complementary opposite. As in my initial remarks on recent elections, conflicting interpretations give rise to different political realities. Or, to use a more scholarly example, there is the massive and inconclusive controversy surrounding Marx. To put the matter in blunt commonsensical language, Marx's writings contain both a sound analysis of nineteenth-century industrialism and a fantastic eschatology that anticipates a revolutionary transformation of human existence. How are these two contrary aspects to be understood? Characteristically, the phenomenologically inclined critic opposes his implicit and fantastic teleology, the spectral shape of communist society, the occult power of an historically inevitable proletarian revolution, the short-cut evocation of socialist man who does not raise embarrassing Aristotelean questions. His followers, demythologizers all, generally do no more than point to the contradictions of industrial capitalism and the dangers of false consciousness. In other words, critics use one interpretative strategy and ignore whatever truths may be found in Marx's use of the other; defenders ignore whatever lies Marx may have told in unmasking illusions. Put more generously, they ignore the limit of demystification and the nature of archaeology as a constituent element of a greater dialectic. Neither critic nor follower moves away from external confrontation to an internalized and self-conscious symbolic meaning.

Let me end by suggesting what a synthesizing strategy entails. On the one hand, a reductive hermeneutic is required for a political science concerned with symbols, since it alone alerts one to the possibility of not falling for idols. But demythologization must be followed by remythization, not in any sort of Averroistic sense of two truths, a speculative one for political science and a mythic one for the remainder of humanity. Rather, it is the symbolism adequate to the concrete and faithful articulation of a reality experienced as beyond one's discursive and conceptual control, beyond the veil, as Weinberg said.

Let me illustrate this rather terse formula with a familiar example from Plato.[18] Plato, we all know, was a philosopher who deliberately created myths. Most philosophers do the opposite and transpose myths into speculative discourse typically using one of the strategies I have been discussing. Assuming Plato knew what he was doing, we may wonder why he thought myth was a better instrument to transmit meaning than discursive argument. Quite plainly, myth is an extremely dangerous instrument. One needs only recall a book with the title *Der Mythus des Zwanzigsten Jahrhunderts*. This question of adequacy is particularly important in Plato because, as it happens, he created two myths with equivalent meanings of which the second was meant to be better or truer. In the *Republic*, Plato's Phoenician tale, the *gennaion pseudos*, as he called it, tells how the three types of citizens, the rulers, the guardians, and the producers, resulted from the gods having mixed gold, or silver, or iron into their souls. The theoretical truth of the myth, that all human beings are brethren as they come from the same mother, the earth, is far overshadowed, as virtually all commentators agree, by its pragmatic usefulness in keeping the unruly mob and merely courageous military types in line.

In the second and truer myth, unencumbered by the need for a pragmatic compromise to hold in a single community the mystic philosopher-king and the lower orders, tells how living creatures are puppets of the gods. The strings of the puppets correspond to the sentiments and apprehensions of life, pulling us in different directions, with different strength, and requiring different responses from us. The gentle pull of the holy golden cord requires the support of man if it is to be effective; the stronger pulls of the other cords likewise must be resisted if men are to lead good lives. In this second myth, the lump-sum distribution of qualities, symbolized by the metals of the Phoenician tale, has been superseded by a myth of the nature of human beings as such: the characters of living things, Plato said in the later myth, is determined by their response to the pulls of the several cords and not, to use a modern term, by their genotype. In the second myth, we can experience as truth the mysteriousness of joy and sorrow in our own actions; nothing like that emotional intensity is found in the Phoenician tale.

The assertion that the story of the cords is truer than the story of the metals contains implicitly an assertion that the road to the truth of experience proceeds by way of reminiscence and that in contrast suspicion serves only as a *via negativa*. In our demotic and rather cowardly age the implications will not command widespread approval. To begin with, political science will have to confront the demands of Platonic or philosophic rhetoric, the skill of speaking in such a way that the arguments put forward are always fit for the psyches to whom they are addressed. That is, the implications of the adjective in Plato's phrase *gennaion pseudos* will have to be faced. Secondly, there is the question of the authority of the one who tells the great lie and thereby persuades his audience of the truth. For this question no theoretical answer exists. All one can do is recall one's own experiences of truth, the actions of searching, and verifying, the emotions of hope, anticipation, and fear. That is, one must clarify through archaeology the manner of one's own response to events just as one is guided in one's search by the attraction of wider horizons. So far as the topic of this paper is concerned, if hermeneutics aims at both the discipline of reduction and the grace of imagination, at both necessity and possibility, political science needs recognize that its own special excellence combines the familiar scientific virtues of discursive clarity and noetic insight with those of character and self-knowledge, much as Aristotle indicated in his *Ethics*.

Notes

[1]On this topic see Charles Taylor, "Interpretation and the Sciences of Man," *Review of Metaphysics* xxiv (1971), pp. 1-51 or Michael Platt, "Interpretation," *Interpretation: A Journal of Political Philosophy*, 5 (1975), pp. 109-130.

[2]Hans-Georg Gadamer, *Philosophical Hermeneutics*, tr. and ed., David E. Linge (Berkeley, University of California Press, 1976), pp. 21, 47.

[3]See Paul Ricoeur, "The Model of the Text: Meaningful Action Considered as a Text," *Social Research*, 38 (1971), pp. 529-562.

[4]Hans Jonas, *Philosophical Essays: From Ancient Creed to Technological Man* (Toronto, Prentice Hall, 1974), p. 263.

[5]Paul Ricoeur, *Freud and Philosophy: An Essay on Interpretation*, tr. Denis Savage (New Haven, Yale University Press, 1970), p. 27.

[6]*What is Political Philosophy? And Other Studies* (Glencoe, The Free Press, 1959), p. 55.

[7]*Technology and Empire: Perspectives on North America* (Toronto, Anansi, 1969), p. 143.

[8]Ricoeur, *Freud*, p. 280.

[9]*Order and History*, vol. iv, *The Ecumenic Age* (Baton Rouge, Louisiana State University Press, 1974), pp. 59-113. I have given an exegesis of this concept in "Voegelin's Concept of Historiogenesis," *Historical Reflexions/Reflexions historiques*, Winter 1977-78.

[10]All quotations are from Marx's *Early Writings*, tr. and ed., T. B. Bottomore (Toronto, McGraw-Hill, 1963), pp. 164-66.

[11]*The First Three Minutes: A Modern View of the Origin of the Universe* (New York, Basic Books, 1977), p. 146. A Russian cosmologist, speaking of the initial phase transitions of the early universe, said: "Of the third stage we know almost nothing, of the second can be said the same, and of the first, that it preceded the other two."

[12]*The Tao of Physics: An Exploration of the Parallels Between Modern Physics and Eastern Mysticism* (Boulder, Shambhala, 1975), pp. 140-41.

[13]*Science*, 161 (May 23, 1968), pp. 762-65.

[14]Capra, *The Tao of Physics*, p. 301.

[15]The sentence reads: "hauton de noei ho nous kata metalepsin tou noetou." No translation I have consulted seems to convey the meaning of Aristotle's words; hence my paraphrase.

[16]Modern cosmologists, like Aristotle, consider their predecessors crude and unsatisfactory. See Weinberg, *op. cit.*, pp. 3-4, but also the grudging respect paid, pp. 8, 153.

[17]*Anamnesis*, tr. and ed., G. Niemeyer, (Notre Dame, University of Notre Dame Press, 1978), pp. 12-13. Voegelin undertook a series of "anamnetic experiments" reported at pp. 36-51 in the translation. The translation is not always reliable; see also, *Anamnesis: Zur Theorie der Geschichte und Politik*, (Munich, Piper, 1966), pp. 61-76.

[18]The texts are *Republic*, 414b-415d and *Laws*, 644d-645b. See also *Anamnesis*, pp. 45-47 (tr., 21-23), and Voegelin, *Order and History*, vol. III, *Plato and Aristotle* (Baton Rouge, Louisiana State University Press, 1957), pp. 104-108, 232-236.

Commentary on
"Hermeneutics and Political Science"

J.M. Porter, University of Saskatchewan

Hermeneutics—the art or science of interpretation—had its
modern origins probably in Vico but its contemporary variations
owe more to German thinkers. In particular, the reaction to the
methodological monism of positivism and the "hard sciences"
lead several thinkers on the continent to propose alternative
interpretative frameworks. Hermeneutics covers a rather diversi-
fied array of these positions. In political and social science, the
efforts to establish a human science, distinct from the natural
sciences, were made by Droysen (who coined the distinction
between understanding and explanation), Dilthey, Simmel, and
Weber. There was also a neo-Kantian wing of Windelband and
Rickert. Closer to the present are such thinkers as Ricoeur and
Godamer, who are relied upon by Professor Cooper. In the
English world one immediately thinks of Collingwood. And,
although the title "hermeneutics" is not used, there are some
thinkers in analytical philosophy who have comparable concerns: Anscombe, Dray, and Winch are examples. Karl-Otto Apel,
a German philosopher, has shown the similarities between the
English and continental philosophers in his excellent book:
*Analytical Philosophy of Language and the Geisteswissen-
schaften* (1967). For most political scientists probably the most
accessible route to this philosophical tradition is through reading
contemporary analytical philosophers rather than through continental sources such as Godamer and Ricoeur with their echoes
of Husserl and Heidegger.

Professor Cooper, if I have understood him properly, argues
that the modern origins of hermeneutics are found in the desire to
find a theoretical justification for political knowledge which
would be analogous to Kant's justification for Newtonian or
Baconian natural scientific knowledge. The difficulty in the task
derives from the difference in the role of the knower in natural
science and the role of the knower in political and social science.
For the latter, we are told, "the knowing subject is a part of the
object he studies. That is, he does not confront history, politics,
society, etc. as a thing. He participates in it; he is a part of a larger
whole."

There are two problems with this formulation of the problem.
First, it is not clear that an "analogous theoretical justification"
was sought. The neo-Kantians may have, but Vico, Dilthey, and

Weber stressed the critical differences between the natural and human worlds. There was no desire to claim the same "objectivity" for both worlds. There was an analogy only in the trivial sense that they too wanted a theoretical justification. Second, it is argued that that the "famous hermeneutical circle" leads to the two strategies of interpretation outlined in the paper. Circularity and paradox are the two descriptions given of the hermeneutic circle. We are told that it is the "participation of the scientist in the things he studies" which is the root of the problem. But the nature of this participation is not clear nor are the arguments that purport to show paradox and circularity. That evidence prescribes at one level, in the forming of a concept, and that the concept then also prescribes as to what is to be included as evidence need not be paradoxical or circular. It depends on what is meant: is observation a neutral variable? how inclusive is the claim made for the encompassing concept? In fact, it is hard to see how Professor Cooper's argument has anything to do with the root of the original problem, participation. If the problem were framed in terms of Winch's form of life, an argument might be developed. But in that case the problem would become one of meaning rather than a problem of evidence. The relationship between evidence and a uniting theory is not in itself paradoxical.

In any case, it is argued that there are two major strategies of interpretation which can be used in attempting to break out of the problem created by the participation of the knower: the strategies of interpretation as reminiscence and of interpretation as demystification. Whether hermeneutics is understood as reminiscence or demystification the key problem, we are told, is the deciphering of symbols. Both strategies are shown to be inadequate and incomplete. In contrast, we are shown a proper use and creation of symbols with brief descriptions of Aristotle, Voegelin, and some contemporary astrophysicists.

It is difficult to relate the various themes in this middle section of the paper—no doubt space is a major factor. After comparing and contrasting, Professor Cooper concludes that either type of interpretation by itself is inadequate and that a synthesizing strategy is needed. The possibility of a synthesis between the two types of hermeneutics seems doubtful, at least as they are presented. One stresses a reductionism and the other remythization. They seem at first glance ontologically distinct. One can synthesize explanatory and statistical models to a substantive model of human life, as thinkers from Vico to Winch have suggested but in these cases the explanatory models are not ontologically separate. Further, it is difficult to see how a synthesis of two flawed approaches will accomplish what Professor Cooper desires. Actually, one is left with the suspicion that Professor Cooper would prefer Plato, Aristotle, and Voegelin's methods to any synthesis.

Nevertheless, one can agree with Professor Cooper on the need to include reflective as well as empirical methods in the human sciences. The limitations for analysis in relying only on the empirical enterprise include the difficulties of knowing when the "reasons" given for action and the symbols used are illusory or rationalizations, or when they can be truly explained by sociological factors, as rust can explain the breakdown of a watch. More importantly, a synthetic hermeneutic could recognize purposes and reasons for human action. Categories such as truth, justice, and morality would not be conceived to be wholly derivative or illusory but would be recognized as real in the life of man. However great the difficulties are in relating this type of ontological statement to others in political science, there seems to be no way to ignore its explanatory usefulness that is not contradictory to much purposive human action. Wittgenstein spoke of this dimension in analysis by saying: "What people accept as a justification—is shown by how they think and live." By citing Wittgenstein I mean to indicate that the "normative content" need not be expressed in the form of universals. Vico, Apel, Winch and many others starting from different premises, have held the view that 'relativism' does not necessarily preclude the sharing of certain common attitudes or 'propensities', sufficient for some degree of understanding between different peoples and generations, regarding the standards to which they ought to aspire as human beings. For the limited epistemological purposes of political science one need claim little more than this.

There are many advantages to an analysis or hermeneutics which recognizes the intrinsic authenticity of the normative element. By taking cognizance of the historical and normative aspects, hermeneutics can allow us to escape from mechanical, static, and wholly functional explanations of political reality. It can emphasize a dynamic understanding of political reality rather than an ultimately static one. The social solipsism found in functional analysis, for example, is escaped by noting that there are values, if differently understood, that take concrete forms and transcend a system. Hermeneutics so conceived restores, lastly, the same level of meaning and significance to political actors and vocabulary that we attach to, and affirm for, our own existence.

The dialectic of negation and affirmation found in the political process derives its sustenance, in part, from the act of knowing itself. In knowing, we both reflect and critically examine; we also affirm and authenticate in the process the never-ending search for understanding. *How* we know witnesses to what is knowable and what is significant and worthy of human pursuit, on the political, or any other level, of human existence.

To conclude, a study of hermeneutics can be valuable to political and social science. I am inclined to think that the approach that is most apt to persuade us is one which starts from the problems of knowing as formulated by some contemporary analytical philosophers and then, as with Karl-Otto Apel, probes the similarities with other traditions.

Towards a
Science of Man

Freedom, Necessity and Human Values in the Social Sciences

E. K. Hunt, University of Utah

Introduction

Social theory always rests, implicitly or explicitly, on ontological, epistemological and axiological foundations. Unfortunately in contemporary academic circles most philosophers show little concern for the human, social, political and economic implications of their philosophical theories, while very few social scientists show any concern with the philosophical foundations of their social theories.

In this paper I shall briefly sketch what I consider to be some of the necessary philosophical assumptions of any truly humanistic social science and to indicate why I believe that most social science is antihumanistic and hence, despite any amount of goodwill on the part of individual social theorists, most social theories are morally objectionable.

The most fundamental dilemma of contemporary social science can be explicated by examining the dualism of Descartes and the naturalistic reaction to Descartes' inadequacies. It is my belief that contemporary social science is the modern embodiment of the ideas of this naturalistic reaction.

Descartes' philosophy was an attempt to reconcile his humanistic concerns about human freedom and creativity, his belief in Catholic Theology, and his enthusiasm for the natural sciences. He posited an ontology in which reality consisted of three irreducible substances, God, mind and material nature. While modern thinkers frequently dismiss Descartes because of his theology, I believe that one should leave this theology aside and examine his problem of reconciling the different ways in which we understand the mental and material aspects of reality.

For Descartes, material nature (including human bodies) was governed by iron laws which made the succession of natural states absolutely necessary. Human understanding of any natural event required the knowledge of other events which temporally preceded the event in question (the *explanandum*) and which constituted the necessary cause (the *explanans*) of the event in question. This conception of the nature of human understanding of the material world was in Descartes' time, and has subsequently proven to be, a practical and effective means for human manipulation and control of inert, material nature.

But Descartes was forcefully aware of the undeniable, ever-present sense of human freedom and creativity that has always characterized human subjective consciousness. He was thus unwilling to reduce an understanding of the mental world to the same principles by which the material world was understood. He realized that this reduction would render human freedom and creativity an illusion.

In the material world, if A causes B which in turn causes C then it is equally correct to say that A is the cause of C or that B is the cause of C. If this principle is applied to the mental world, and if B represents states of an individual's consciousness while A represents the set of causes of these mental states and C represents the consequences of the mental choices and acts of creativity that result from these mental states, then all human accomplishments are the inevitable effects of causes external to the individual. The human self or identity is of no "scientific" consequence in this explanation of human behavior, the feelings of genuinely free human choice and creativity are illusions based upon ignorance of the relevant causes. Hence, Descartes insisted that because human freedom and creativity had real, ontological status the method of understanding material nature was insufficient for understanding mental phenomena.

He was aware, however, that material and mental states frequently seemed to be interconnected and wanted to understand the nature of this interconnection. He was unable to conceive of any comprehensible interconnection that was not couched in mechanistic cause-effect terms. As a result he offered two speculative explanations. The first was biological and was not satisfactory to Descartes himself because biological explanations relied upon the notion of material causation and hence could not preserve the free will and creativity of the mental world. So he fell back on his second explanation: human ideas, choice and free will could only be subject to causation if one posited God's existence.

Descartes' dilemma was very real and very important. His failure consisted in his insistence that if material events could never be the necessary and sufficient causes of mental events then some other realm of necessary causation had to be posited to account for mental events.

The inadequacy of both of his explanations of mental events is nearly universally conceded. But in rejecting Descartes' explanations of the interconnection of the mental and physical aspects of reality, most subsequent thinkers at least implicitly have rejected as meaningless the problem with which he was grappling. I believe that this was one of the most unfortunate mistakes in intellectual history and shall indicate why. Subsequently I shall argue that Karl Marx was one of the very few important social scientists to have taken Descartes' problem seriously; but that while Marx's writings exemplify the only satisfactory resolution to the problem, he did not make explicit the epistemological foundation of his solution. I shall conclude the paper by indicating premises I believe to be necessary to a successful resolution to Descartes' problem. Such a resolution seems to me to be an absolute prerequisite for the development of humanistic social science.

The Naturalistic Conception of Plastic Man

Naturalism and what is paradoxically called enlightenment "humanism" emerged as a reaction to the influence of the Cartesian philosophy. Naturalists rejected Descartes' claim that the methodology appropriate for understanding the material aspects of nature was inadequate for understanding the mental aspects of nature. They insisted that human beings were continuous with all nature and that a single mode of understanding was appropriate for all reality. Although naturalism per se does not imply materialism, empiricism or determinism, in the social sciences naturalism has generally gone hand in hand with all three. For most naturalists, the only form of human understanding was the cause-effect relationship. An understanding of event B (whether material or mental) consisted of recognition that it was the inevitable consequence of event A. Hence the determinism of naturalism.

Although philosophers often speak of "hard" and "soft" determinism, the distinction seems to me to have no practical importance in the social sciences. To simplify, "hard" determinism generally means that effect B follows from cause A with the same certainty with which the conclusions of deductive logic follow from the premises, i.e. if A and B are both correctly and completely understood then we cannot even conceive that B will not always be the effect of A. "Soft" determinism asserts that we cannot understand any event B unless we can find a cause A of which it is the effect, but it is always *conceivable* that some other event C rather than B could follow event A.

In other words, "soft" determinists admit the possibility of random, inexplicable, incomprehensible events. But because the only mode of human understanding of an event is the identification of the prior, external cause of that event, such random events can never be among the objects understood by the social sciences. Therefore the principal practical difference between "hard" determinism and "soft" determinism is that the one holds that every aspect of reality is, in principle, comprehensible within the cause-effect mode of explanation, whereas the other admits the possibility of incomprehensible events. In so far as human reality is understood, i.e. in so far as there is a social science, human beings are understood as the passive effects of prior external causes by both "hard" and "soft" determinists. When humans are so conceived, social scientists can make the claim of having a value free science. If event B (e.g. some state or aspect of human experience) is merely the inevitable, deterministic, passive effect of event A, then the naturalist *qua* social scientist simply asserts that the scientific validity of the causal connection between A and B is independent of his own emotions and values and then he is merely reporting a scientific truth. This is what is usually meant when orthodox social scientists assert that social theory is value free.

The Achilles heel of this conception of plastic man as the passive outcome of prior external causes is epistemological. If, as is generally the case in orthodox social science, the theorist uses an empiricist methodology and a correspondence theory of truth, theories of human behavior are true if they correspond to that portion of sense perceptions which in turn corresponds to the real ontological reality being perceived. Such an epistemological-methodological approach, however, demands an Archimedean point from which the evaluator of the truth or falsity of a theory simultaneously comprehends the theory, perceives the perception of reality to which the theory must correspond and intuits in an unmediated and absolute manner (i.e. without the aid of the sense organs which can give distorted impressions) the true ontological reality to which the perception must correspond. Moreover, the evaluator, having found his Archemedean point must not have already been determined in his evaluation by prior causes. He must *freely* decide if the appropriate correspondences hold and the theory is true. Therefore, the intellectuals who evaluate the truth or falsity of the theory must themselves be exceptions to the theory. Otherwise, statements about scientific truth or falsity, being wholly determined by prior external causes, do not differ in ontological status from a person having the mumps, or a leaf falling to the ground or any other natural event. In other words, the ontology implicit in the deterministic conception destroys the epistemology.

The deterministic view of plastic man fares no better with a rationalist epistemology because determinism is compatible with rationalism only on the assumption that *a priori* knowledge that stands independent of sensuous experience is causally determined (as e.g. through the laws of genetics). In this case, judgements about truth and falsity have the same status as the color of one's skin and eyes. Again the ontology destroys the epistemology. The evaluator of truth and falsity must be one of an elite that has escaped the determinism and can evaluate and freely choose truth.

This elitism implicit in the cause-effect conception of plastic man can be clearly seen in the usual manner in which most social scientists use their theories as a basis for policy recommendations. Such recommendations are usually based on three (generally implicit) premises: First, that there is a human nature which ought to be realized but that nature is attained or thwarted independently of individuals' free wills by the effects of the social environment that determines the individuals (e.g., for neoclassical economists social obstructions of the free market thwart human nature, while for some Marxists the market thwarts human nature); second, that there is an intellectual elite that is above the deterministic, plastic nature of the masses, and is therefore able to freely understand the laws of social science and to use this understanding to manipulate the environment through social engineering; third, that once this environment is correctly manipulated the plastic masses will be deterministically created in a manner consistent with their true nature as conceived by the intellectual elite.

This brief description of the policy orientation of deterministic social science is, I believe, equally descriptive of neoclassical economics and that portion of Marxist economics which is under the influence of Stalinism. Both are inherently elitist, anti-humanist and repressive. The intellectual premise on which this elitist rests seems to me to be the rejection of Descartes' notion that human freedom and creativity while comprehensible cannot be understood within the cause-effect framework of natural science. By insisting that the cause-effect relationship is the only mode of scientific understanding, determinists make all human choices and actions the effect of prior causes and hence destroy human free-will as it is commonly conceived, or they make any human freedom that might exist appear to be random, incomprehensible and hence intellectually meaningless.

At the other end of the intellectual spectrum from naturalistic determinism is another conception of plastic man which I shall mention only to dismiss. This is the radically free human being portrayed in Sartre's *Being and Nothingness*. Sartre's plastic man has no inherent nature but creates himself entirely through free acts of will. I shall simply assert, without defense, that this notion of plastic man leaves no possibility whatsoever for any social science. This is because Sartre's conception of human beings is that they have no common essence. Each person begins as a "creative vacuum" who creates his or her self. This precludes the possibility of making any valid generalizations about human nature and ultimately leads to intellectual relativism that is nihilistic. Although Sartre attempts to moderate this by insisting that the social world constitutes constraints on the individual, the effects of such constraints can never be generally understood if they act on human beings who have no general nature. Moreover his distinction between being-in-itself and being-for-itself must remain forever incomprehensible if there is absolutely no nature to the "creative vacuum" that becomes by its own choice. Social science simply is not possible with this extreme relativism. Thus Sartre like the naturalistic determinists "resolves" Descartes' dilemma by denying one of the horns of the dilemma. Both resolutions render incomprehensible and thereby make insignificant an integral and important aspect of human reality. Neither the resolution of the naturalists nor that of Sartre permits the possibility of humanist social science.

Humanistic Social Science and the Epistemological Dilemma

In order for social science to be humanist, by my definition, it must face Descartes' dilemma. It must posit that human beings are simultaneously (1) part of material nature and at least partially the passive effects of prior, external causes, and (2) the possessors of consciousness, intelligence, creativity and free-will which renders them in part self-caused causes. In other words, human beings are some complex combination of determined passive aspects and free autonomous aspects. The intellectual tension between simultaneous conceptions of man as plastic and autonomous is a difficult one to maintain, but it seems to me that the only alternatives are the naturalistic determinism which I have argued results in antihumanist elitism and insuperable epistemological problems or the intellectual nihilism of Sartre's *Being and Nothingness*.

Only by maintaining this intellectual tension can one simultaneously argue that (1) there is a human nature which involves the potential for substantial improvements in human creative, esthetic, intellectual and physical development, and that (2) these ends can be democratically pursued through the free use of human intelligence by everyone rather than having these ends pursuable only through the repressive, manipulative control of the majority by an elite minority (whether that control is exercised through the medium of the market and ballot box or through other means). Nothing short of this seems to me to warrant the name 'humanism'.

But such an approach demands that, following Descartes, we formulate an epistemological framework such that we can show that cause-effect reasoning permits comprehension and explanation of those aspects of human behavior that are passively determined and that free, autonomous behavior is comprehensible but not amenable to the mechanistic cause-effect explanation. The remainder of this section will consist of a brief outline of the epistemological framework within which I believe this problem must be solved. The next section will consist of a defense of my earlier assertion that Karl Marx had a social philosophy that requires a resolution of this epistemological dilemma. The concluding section will outline my opinions on what seems to me to be the only possible resolution of this dilemma.

The principal problem of epistemology is the relation between thinking and being. Thinking is thinking about things or relations among things. The "things", "material" or "substance" of our thoughts is "given" to us through experience. In experience we perceive the sensuous qualities of things. These things, their qualities, and relations among them *then* become the objects of thought. Common sense as well as most of what we call "science" simply assumes as immediately and intuitively obvious that the sensuous world which perception makes known to us exists outside of, and independently of, its being perceived or conceived by a human being. The existence of a material thing is taken to be a fact which is quite different from the fact of that same thing being the object of either perception or conception.

The common sense view is that through perception we gain immediate awareness of qualities of things (hardness, shape, color, odor, etc.) and hence of the existence of these things, but a perception of a thing is generally not considered to be identical to the total existential reality of the thing itself. Perception (or experience) then furnishes the mind with the qualities of the objects about which the mind forms concepts. But a thing's existence is generally considered to involve something "more" than simply those qualities of the thing that appear immediately in the subjective sense perception, or those aspects of the thing as they are objectified mentally in the thought process.

This common sense view is the basis for both empiricism and Marx's materialism. Marx's consistent use of the word "materialism" to describe his philosophy has led to a significant semantic misunderstanding. Materialism prior to Marx and in contemporary usage refers to the notion that material nature is ontologically prior to mental states, i.e. mental states are reducible to material states. Marx's materialism, which is generally called "common sense realism" in contemporary philosophy, preserves the ontological irreducibility of both mental and material reality. But despite the fact that empiricism and Marx's materialism both derive from this common sense view, they are by no means identical. Nor does acceptance of one of them imply acceptance of the other. In fact, I shall argue that they are incompatible. Empiricism is the view that sense perceptions represent the sole origins of knowledge. For an empiricist, ideas or concepts are true to the degree that the object as represented in the concept or idea accurately reflects or corresponds to the object as it is given in immediate sensual experience. Marx's materialism is simply the view that existence is not reducible to mental states (either perception or conception). While mental states are a part of the total of existing reality, there is another part of reality that is non-mental—i.e. material—which can never simply be reduced or collapsed into a mental state.

The fundamental problem of epistemology is to explain the transition from sense perception (which, for empiricism, is the only source of knowledge) to ideas and general concepts. It is ironic that while David Hume is frequently seen as the father of modern empiricism, it was he who convincingly demonstrated the impossibility of empiricism. He showed that sense perception itself can never be the sole source of our *idea* of the distinction between the objective and subjective elements of experience. It never reveals a subjective self, it never reveals anything corresponding to the idea of causality that is found in thought, nor (most importantly) does it ever reveal the source of generalization which is the most distinctive characterization of thought.

Sense perception simply cannot, by itself, account for thought. Sense perception is always immediately *organized* by the mind. We immediately and intuitively *know* that the objects we perceive are *our* perceptions and that *we* are something other than or more than our sense perceptions and that the sense perceptions are of things that are other than (and outside of) us. If we examine the material revealed solely by the senses we *see* nothing but a continuous collage of colors of various shades, hues, etc., one shading off into the next, sometimes gradually, sometimes abruptly; we hear nothing but intermittent or overlapping sounds of varying pitch, loudness, duration, etc.; we feel, with the tactile sense, smoothness, hardness, softness, texture, etc.; and so forth for all of the senses. The senses by themselves would give us nothing but innumerable, heterogeneous qualities with no inherent order, form or intelligibility—in a word, utterly non-rational, infinitely complex chaos.

But experience contains more than a random, unconnected, nonrational welter of colors, sounds, smells, etc. Experience *is* organized. We are aware of the self having the experiences as being distinct and in some way constituting "more than" simply these qualities of sensations. We are aware of the self as subjectivity and the experience as an experience of objective reality which is other than the self. We are immediately aware that these qualities which we sense "coalesce" around or in distinct things. We are aware that these things are different existences each with its own identity. We are also aware of differences, similarities and other relations among these things. Yet we do not have a separate sense faculty which distinguishes subjectivity and objectivity, identity and nonidentity, similarity and difference, etc., in the same way that the eye sees colors, the ear hears sounds, and the nose smells odors. These aspects of experience, which are aspects of all human experience, are simply not the direct objects of the senses. The self, the other-than-self, the principle of identity and difference are *all ideas*—not sense perceptions. Therefore, sense perception by itself can never furnish the objects of thought simply because the perceptions themselves are *actively organized* in accordance with complex conceptual categories already present in our immediate apprehension of sensual reality.

Thus, the conundrum of epistemology: thought can have no substance or object without the prior passive reception of the sensual data of experience, but experience can only become the substance of thought if it is prearranged and *understood* in terms of general abstract categories which are not themselves given in experience, and which must therefore be known and understood prior to experience for that experience to have any meaning. Therefore, it appears that before the individual can become the active agent (the thinker) he must first be the passive receiver (the perceiver). But before he can be the passive perceiver of intelligible experience, he must first be capable of assimilating experience in terms of preexistent conceptual categories. It would thus appear both that intelligible experience must precede thought and that abstract conceptual categories (i.e. thought) must precede intelligible experience.

Naive materialism and empiricism simply assume away the problem of the intelligibility of experience. This naive avoidance of the problem probably explains (in part, at least) why most of the great philosophical minds have tended toward an idealist form of epistemology. The very quest of epistemology is *thought* trying to *understand* its own origins, not perception trying to sense or perceive its own origins. Therefore, even if a materialist states that thought is merely the passive reflection of material reality, his notion of the foundation of thought originated in (or was caused by) the very process of thought itself. Nowhere in material reality does one perceive the material existential referent of thought thinking about thought itself. Hence, if one is unable to resolve (or accept the unresolved nature of) the dilemma that thought requires previous sensual experience but sensual experience can only be intelligible if one presupposes a prior abstract mental understanding, then anyone who thinks seriously about epistemology is led toward idealism. In idealism the dilemma is resolved by collapsing all reality into mental states and rejecting the common sense notion that existence includes not only mental states but nonmental, material things whose existence always involves something more than or additional to our perceptions and conceptions of these things.

Most materialists writing prior to Marx had, in rejecting idealism, made thinking itself less real than material existence (i.e. they had made thought an epiphenomenal, shadowy, less real, ideal "reflection" of the truly real—matter). These materialists were nearly always epistemological empiricists. For them, non-human matter reacting on passive human matter (the physical sense apparatus and the physical brain) constituted the material causes of which the epiphenomenal or shadowy "mental" images of the real (manifested in perceptions and conceptions) were the effects. Monistic materialism has always been unable to explain how consciousness itself (as opposed to the material organs which are necessary for consciousness) exists at all since it is not matter. However definitively we can prove that sight is impossible without a physical, material eye, the subjective experience of seeing is always (and immediately known to be) something other than simply the material eye and external material objects reflecting light, etc., just as we know that the object seen is something more than the mere experience of seeing the object. Consequently most pre-Marxian materialists (with some notable exceptions such as Kant) simply relegated thought to a vague, quasi-real existential status much as Hegel relegated matter to an unreal, illusory status.

For most pre-Marxian materialists, thought had greater reality, or more truth value, the more accurately it reflected material reality and had a lesser reality, or less truth value, the more it differed from or distorted material reality. Crude or naive materialism and empiricism base their epistemological definition of truth on the belief that thought is passive effect and material reality is cause. Truth consists in material reality acting in such a manner as to effect a mental image that accurately reflects that material reality which is its cause. The greatest difficulty for this point of view, of course, is to explain subjectivity at all. Subjectivity appears as material effect (i.e. as object) of material cause. Everything appears to be in danger of being collapsed into nothing but matter in motion. The distinctions between subjectivity and objectivity, between human and non-human matter have no basis and ultimately *appear* to be illusory.

The word *appear* in the previous sentence is important. Obviously the materialist theoretician is thinking and perceiving. The notion that thought merely reflects matter is just that—a notion, a product of thought. The strict materialist monist is always forced into an impossible dilemma. He knows he is think-ing about thinking but perceives no material existence whose reflection consists of thinking about thinking. Thinking itself must be made into matter. Otherwise how is the searcher for truth to perceive both the material entity and the thought of the materi-al entity and to compare them as to similarity or lack of similarity. And thinking about thinking (epistemology) must be another different material entity if the thinker is to compare it with the material thing of which it is a reflection and to ascertain its truth value. But then we are in an infinite regress because we can think about differing epistemologies, i.e. we can think about thinking about thinking, and so forth, ad infinitum. Strict monistic materialism can give no more reality to subjectivity and thought than strict idealism can give to material things. We are still left with our original dilemma of epistemology: experience of material reality presupposes certain subjective thought processes before it can be intelligible and thought requires the experiencing of an external material reality before it can have objective content.

Mind and Matter in the Writings of Marx

It is my contention that Marx accepted both sides of the epistemological paradox and hence neither attempted to reduce thought to matter nor matter to thought. There was for Marx only one reality. But reality was made up of two irreducible, but inter-related and interacting components: matter and thought. In Marx's theory the basic existential facts, or ontological premises, are men who are perceiving, thinking, and acting in a material world whose ontological status is not dependent on these perceptions and thoughts. As material beings, men act in and upon a material world and are acted upon by a material world. But men are also thinking beings. And it is in human action that thought and matter interpenetrate each other. Human action both affects and is affected by thought. Human thought both affects and is affected by matter through human action. In short, Marx rejects both empiricism and idealism. His theory

> starts out from the real premises [of the existence of concrete real human beings and concrete material objects in various relations] and does not abandon them for a moment. Its premises are men, not in fantastic isolation and fixity, but in

their actual, empirically perceptible process of development
under definite conditions. As soon as this active life-process
is described, history ceases to be a collection of dead facts, *as
it is with the empiricists*..., or an imagined activity of
imagined subjects, as with the idealists.[1]

When materialism considers *all reality* to be simply matter in
motion, then as we have seen everything is reduced (at least
implicitly) to non-human matter. Non-human matter, in so far as
it is intelligible to us, is governed by mechanistic, material
causation. Each link in the chain of causes and effects is the
passive recipient of a prior cause and in turn this link becomes a
cause whose effect again becomes a cause which acts on other inert
matter. In the world of non-human material nature there are no
active causes only passive causes. Thus for the monistic materialist, if one man shoots and kills another man, then the cause of
the death can be said to be the mental and emotional state of the
killer, the killer's *intention* of killing, the killer's decision to kill,
and finally the killer's *goal oriented* action (the aiming of the gun
and the pulling of the trigger). The cause of the death can, with
equal truth, also be said to be the bullet which flew through the
air and entered the man's body. For monistic materialism there is
absolutely no qualitative difference between goal oriented human
behavior as cause and inert matter being acted upon and in turn
"acting" as the cause. There is no difference because, as we have
seen, monistic materialism reduces human beings to inert matter.
  For Marx there is a difference between these two types of causes.
Human beings are both inert matter and conscious, goal oriented
subjective consciousness. And neither of these aspects of human
beings can be reduced to the other. The two interpenetrate and
affect each other, but the subjective goal oriented consciousness
and the material objectivity of a human being are irreducibly
different aspects of human existence. To understand the reciprocal relationship of these two facets of human behavior is, for
Marx, the methodological starting point for understanding
human beings, human society and human history. Prior to Marx,
that part of human behavior which was goal oriented consciousness was recognized only by idealists (with a few exceptions). But
they made that aspect the whole of human reality and ignored the
passive, inert material side of human beings. Most pre-Marxian
materialists simply reversed this one-sidedness. Human life is in
reality, Marx insisted, a reciprocally interrelated unity of these
irreducibly different aspects of human existence. Thus, in the
"Theses on Feuerbach" Marx wrote:

> The chief defect of all previous materialism—that of Feuerbach included—is that things, reality, sensuousness, are conceived only in the form of the object, ... but not as human *sensuous activity, practice,* and not subjectively. Hence it happened that the *active* side, in contradiction to materialism, was set forth by idealism—but only abstractly, since, of course, idealism does not know real, sensuous activity as such.[7]

Thus Marx departed radically from previous materialists and from all idealists and from all monist philosophy which has sought or seeks to collapse all reality into a single substance—be that substance mental or physical. And yet Marx was not a dualist in the sense that Descartes was. He did not posit two equally real, but separated and independent "worlds" of mental and material reality. Marx was the most important modern thinker to preserve the irreducible integrity of both thought and matter and yet to recognize the complex reciprocity of thought and matter in one single existential reality. Much of Marx's writing assumes this epistemological premise. But while the premise is implicit in many of Marx's writings only occasionally is it explicitly stated as it is, for example, in the *1844 Manuscripts*: "Thinking and being are thus certainly distinct from each other, but at the same time they are in *unity* with each other."[3] Marx was, perhaps, the most important thinker to investigate human thought as an aspect of human behavior in the material world, without putting either thought or matter into an unreal, epiphenomenal limbo or into a hermetically sealed region where either would be unaffected by the other.

The mental and the material reciprocally unite in the *practical activity* of human beings. One cannot understand Marx until one accepts and *understands* the seemingly paradoxical fact that every human being is at one and the same time partly the free active creator of himself and his world (as objective extensions of his self) and partly the unfree, passive, inert effect of his environment as it acts on and conditions him. Non-human matter in motion can be comprehended strictly in terms of passive, inert, material causation. Human activity must be understood in terms of *both* material causation and free, conscious, purposive (or teleological), self-caused causation.

Human beings are both cause and effect of both of these types of causation. People work with matter and in so doing must exert their own material being (physical hand, fingers, etc.) on matter in accordance with the principles of material causation (hence they act as material cause for the transformation of matter) but they do so as a consequence of a conscious image of that into which they wish to transform the matter and a mental desire or act of will to transform the matter (hence they act as conscious, purposive, teleological cause). People can also, of course, act as both material and teleological causes on other human beings as mental and material objects. Hence human beings are also effects of both kinds of causes (it goes without saying that human beings can be materially affected by non-human matter, as, e.g. being caught in a snow storm or being struck by lightning, etc.).

In acting *creatively* as both material and teleological cause men become conscious of reality and objectify their consciousness by molding reality according to their consciousness. It is this human activity (as teleological and material cause) through which, in Marx's view, human beings *create* themselves, both subjectively and objectively. Human reason, by virtue of which man is creative, also defines man as a species-being. He is mentally able to appropriate (consciously understand) the essential features of all other human beings as well as all other forms of material existences (organic and inorganic) and to act upon them and influence, mold or condition them in accordance with these principles of understanding. In that way he is able to make features of all existence a part of himself subjectively and to objectify himself in all existence. This is what Marx meant by human beings as species-beings. And as species-beings, human beings actively and freely create themselves and their environment. In Marx's words:

> Man is a species-being, not only because in practice and in theory he adopts the species (his own as well as those of other things) as his object, but—and this is only another way of expressing it—also because he treats himself as the actual, living species; because he treats himself as a *universal* and therefore a free being.
>
> The life of the species, both in man and in animals, consists physically in the fact that man (like the animal) lives on inorganic nature; and the more universal man (or the animal) is, the more universal is the sphere of inorganic nature on which he lives. Just as plants, animals, stones, air, light, etc., constitute theoretically a part of human consciousness, partly as objects of natural science, partly as art— his spiritual inorganic nature, spiritual nature, spiritual nourishment which he must first prepare to make palatable and digestible—so also in the realm of practice they constitute a part of human life and human activity. Physically man lives only on these products of nature, whether they appear

in the form of food, heating, clothes, a dwelling, etc. The universality of man appears in practice precisely in the universality which makes all nature his inorganic body—both inasmuch as nature is (1) his direct means of life, and (2) the material, the object, and the instrument of his life activity. Nature is man's inorganic *body*—nature, that is, insofar as it is not itself human body. Man *lives* on nature—means that nature is his *body*, with which he must remain in continuous interchange if he is not to die. That man's physical and spiritual life is linked to nature means simply that nature is linked to itself, for man is a part of nature.[4]

Thus man's labor (his entire sensuous activity) in transforming nature is a process in which *he creates himself*. But it is central to Marx's conception of man that human beings are a *social* species. To be human is to be social:

> The production [creation] of life, both of one's own in labour and of fresh life in procreation, now appears as a twofold relation: on the one hand as a natural [i.e. a relation with nature], on the other hand as a social relation—social in the sense that it denotes the co-operation of several individuals, no matter under what conditions, in what manner and to what end.[5]

Man is, for Marx, both a natural biological being and a social being. Man's nature has a biological foundation which consists of innate *needs* and potential powers. It is only through *social activity* that these needs take on a specific form, that is become concrete, conscious desires. And it is only through social activity that these needs can be satisfied. Furthermore the nature and extent of the particular means used to satisfy these needs are social. For example, hunger has a biological foundation, but only in social intercourse does hunger become the desire for a particular kind of food; and the means for procuring this kind of food are social. Moreover, not all human needs are satisfied by material substances. There are various social, psychological, or spiritual needs which have some biological basis, but which develop into conscious desires (for affection, approval, belongingness, etc., in general and, for example, for a husband, a friend, membership in a club, etc. etc., for a few of the nearly infinite number of specific examples that could be found in different social settings) only within a specific social context. Needless to say, the means of satisfying these needs are entirely social.

Needs are satisfied through social activities (through which they are also concretized into actual conscious desires). The social activities are also the only means by which potential human powers—which exist in original biological form as mere potential—become actual powers of an individual. The powers or faculties which an individual develops are *social*. Only their potential is biological. The satisfaction of human (social) needs and the development of human (social) powers are, in reality, only one interconnected process of social practice in which the individual creates himself as an individual. This doctrine is so important (and so widely misunderstood) in Marx's writings that we shall quote him at length:

> Activity and enjoyment, both in their content and in their *mode of existence* are *social*: *social* activity and *social* enjoyment. The *human* aspect of nature exists only for *social* man; for only then does nature exist for him as a *bond* with *man*— as his existence for the other [human being] and the other's existence for him—and as the life-element in human reality. Only then does nature exist as the *foundation* of his own *human* experience. Only here has what is to him his *natural* existence become his *human* existence, and nature become man for him.[6]

> ...[The] *perceptible* appropriation for and by man of the human essence and of human life, of objective man, of human *achievements*...should not be conceived merely in the sense of immediate one-sided enjoyment, merely in the sense of *possessing* or *having*. Man appropriates his comprehensive essence in a comprehensive manner, that is to say, as a whole man. Each of his *human* relations to the world— seeing, hearing, smelling, tasting, feeling, thinking, observing, experiencing, wanting, acting, loving—in short, all the organs of his individual being...are in their *objective* orientation, or in their *orientation to the object*,...the appropriation of *human* reality. Their orientation to their object is the *manifestation of the human reality*, it is human activity...[7]

It is obvious that the *human* eye enjoys things in a way different from the crude, non-human eye; the human ear different from the crude ear etc....

On the one hand, therefore, it is only when the objective world becomes everywhere for man in society the world of man's essential powers—that all objects become for him the *objectification* of himself, become objects which confirm and realize his individuality, become *his* objects: that is, *man himself* becomes the object. The *manner* in which they become *his* depends on the nature of the *objects* and on the nature of the *essential power* corresponding to it; for it is precisely the *determinate nature* of this relationship which shapes the particular, *real* mode of affirmation. To the eye an object comes to be other than it is to the *ear*, and the object of the eye *is* another object than the object of the *ear*. The specific character of each essential power is precisely its specific mode of its objectification, of its *objectively actual, living being*. Thus man is affirmed in the objective world not only in the act of thinking, but with *all* his senses.

On the other hand, let us look at this in its subjective aspect. Just as only music awakens in man the sense of music, and just as the most beautiful music has *no* sense for the unmusical ear—is no object for it, because my object can only be the confirmation of one of my essential powers—it can therefore only exist for me insofar as my essential power exists for itself as a subjective capacity; because the meaning of an object for me goes only so far as my *sense* goes (has only a meaning for a sense corresponding to that object)—for this reason the *senses* of the social man *differ* from those of the non-social man. Only through the objectively unfolding richness of man's essential being is the richness of subjective *human* sensibility (a musical ear, an eye for beauty of form—in short, *senses* capable of human gratification, senses affirming themselves as essential powers of *man*) either cultivated or brought into being. For not only the five senses but also so-called mental senses, the practical senses (will, love, etc.), in a word, *human* sense, the human nature of the senses, comes to be by virtue of *its* object, by virtue of humanized nature.[8]

Several important points from our previous discussion are forcefully stated in this lengthy quotation. First, the human knowing process *requires* an independently given, external, material world. Second, direct human experience of that world becomes *intelligible* only because of specific creative mental powers within the individual. An external material world certainly exists prior to any human being's knowing of its existence. And that external world is the necessary source of the objects of human consciousness. But in another very important sense human subjectivity actively *creates* the form or the qualities which that external world will have if the external world is to be a conceptual (or perceptual) object *for a human being*. Thus, Marx clearly retains (in contrast to monistic materialism or monistic idealism) both sides of what we described as the epistemological dilemma.

The important distinction which we drew earlier between teleological and material causation, and hence between a human being as an *active, creative* causal force and as a passive inert effect of other environmental conditions or causes (both human and non-human) does not seem to be clearly spelled out in this and the previous several quotations. Rather, these quotations seem to focus more clearly on man as active creator of both himself and his environment. But to emphasize only this aspect of Marx to the exclusion of this theory of man as passive inert effect would be to severely distort his social philosophy (although the majority of the accounts of Marx go to the opposite extreme and emphasize the passive inert side of human existence to the exclusion of the free, active, and creative side of human beings).

For Marx human beings living and acting in society are simultaneously the active subjective creators of themselves and their society as well as the passive conditioned objective products of their society. This point is central to an understanding of Marx's critique of capitalism as well as his vision of socialism. He wrote: "just as society itself produces man as man, so is society produced by him."[9] This is because when man acts as an active, creative force the objects which he molds, shapes, affects, etc., are not simply inorganic material objects, they include human objects as well. Insofar as you are an object of my conscious will and actions (that is insofar as you are the material objectification of my human powers), you are passive inert effect. Insofar as I am the objectification of your human powers I am passive inert effect.

Thus, in Marx's notion of a mode of production, the physical techniques by which inorganic nature is reshaped or molded are not as significant as the relations among people whereby the social reshaping of nature by human beings is simultaneously a process of people acting upon (and being acted upon by) other people. In other words, the concept of the social relations of production incorporates the notion of human beings as active, conscious, teleological causal agents with the notion of human beings as passive recipients of external causes, i.e. as conditioned, effected objects. Thus, human productive activity always has two aspects: "one aspect of human activity [is] the *reshaping of nature by men*. The other aspect [is] the *reshaping of men by men*."[10]

The most significant error, in Marx's view, of those humanists (including Feuerbach) who viewed man *only* as active creator of his own life and circumstance, was that they forgot that man is always a social being, and hence always *effect* as well as *cause*. The particular nature of the social relations of production determines the degree to which man as passive effect of other men dominates man as active free cause, in other words, the degree to which the effects on me of other men's activities systematically prevent my own free development of all of my potential powers as a free, whole, human being. To just that degree, my work (or creative activity) will not be free, will occur against my will, and can stultify rather than develop my subjective powers, and prevent me from creating myself objectively through my activity:

> The fact is, therefore, that definite individuals who are productive in a definite way enter into these definite social and political relations... The social structure and the state are continually evolving out of the life-process of definite individuals... as they act, produce materially, and hence as they work under definite material limits, presuppositions and conditions independent of their will.[11]

This distinction of human beings as active, conscious, free creators and passive, conditioned products of social forces is generally misunderstood in Marx's writings. For Marx, so far as economics (or social science generally) functions as *science*, it takes human beings as pure objects, i.e. it considers them merely effects of material and social causes. The view that this notion of science is all there is in Marx's writings accounts for the widely held misconception that he has a rigidly deterministic theory. Marx himself was well aware that this approach was abstractly one-sided as is evidenced in the following quotation from the "Preface" to the first German edition of *Capital*:

> ...here individuals are dealt with only in so far as they are the personifications of economic categories, embodiments of particular class-relations and class interests. My standpoint, from which the evaluation of the economic formation is viewed as a process of natural history, can less than any other make the individual responsible for the relations whose creature he socially remains, however much he may subjectively raise himself above them.[12]

Here Marx is stating that he is *not* considering whole, real, living, actual individuals, but only individuals who are the "personifications" of intellectual categories, or mental abstractions. This appears to be precisely what he condemned Hegel for doing. But it is not. Only when we understand that aspect of our selves which is passive inert effect can we *use* this understanding as a means of functioning as free active creators of our own lives, of our own society. As Marx proclaimed in one of his most famous passages: "The philosophers have only *interpreted* the world in various ways; the *point is* to *change* it."[13]

This is a point of the utmost significance because it is here that Marx is most widely misunderstood. For Marx, as we have seen, human beings are both active creators of their own society and passively created products of that society. This represents in Marx a perpetually unresolved intellectual tension, because to the degree that human beings appear to be free creators they appear as other than unfree products or objects and to the degree that they appear as created objects they appear as other than free creators. Most thinkers (including most disciples of Marx) cannot maintain this intellectual tension, cannot see free creative human being and unfree created human being as separate and distinct (although reciprocally interrelated) but *equally real facets* of every human being. Most thinkers collapse one of these facets into the other, so that if free creative human being is given primacy, idealism is the result, and if unfree created human being is given primacy, mechanistic, scientistic materialism is the result.

Marx insisted on retaining this intellectual tension of accepting *both* aspects of human existence as equally real. He believed that the very nature of scientific theory was to see the objects of the theory as passive effects of prior causes. Therefore social science (including Marx's own) would always have to view human beings in an *abstract one-sided manner as determined objects*. Therefore in the above quotation from the "Preface" to *Capital*, he acknowledges that, *as social science*, his theory views individuals in their abstract one-sidedness.

But in so doing Marx was not reducing people to socially determined objects. He was *freely and creatively* attempting to understand one aspect of human existence in order that he and others in the socialist movement could *freely and creatively use* this understanding to change their social circumstances. So for Marx, the very impulse toward social scientific understanding can be an *instance* of free creative activity and the ultimate action-oriented end or purpose to which the understanding is put can be an instance of free creative activity.

The Epistemological Dualism Required for Theories of Human Freedom

Marx never formulated an epistemological theory upon which to base his social theory. By accepting the prevailing notion that social science could only understand human beings as passive effects of prior causes, he was, in effect, leaving all of his perceptive statements about free, active human creativity without an epistemological foundation. One of Marx's greatest merits, however, was his insistence on maintaining that human beings were simultaneously determined by external causes and active, free, creative, self-caused causes. He realized that the only possible solution to the epistemological dilemma was to leave this intellectual tension unresolved.

In this concluding section of my paper I shall assert that epistemological rationalism is the only possible foundation for humanistic social theory which retains the dilemma of the simultaneous concepts of plastic, passively created man and active, creative, autonomous man.

I have argued elsewhere that (1) most economic theories rest either explicitly or implicitly on rationalistic foundations, and that (2) rationalism provides an epistemological basis for the social sciences that is superior to empiricism.[14] While space limitations prevent me from making a case for rationalism in this paper, I shall merely state a few tenets of rationalism and briefly discuss their significance for humanistic social science.

First, all human rational cognitive activity is structured and the logical and linguistic forms of the structuring are amenable to *a priori* understanding. We can never understand these structural forms as the effects of environmental causes because an understanding of environmental objects and relationships requires these forms as a necessary precondition.

Second, sense perceptions that are comprehensible are mentally structured as a necessary precondition for their being objects of cognition. Again, empiricism or cause-effect analysis cannot explain that which is its own necessary precondition. The principles by which these perceptions are structured are amenable to *a priori* understanding.

Third, since the material environment within which humans function is only knowable through perception and cognition, and since our knowledge of the forms of comprehensible perception and correct cognitive processes is *a priori*, it follows that priori reason gives us some knowledge about the material world insofar as that world is comprehensible to us. In other words, I fully accept the age-old philosophical argument for *a priori* synthetic statements. Only because rationalism has been so caricatured and maligned is it necessary for me to add the obvious statement that most knowledge about the material world is also dependent upon contingent, sensuous experience, i.e. has an important *a posteriori* element.

Fourth, since some forms of human thought, such as, e.g., mathematics and logic, have both analytic and synthetic implications while being comprehensible *a priori,* and since these forms of thought are necessary for rational thinking and rational acting in the world, there is an important element in the rational thoughts or actions of other human beings which we can comprehend directly *without any knowledge whatsoever of empirical cause-effect relations.* Reason is its own explanation.

This fourth principle is of particular importance for my conclusion so I shall give one brief illustration. At the time of the writing of this paper the world chess championship is being played. Dozens of chess experts analyse and try to comprehend each move of each contender. When a contender makes a nonrational or an irrational move (i.e. a bad move) the experts attempt to explain the move by speculation about the causes of the move. The player was overly fatigued and so not thinking clearly; emotional stress resulted in the error, etc. But when a player makes the best possible move logic alone explains why it was the best possible move and hence why he made the move. Thus, rational thinking is its own explanation.

No amount of cause-effect analysis can explain rationality. Certainly we can give necessary conditions for rationality (e.g. certain necessary physiological functioning of the brain) but these conditions are never sufficient to be said to be the cause of rationality. People with perfectly healthy brains sometimes function irrationally.

Thus, we can return to Descartes' dilemma. We can understand human freedom and creativity without resorting to cause-effect explanations because rationality is its own explanation.

Humans are free to act rationally or not act rationally. When they act nonrationally or irrationally we can use cause-effect analysis to explain why their nonrational or irrational act took the particular form that it did (e.g. we may explain it as the effect of social-psychological conditioning). When they act rationally, however, we can directly comprehend the act because of our immediate *a priori* understanding of rationality.

What we can never fully comprehend, however, is the actual choice in which one freely acts rationally or fails to do so. To demand an explanation of this within my epistemological framework is to demand what is inherently impossible. This is because an explanation of the choice itself would have to be either a cause-effect explanation (which would render the free choice an illusion) or a rational explanation (which would obliterate the distinction between the rational and the irrational by making the irrational amenable to *a priori* rational understanding, i.e. making the irrational rational).

Thus, we may conclude that we understand free, creative acts because they are rational. Although, there does remain the problem of identifiability. A person may be acting as the passive effect of a prior cause and do the rational thing. For example, the chess player in his fatigue and anxiety may hurriedly move the first piece he can get his hand on without knowing that his move was the logically best move. This does not seem to me to be a very damaging problem, however. At worst we may occasionally erroneously identify an act as a free, rational act. The problem of identification is at least as great, if not greater, in understanding empirical cause-effect relationships.

My notion of rationality is drastically different from that encountered in conventional neoclassical economics. First, I believe that there is a crucial difference between means-rationality and end-rationality (which I shall discuss more fully below). Neo-classical rationality is limited entirely to means-rationality, i.e. *given* some end (or ends) and alternative means of achieving this end, neoclassical economists are concerned only with ascertaining the most rational means. Means-rationality generally reduces to the logic of constrained optima where the ends are given and means involve either explicit or implicit opportunity costs. Second, neoclassical means-rationality generally leaves no room for human freedom because this theory tautologically defines all action as rational. It may be the case that the consumer's over-riding end is to maximize his utility from his purchases or that the businessman's end is to maximize profit. Regardless of how elegantly the neoclassical economist logically deduces the necessary conditions for this maximization it remains possible (contrary to neoclassical textbooks) that the consumer or the businessman will not act rationally. Neoclassical theory explains only behavior in which (1) the agent's ends are narrowly predetermined, and (2) the agent inevitably chooses to act rationally.

Insofar as one is concerned with means-rationality only, neoclassical economists have done a great service by developing the abstract logic of constrained optima. But they have ignored the problem of freedom and, more importantly, they have ignored the problem of end-rationality. In doing so they have implicitly endorsed utility maximization and profit maximization as rational ends. The concern with these ends certainly has no empirical justification. We cannot say empirically whether people maximize utility because utility has no empirically identifiable meaning. Indeed, most neoclassical theory is so circular that utility is an imaginary abstraction which is always and constantly being maximized so that no institutional or descriptive data need ever enter their pure deductive theory of constrained optima. Empirically it is clear that some businessmen have profit maximization as their overriding end while others do not. Neo-classical economics gives no reason for exclusively concerning itself with the means-rationality of the profit maximizers and ignoring the others as either nonexistent or irrational.

Neoclassical economics gives little understanding of human behavior because (1) its version of means-rationality denies the agent the capacity to freely choose the rational means, and (2) it ignores end-rationality. Most other social scientists completely ignore rationality as an explanation of human action and rely on "hard" or "soft" models of plastic, determined man.

As soon as rationality is used as an explanation in the social sciences human ends and values become the foundation of social theory. When neoclassical economists take ends as given the normative importance given to rationality and efficiency impli-citly confers ethical and moral legitimacy to whatever ends are actually pursued as well as to the relative distribution of power and to the social-institutional means by which these ends are pursued in any given social situation. This is one of the primary reasons that neoclassical theory consistently supports the status quo. Thus, when the status quo is repressive or ethically repug-nant neoclassical theory becomes repressive and ethically re-pugnant. This is the consequence of the neoclassical theorists' refusal to admit end-rationality.

The distinction between means-rationality and end-rationality is a cognitive and a moral distinction of such significance that it is unfortunate that the word rationality is generally used in both cases. Thus, when an agent uses the most rational means of pursuing an irrational end, his action is means-rational and end-irrational. While means-rationality implies freedom and re-mains, at least in part, its own explanation, it implies a quali-tatively different form of freedom than is implied in end-ration-ality.

The person's ends, for example, may be dictated by the socially inculcated desire to always submit to and please those in authority. But regardless of how rationally the person pursues the means to these ends, if the ends are irrational there is always some moral sense in which the means share in the irrationality of the ends. Social scientists, for example, spend countless thousands of hours devising rational means of effecting human oppression and destruction. Surely from the standpoint of humanity such actions are irrational.

End-rationality is, in my view, epistemologically similar to means-rationality in that our knowledge of it is partly *a priori* and partly *a posterori*. The form of rational human ends is knowable *a priori* while much of the particular empirical content of the form can only be known *a posteriori*.

Because it would require a treatise on ethics to adequately defend this view, I shall merely indicate what I consider to be the *a priori* form of end-rationality and briefly discuss the implications for social theory. My view of the general form of the *a priori* content of end-rationalism is that every human being ought to, and ought to have the means to, freely create herself or himself such that she or he realizes fully all of the physical, emotional, esthetic and intellectual potential inherent in being human generally and inherent in being the particular individual human being that she or he is.

 I would argue that some version of this principle of *a priori* end-rationalism can be found in a whole succession of philosophers from Aristotle to John Dewey and Bertrand Russell. Even J. S. Mill who seemingly made utility maximization the ultimate human end implicitly accepted this principle when he wrote that famous caveat to his utilitarianism that it is better to be an unhappy Socrates than a satisfied fool. A large number of influential psychological theorists—including, among others, Carl Jung, Alfred Adler, Karen Horney, Erich Fromm, Carl Rogers, G. W. Allport, and Abraham Maslow—have concluded that no amount of simple, direct empirical observation can furnish an adequate scientific foundation for a theory of human behavior. Certain first principles, all of these theorists agree, must be given *a priori* and must come from introspection and immediate intuition. Moreover, several of these theorists agree that some notion (which is not derivable empirically) of a self-created, fully developed human being is a necessary prerequisite for a psychological understanding of human behavior. Maslow has, perhaps, given the greatest importance in his work to the notion of a self-created, fully developed human being. And while Maslow's empirical work on the characteristics of actual people who are "self-actualizing" and more fully developed might suggest that he has an empirically derived norm, it is clear that his choice of people to investigate required a pre-existing *a priori* model (however vaguely defined) of a self-created, fully developed human being.

The implications of this view for the social sciences should be obvious: First, rationality is its own explanation and the free human choice to act rationally can be explained in part simply by the rationality of the act (whether the rationality refers to means or ends). Second, social scientists are not an elite who freely study and evaluate the passive, determined responses of the plastic masses. Like all other human beings, social scientists sometimes act freely and rationally and sometimes behave and think as a passive consequence of prior causes. Third, because free, creative, self-actualization is, by definition, not merely the passive effect of external causes, social institutions can never cause a person to act freely, creatively and rationally. Social institutions may thwart freedom and rationality by making free, rational acts the object of harsh social consequences. But in doing so social institutions can be used to explain only the form of unfree and nonrational acts that are fostered by the institutions. Fourth, it follows that social engineering can only eliminate the social barriers to freedom and creativity. The freely self-actualized person is not the passive effect or the creation of an elite. End-rationality requires a much more radical democracy than is envisioned by most social scientists. Fifth, since human beings are social and as such are always both passive effects of the actions of other people and free active creators of their own selves and environments, the tension, antagonism, or contradiction between these two aspects of human existence can only be satisfactorily resolved if a communal, co-operative social setting in which the two antagonistic aspects of human nature are in harmony is conceived as an empirical possibility and a moral necessity—in an individualistic, competitive world one person's freedom generally rests on another person or persons' restrictions or lack of freedom.

If this view is accepted then social scientists can hope to understand both that human behavior which is the effect of prior causes and that human behavior which is free, creative and rational. Moreover, the understanding of rational behavior necessitates extensive inquiry into the human values implicit in end-rationality. And finally, the conclusion that is most likely to evoke the displeasure of my colleagues in the social sciences is that if the inquiries of the social scientists themselves are to be free, rational inquiries (having both means-rationality and end-rationality) they must be explicitly value laden; the social scientist must choose whether to adopt the mechanistic plastic man approach, the Sartrian plastic man approach of nihilistic relativism, or what I have called the humanist approach, and such a choice is a value judgement with enormously important practical and ethical implications; moreover, the theorist's inquiry, if it is truly free, must be but a part of a choice of the social scientist to freely act rationally in the world—which means it must be a part of an active effort to create those social conditions and institutions most conducive to end-rational, free human creativity. In the words of Karl Marx: "The philosophers have only *interpreted* the world in various ways; the *point is* to *change* it."

Notes

[1]Karl Marx and Frederick Engels, *The German Ideology*, in *Karl Marx, Frederick Engels, Collected Works (MECW)*, (New York: International Publishers, 1976), Vol. 5, p. 37.

[2]Karl Marx, "Theses on Feuerbach," in *MECW*, Vol. 5, 6.

[3]Karl Marx, *Economic and Philosophic Manuscripts of 1844, MECW*, Vol. 3, p. 299.

[4]*Ibid.*, pp. 275-276.

[5]*The German Ideology, op. cit.*, p. 42.

[6]*1844 Manuscripts, op. cit.*, p. 298.

[7]*Ibid.*, pp. 299-300.

[8]*Ibid.*, pp. 301-302.

[9]*Ibid.*, p. 298.

[10]*The German Ideology, op. cit.*, p. 50.

[11]*Ibid.*, pp. 35-36.

[12]Karl Marx, *Capital* (Moscow: Foreign Language Publishing House, 1961), Vol. 1, p. 10.

[13]"Theses on Feuerbach," *op. cit.*, p. 5.

[14]E. K. Hunt, "Rationalism and Empiricism in Economic Theories of Value", *The Social Science Journal*, Vol. 14, Oct., 1977, pp. 11-25.

On Marx and
Moralizing Social Science

Kai Nielsen, The University of Calgary

"D'où Venons-Nous? Que Sommes-Nous? Où Allons-Nous?"
Paul Gauguin

I

During the decade after the Second World War, in what might well be called the Stalinist phase of ordinary language philosophy, it was John Wisdom, I believe, who said of much traditional philosophy, that it was the manner, not the matter that stultifies. While I indeed feel somewhat edgy about the matter as well, it was just Wisdom's feeling about a certain kind of philosophy that overwhelmed me as I read Professor Hunt's article. It struck me, again and again, as being 'too philosophical', in the way that analytical philosophers, particularly during the therapeutic era, sought to expose and diagnose. I wish that Hunt had been more of a social scientist and had indulged in fewer philosophical meanderings, for I think when he grows philosophically expansive, he is, for the most part, simply badly confused and that these confusions obscure what perhaps has the potential of being a series of important points about some ways of proceeding in the social sciences.

Hunt's article is so replete with ambiguities, mischaracterizations of philosophical positions, unclarities and confusions, that to sort all this out would take an article even longer than his. I will spare you that, contenting myself with isolating two major philosophical perplexities which have so taken hold of him that he has created unnecessary problems for himself concerning the social sciences. I shall, in conclusion, turning to a quite different matter, point to a facet of Marx's work, which, if Hunt had taken it to heart, might have made him more cautious in making the claims he makes about social science and values.

It is evident enough from my tone that I am not in extensive sympathy with Hunt's account. This is surely true principally about his methodology and manner. There is in his essay simply too much bad metaphysics parading as a reflective elucidation of how to do social science. But in another way it is not so. We share a common conviction concerning the crucial importance of Marx and more specifically a common recognition of the importance of carefully cashing in on Marx's recognition that "human beings are both active creators of their own society and passively created products of that society". I also agree that social science, where it has any systematic or theoretical pretensions at all, cannot be *wertfrei*, that the exclusive concern with instrumental rationality has hobbled it, that its obsession with certain formalisms has often trivialized it, that human beings can in a perfectly straight-forward way act rationally and with self-consciousness control their own destinies, that it is crucial to understand man as a creator of his own self-conceptions and of his social environment and that the extent and way in which that is so is not unrelated to the distinctive kind of relations of production dominant in the society in which he lives.[1] Finally, I am in sympathy with Hunt's stress on developing a social science with a human face, a social science that will be a genuinely critical science of society and would not maintain a normatively neutral posture toward even the most deeply embedded social structures.[1] But I also believe that social scientists who tend to reject any or all of those positions would not likely be persuaded by Hunt's argumentation. We need far more in the way of argument and the marshalling of evidence and considerably less moralizing and freewheeling rhapsodizing.

Hunt's preoccupations with and confusions about a) deter-minism and what he calls 'rationalism' and b) about materialism/idealism (mind and body) lead him down the garden path. The former, I believe, is more crucial for us, but I shall first look at the latter briefly.

II

Descartes' dualism provides Hunt with his *entré* into his subject and he seeks to show how in Marx, thought not in the earlier mechanistic materialists, we finally resolve that problem. But it seems to me that it is in these domains, as well as in the discussion of the is/ought problem, where Marx is the least helpful. Here Marx, deeply indebted to Hegel, is not so much wrong as frustratingly obscure. Marx is important for what he said about alienation and human nature, method (his historical materialism), the specification and critique of ideology, the labour theory of value, for his dissection and critique of capital-ism, his theory of classes and class struggle, his revolutionary strategy and his conception of the relation of theory to practice. Marx's remarks about materialism, dualism, the problems Hunt flags as 'Descartes dilemma', a theory of truth and 'the conun-drum of epistemology' are all so vague and metaphorical and so cluttered with unexplicated metaphysical conceptions, that they are of no very great significance in thinking about these problems.

Hunt doesn't help us here. Consider just one of his allegedly elucidatory remarks. "Marx's materialism is simply the view that existence is not reducible to mental states. . . . While mental states are a part of the total of existing reality, there is another part of reality that is non-mental—i.e. material—which can never be reduced or collapsed into a mental state."[2] Surely, it is a commonplace to say that mental states are part of the total of existing reality and that there is another sort of reality that is non-mental. It is evident, as anything can be, that my thinking as I am writing this is one sort of thing—I didn't say 'one sort of stuff'—and the chair I am sitting in is another. But is my thinking a disposition to behave in a certain way, a certain firing of my central nervous system or what? What is it 'for mental states to be part of the existing reality'? Are they epiphenomenal to matter? Are they brain states? And what is this 'existing reality' anyway? Marx's thoughts were quite properly elsewhere and when he did say a few things about these matters, they were, as one might expect, unhelpful. And Engels was no improvement.

In spite of Wittgenstein, in spite of Austin, either the ghost *in* or *of* the machine has continued to haunt philosophers and, so it seems, certain social scientists. It is anything but clear what exactly should be said. Many of us have an abiding conviction that some form of materialism must be correct, if only we could say what that form is. But that may be the *Weltgeist* working on us. What is crucial to recognize is that such questions should not intrude into questions about proper method in the social sciences. (I am inclined, though somewhat more hesitantly, to believe that they should not even intrude into questions about the foundations of the social sciences, where questions concerning methodology and foundations are taken to be distinct.)

Hunt recognizes that there is a myth of the given and he rightly sees it as a myth. The classical empiricists were mistaken in thinking impressions came neat. Without conceptions they are blind, just as conceptions without impressions are empty. These, by now, Kantian commonplaces crank the machinery of metaphysics for Hunt. But why is it not enough for social scientists to say something like the following? Man is a language-using animal and the language he has reflects his needs and interests, just as his interests and needs are in turn for the most part not independent of his language (the ensemble of concepts he employs). In such a situation, the human animal categorizes his/her experience in certain distinctive ways, though this categorized experience—there is no pure given—in turn modifies his/her categories. Thinking and thought—or rather a large part of it—is reflected in, or perhaps even constituted by, the purposive activities of language-users and these activities are importantly different from matter in motion, e.g. working out a stratagem is very different than a ball rolling down an inclined plane. (It is over such issues that the work of Wittgenstein and the perspective he brings to philosophy is of inestimable importance. It is also work which is here, at least in large measure, perfectly assimilable by the Marxist tradition.)

There are, of course, a host of questions swept under the rug here—questions that, for certain philosophical purposes, we might want to probe, but, for the purposes of what Hunt calls a humanistic social science or indeed, for any social science at all, why can we not, and why should we not, rest content with such a rather minimal picture and ignore the great metaphysical questions concerning the nature of mind and matter?

III

I turn now to determinism, for I suspect that this is what really bothers Hunt, raising in him the fear that if we are determinists, we must also be fatalists denying freedom and rationality and the very possibility of an unalienated society.

Determinism is crudely the doctrine that every event and every action has a cause, or, slightly less crudely, the claim that for every state of affairs, as, for example, for every state of affairs of type D, there is some antecedent state of affairs of type C or states of affairs of types C, B and A, such that when states of affairs of type C occur or of C, B and A occur, then states of affairs of type D must occur, where the 'must' has the same force as the 'must' in 'If you decapitate a human being he must die'.

Hunt proceeds to confuse utterly what hard-determinism and soft-determinism are. In another jargon, he fails to distinguish between incompatibilism and compatibilism. Determinism, unlike compulsion or coercion or even being neurotic, does not admit of degrees. An event cannot be more or less determined. It is either determined or it is not, so it is nonsense to speak, as Hunt does, of 'rigid determinism'. 'Non-rigid determinism' is a contradiction in terms. Hard and soft determinists are equally determinists. They both agree that every event and every action has a cause. Where they disagree—something Hunt completely misses—is over the implications for freedom and autonomy which follow from determinism. Hard-determinists, such as Holbach and Schopenhauer, say that since determinism is true, freedom is an illusion. Soft-determinists, such as Hobbes, Hume and J. S. Mill, say that the determinism/indeterminism conflict has nothing to do with freedom of conduct or moral autonomy. Our actions can, and indeed do, have causal antecedents and we can be free, in the only sense that matters, for all of that. What makes us unfree—and this, unlike determinism or indeterminism, does admit of degrees

—is being coerced, compelled or constrained to do one thing rather than another. No doubt my preference for Burgundy over Bordeaux has causes but those causes do not compel. But when I cannot but have a drink, no matter what I resolve, those causes are, as well, compelling causes. I am, again, to put it roughly and in a way oversimply, free when I have a rational understanding of my wants and I am able to do what I want to do. When I have no such understanding or cannot do what I want to do because of coercion, constraint, compulsion, neurosis or ideological bamboozlement, I am not free. Again these things admit of degrees and there are varieties of constraints and different forms of compulsion. But the point is that all of this practical freedom of action and thought could take place even in a completely deterministic universe. As I remarked, these views were developed with considerable clarity by Hobbes, Hume and Mill. But, significantly enough for our purposes, rather more metaphysically ramified, though more obscure, versions of soft-determinism were developed by Spinoza and Hegel and it is these versions that would have more deeply influenced Marx. Marx's dominant interests were quite properly elsewhere and he is not very clear about these issues. But, as far as I can make out, Marx should be read as another soft-determinist.

Given what he says in his article, Hunt should respond that my above characterization of soft-determinism shows that soft-determinism isn't really genuinely deterministic, for in my analysis I appealed to the concept of rationality but that concept cannot be understood in deterministic terms.

However, that seems to me a mistake, and a rather important one at that, when we think of the logic of explanation in the social sciences. "Reason", Hunt tells us, "is its own explanation".[3] He points out, quite rightly, that typically we seek causal explanations for irrational acts or non-rational reactions but not for rational acts. When the great chess masters compete, chess experts analyze and try to comprehend each move of each contender. When a contender makes an obviously bad move—a move that is. irrational for him to make—the experts typically, quite properly seek a causal explanation. He was overly fatigued, rattled, distracted, the emotional stress was too great and the like. We typically look for things like that, utilizing in our pattern of explanation a causal account. But, Hunt rightly, though somewhat metaphorically, remarks that when "a player makes the best possible move, logic alone explains why it was the best possible move and hence why he made the move".[4] We use here, what Dray and Winch have called rational explanations rather than causal explanations.[5] We display, that is, the rationale of the action or cluster of actions. But that, given our distinctive explanatory interests in such contexts, we do not give causal explanations doesn't mean that we can't. We can, but typically don't, for there is no *point* in doing so. But this shows that we need not assume that these rational actions are really indeterministic and are without antecedent conditions sufficient to bring them about. Presumably there are certain antecedent conditions determining why one chap becomes rattled and acts irrationally and another chap does not but thinks out calmly what to do and does it. Hunt says 'No amount of cause-effect analysis can explain rationality'. But that needs, as Hunt partially recognizes, disambiguation. What would often be meant in such a context by 'understanding rationality' is just the ability to display a certain set of logical relations and, where that was not already understood, to exhibit the point of what was being done. This explaining of rationality is neither a causal nor a counter-causal notion. Such talk just doesn't apply in that context anymore than being red or green applies to heat. But there are causal conditions for the capacity to understand rationality and to respond rationally. In that way rationality—the occurrence and persistence of rationality—can be causally explained. There is no act or event or occurrence linked with the phenomena of rationality that is out of the causal network such that it would constitute a disconfirming instance of determinism. That A can understand a logical inference while B cannot has just as much a cause as the fact that A has pimples while B does not. And that there are causes here does not at all effect, one way or another, the validity of the pattern of inferences. It is simply not true that if determinism is true rationality totters. And it is simply false that it is inherently impossible, as Hunt believes, to causally explain why A acts rationally and B does not. There is nothing in principle at least standing in the way of doing so. If we understand the canons of rationality, we can, *a priori*, if you will, see that such and such follows from such and such. But why A has that capacity and B does not is, as I have remarked, under the causal net.

So Hunt has failed to establish that there are certain free, creative acts, the rational acts of autonomous human beings, which are acts which could not be causally explained. And so he has not shown that, because humans do characteristically act in this rational fashion, a) determinism is false and b) a humanistic social science must make non-deterministic assumptions. Moreover, it is his failure to understand soft-determinism which blinds him to the fact that such determinists can, perfectly consistently, accept moral autonomy—the kind of freedom we prize—and utilize patterns of explanation—explanations in terms of reasons

—without at all compromising their determinism. It is such patterns of explanation and interpretation that social science requires and not, as Hunt believes, a rejection of determinism.

IV

Finally, I want to touch on a quite different matter. Toward the end of his article, Hunt provides what he takes to be something of a 'moral foundation for Marxism' or, at least of as much of Marx's analysis as he wishes to appropriate. However, it is one thing to say that various social theories, if they have any pretensions at all to completeness, will have a schedule of values built into various parts of their theories, it is another thing again to stress that it is crucial for a social scientist to construct a treatise on ethics or at least on justice or, alternatively, to work, perhaps fresh from the philosopher's shop, such accounts into their social theories. It is also, as far as I can see, not particularly important, simply because the point is to change the world and not just to understand it, to commit oneself, as a fundamental postulate of practical reason, to the claim, articulated by Hunt, that "every human being ought to, and ought to have the means to, freely create herself or himself such that she or he realizes fully all of the physical, emotional, esthetic and intellectual potential inherent in being human generally and inherent in being the particular individual human being she or he is".[6] This is an expression of a fine moral sentiment, and as such, I, of course, have nothing but sympathy for it. But except perhaps as background beliefs, we do not, in doing social science, need to concern ourselves about articulating such ethical axioms. There is room in social science for a moral critique of capitalism and it is indeed important to make the case for the moral illegitimacy of capitalism. This is often too easily assumed on the Left. It is, moreover, a very scientific conception of social science which assumes that a moral critique of capitalism has no place in the domain of social science. But, unless it is integrated into a critical social theory, moral axioms such as Hunt's are wheels that turn no social science machinery.

Moreover, such a stress entirely neglects Marx's analysis of morality as ideology and his derisive remarks about certain political economists' twaddle about justice. Marx recognizes that, in very subtle ways, even 'progressive moral talk' often tends to have a pacifying effect which unwittingly supports the interests of the dominant class and he also realizes that moral talk typically more directly reflects the class interests of the dominant class. Even more to the point here, preoccupation with values deflects the social scientist's interests from what, both theoretically and practically, it is crucial for him to know, particularly if he wants to play as effective a role as possible in transforming society. I refer to his need to come to understand how capitalism works; that is, to expand on this and extend it a bit, he needs to know, if such knowledge can be had, how capitalism got to be what it is, what it is like now and how it is changing and under what conditions it will come tumbling down or can be made to come tumbling down and what general kind of society will, most likely, arise from its ruins. Preoccupation with norms and values—with ethics—tends to distract him from what is, or at least should be, most distinctively the work of at least one major branch of social science. Surely, Marx and Engels made value judgements all over the place, and many of them appear at least not to be excisable from their theories. (I am not suggesting it would be desirable to do so even if we could.) But this doesn't require an ethical theory or (perhaps) even a justification of a set of end-rational principles. It is enough to take the bourgeois at his word—to take, for example, very seriously the Rawlsian principle of equal respect for all persons—and then to ask under what conditions such a principle could be satisfied, to ask under what conditions we could have a society which maximizes equal liberty for all, including equal worth of liberty. The social scientist had better worry about whether some form of class society is really inevitable and whether, a la Michels, democracy is impossible in Twentieth Century Industrial Society. What we need, in thinking about what to do and how to live, are answers, if we can get them, to such questions. With such answers in hand, ordinary moral sensitivity, with or without moral theory, and ideological though it be, will, I suspect, suffice.

Notes

[1] I have argued some of these things in my "Is there an Emancipatory Rationality?", *Critica*, Vol. VIII, No. 24 (December, 1976) and my "Rationality, Needs and Politics", *Cultural Hermeneutics*, Vol. 4 (1977).

[2] E. K. Hunt, *Freedom, Necessity and Human Values*, p. 11.

[3] *Ibid.*, p. 30.

[4] *Ibid.*

[5] William Dray, *Laws and Explanation in History*, (Oxford, England: Oxford University Press, 1957), Peter Winch, *The Idea of a Social Science* (London, England: Routledge and Kegan Paul, 1958).

See as well the articles by Dray, Hempel, Nielsen and Scriven in Sidney Hook (ed.), *Philosophy and History*, (New York, New York: New York University Press, 1963).

[6] E. K. Hunt, *op. cit.*, pp. 34-5.

On the Self-Proclaimed Poverty of Philosophy

E. K. Hunt

*Thus the philosophers feel safe from all annoyances—the arro-
gance of inelegant classifications, for example. Thus, these Olympi-
ans conduct their affairs inside their patches of damp fog, so
conducive to mysteries and magical transmutations. If we do not
understand, they murmur: O cloud, my beautiful little cloud!*

———————————————————————————

*The philosopher would no doubt reply that the crude concrete
realities I have in mind—war, prostitution, work in the chemical
factories and in the mines—are not, strictly speaking, philosophical
and that, unfortunately, the laws of his profession prohibit him
from dealing with these subjects in any way. But on this point we
must be adamant. For the true objects of philosophy are none other
than the dangerous ones: the very realities the philosophers themselves refuse to pass judgement on.*

Paul Nizan, The Watchdogs: Philosophers
and the Established Order

It is not surprising that on the first page of his critique Professor
Nielsen characterizes my paper as ambiguous, misinformed,
unclear and confused because the remainder of his critique shows
that the issues discussed in my paper reached his consciousness in
a very confused, ambiguous and unclear state. It is possible that
some part of this utterly confused response originated in the
inadequacy of the initial communication. I leave it to the reader of
the paper, the critique and this response to decide that issue.

The objections to my paper are, in virtually every instance,
quite unrelated to the points I was endeavoring to make (indeed in
one place or another and in a most contradictory manner Professor Nielsen seems to concede agreement with most of my points).
For example, on page 7 he chides me for not giving the definition
of soft-determinism which he prefers and asserts I fail to understand the distinction between hard and soft-determinism. How
could I have failed to understand the distinction when the whole
purpose in discussing the two approaches in the original paper
was explicitly to deny that the commonly held notion of the distinction (of which Professor Nielsen strangely tells the reader I
was unaware) was of no practical consequence in social theory.
He then attempts to make the point (which he characterizes as
soft-determinism) "that the determinism/indeterminism conflict
has nothing to do with freedom of conduct or moral autonomy."
My supposed failure to understand Professor Nielsen's point is
taken as an illustration of my ignorance of philosophical Truth.

Indeed in his critique, the disciple of Moritz Schlick has elevated his master's opinion to an absolute philosophical Truth, not knowing that innumerable people, including myself and many philosophers utterly reject his master's opinion that all of this is a "pseudo-issue." Indeed his criticism could not have been leveled at me unless he believed that Schlick's position was an absolute Truth or unless he failed completely to comprehend what I was trying to communicate.

Another example of Nielsen's failure to even vaguely comprehend the issues with which I was grappling occurs on page 3, where he portrays me as grappling with Descartes' dualism. What I was in fact trying to communicate is that the issues that drove Descartes to his dualism are as important (and as generally unresolved) today as they were in Descartes' time. He utterly fails to comprehend the point I tried to make. He writes: "Surely, it is a commonplace to say that mental states are part of the total of existing reality and that there is another sort of reality that is non-mental." Of course it is commonplace. It is common sense. Every child knows it. What is *not* commonplace, and what Nielsen misses entirely is that this commonplace distinction has very important philosophical, theoretical and practical implications and that philosophers rarely (and social scientists even more rarely) explore the full meaning of these implications. Having missed this it is not surprising that he fails to appreciate my own modest attempt to explore some of these implications.

Nielsen's failure to comprehend the issues I was discussing would seem to call for a fairly short response in which the failure is simply pointed out, as I have done in the two previous paragraphs. His critique, however, is quite typical of a broader intellectual phenomenon which must be at least briefly discussed.

It is quite clear throughout his critique that he believes that social scientists do not need to concern themselves with ontology, axiology and epistemology, i.e., with the core of philosophy. But, as I have argued in my paper, since every theory rests on ontological, axiological and epistemological foundations, Professor Nielsen's point of view reduces to the view that these foundations are unimportant. And since these foundations generally have no significance except for that derived from the significance of the theories they support, this view is tantamount to asserting the insignificance and triviality of philosophy. I assert that the traditional concerns of philosophy are of very great significance, although if philosophy is defined empirically as being merely the typical concerns of contemporary academic professors of philosophy then in general (but by no means always) I think Professor Nielsen's low opinion is empirically justified. But I believe that this involves a confusion, however, between contemporary academic philosophy and traditional philosophical concerns.

Having been institutionally "stripped" of much of the concrete subject matter of traditional philosophy by the physical and social sciences, academic philosophers were "left" with only the issues of the ontological, axiological and epistemological foundations of ideas dealt with in other disciplines (and indeed academic sociology and psychology have largely taken over many of the traditional epistemological issues).

But academic specialization has resulted in such a drastic separation of theory from its philosophical foundations that philosophers have, by and large, treated the study of ontology, axiology and epistemology as an end in itself quite unrelated to any superstructure of theory.

Within this impoverished intellectual context, philosophers have found that penetrating objections can be leveled against, and numerous conundrums are encountered within, virtually every approach to ontology, axiology and epistemology. Without recourse to the superstructure of theory, such objections and conundrums seem decisive for every approach to these issues. Consequently every good, sophisticated academic philosopher studies these various approaches together with the relevant objections and conundrums and concludes that only the naive person unschooled in academic philosophy ever adopts and defends any intellectual position in ontological, axiological and epistemological questions.

For them the very study of philosophy destroys its claim to any significance and they are typically reduced to players of esoteric, logical games or linguistic nitpickers preoccupied with definitions, semantics, syntax, etc., seemingly convinced that philosophical desputation would cease if we all used good logic and communicated effectively.

Within the context of criticizing my views on the epistemological and axiological implications of ontological presuppositions Professor Nielsen writes that "What is crucial is that such questions should not intrude into questions about proper method in the social sciences." We are given no reason why these issues *"should not"* be "proper". Obviously Professor Nielsen's use of these normative terms does not reflect his view that "preoccupation with norms and values—with ethics tends to distract...[one] from what... *should be* most distinctively the work of at least one major branch of social science." Why *should* it? Did Professor Nielsen have a religious vision? It would seem so because he is convinced that good Marxist theory "doesn't require an ethical theory or (perhaps) even a justification of a set of end-rational principles."

One line of his critique sums up Professor Nielsen's overall attitude toward inquiry into the philosophical foundations of social theory: "... for any social science at all, why can we not, and why should we not, rest content with ... a rather minimal picture and ignore the great metaphysical questions ...?" In other words, of what practical importance is philosophy? Why, of none at all!

I have briefly indicated in my paper what I consider to be some of the significant practical and theoretical outcomes of determinism in the social sciences. And Professor Nielsen's defense of determinism combined with the general tenor of the remainder of his comments reconfirms my conviction. Thinkers who assert that the philosophical foundations of social theory should go unexamined because they are unimportant generally desire simply to avoid serious criticism of their own ontological, axiological and epistemological premises.

It is obvious to anyone who has read any of Marx's works, including the *Poverty of Philosophy*, that he took philosophical issues very seriously—despite Professor Nielsen's assertion to the contrary. Like Marx I believe that ontological, epistemological and axiological premises are of central importance in any social theory. For this reason I believe that to the degree that Professor Nielsen is at all typical of academic philosophers, social scientists must conclude that philosophy is much too important to be left to the philosophers.

The Notion of a Social Science

I. C. Jarvie, York University

As a philosopher of the social sciences, addressing a symposium
on recent approaches to the social sciences, I reflexively ask, what
is it about the social sciences that leads them again and again to
reflect upon themselves, that has even given rise to specialists in
such self-reflection, for example myself, and frequent invitations
to them to renew and restate their inquiry? My answer to this
question is that the social sciences are haunted by the example of
the natural sciences, and the philosopher of the social sciences is
an exorcist, a specialist in getting rid of ghosts, who performs an
exorcism ceremony consisting of reflections on the state of the art.
However ironic this sounds, it is seriously meant. In the course of
today's exorcism ceremony I hope to invoke some exciting recent
work in the philosophy of the social sciences, work which helps
me at least to combat and dispel the haunting effect of the natural
sciences. Such recent work is important less because it devises new
positions and more because it breaks down some old polarities
and distinctions, one of the most pernicious of which is the very
demarcation between the natural and the social. To stop the
haunting it is necessary to show that the ghostly phenomena are
perfectly understandable, unmysterious events in this world.

My paper advances through several distinct stages. To begin
with, I want to back up my claim that we in the social sciences are
haunted by the example of the natural sciences. Following that I
shall sketch various observable reactions to that haunting. Only
then shall I be in a position to attempt my exorcism. This will
consist in various arguments that criticize the usual distinction
between the natural and the social sciences. Instead, I suggest we
should view the scientific enterprise as a unified whole, and hence
draw any distinction between what is natural and what is social
within the unified enterprise of science. The differences, if any,
between the natural and the social then become a subject of
empirical investigation, rather than an *a priori* or metaphysical
demarcation between two sorts of sciences, natural and social.
Moving between methodological, metaphysical, and quasi-
historical arguments, the paper may not always strike you as
decisive. So be it. To add what plausibility I can I shall also
endeavour to show how what are conventionally thought of as the
natural and the social constantly intermingle, and that the
distinction between them, if any, has as a matter of fact to be
worked out in any science as it goes along.

I
Haunted by Natural Science

Throughout the modern era all of man's cognitive efforts have been undertaken in the dominating shadow of the success of the natural sciences—in a situation somewhat similar to that in which some scholars claim Greek thinkers laboured under the shadow of the success of mathematics.[1] By almost any criterion you cared to set up, physics, chemistry and biology were in their turn successful: by criteria of practical applicability, predictive power, simplicity, abstraction, mechanization, explanation of the puzzling, whatever. Accepting for the sake of the argument the received view of the Middle Ages as a time of social, political and cognitive stagnation; and also the received view of the sixteenth and subsequent centuries as ones of great social, political and cognitive change; we cannot but notice the vast number of books, pamphlets and broadsheets that appeared in the post-Medieval period. It was a time of religious, social and political upheaval, that was expressed in these writings, writings to which much of contemporary political science, economics, anthropology, psychology and sociology can be traced back. Despite these roots into the fairly distant past, it is often said that our cognitive endeavours in the social field are feeble compared to those in the natural sciences. Sometimes, in a spirit of charity, an exception to this generalization is made for economics. Otherwise, the social sciences are often declared to fall short of the natural sciences by the same criteria of success: practical applicability, predictive power, simplicity, abstraction, mechanization, explanation of the puzzling, etc. Above all, by the criterion of cumulative progress, it is held that the social sciences compare poorly to the natural sciences.[2] More *natural* phenomena are explainable today than was the case in 1578; it is at least arguable whether more *social* phenomena are explainable today than in 1578. To offer the excuse that these subjects are new is scarcely credible, since their problems and therefore speculation on their problems has to be as old as speculation of any kind. To explain their poor performance by their youth may be to put the cart before the horse. They appear not to be mature, but since they have longevity we cannot infer to their youth.

Several responses to this perceived state of affairs are possible, and each of them has from time to time been adopted. One is to endeavour to build social sciences that meet some or all of the criteria for success mentioned above. This is *naturalism*. It accepts that the criteria for success in natural science are applicable *pari passu* to the social sciences. Another response is to question the

appropriateness of these criteria for success and hence of the use of
the natural sciences as a model for the social sciences. *This is anti-
naturalism.* A third response is very radical: to suggest that the
way the social is studied, albeit fragmentary as yet, might be taken
as a model for the natural sciences, rather than *vice versa*. Different criteria of success may be invoked; indeed, treating success
as a virtue may be questioned. Science is a human activity,
perhaps, and should be judged as such, not be encouraged to be a
cold and mechanical calculation. If I were a punster I would call
this holding up of the social as a model for the study of the
natural—parallelling naturalism—socialism. However, that
word having been preempted for other purposes, I will choose
humanism.

I have started with the historical situation created for social
studies by the existence of developed natural sciences. That is
supposed to be the situation of the modern period, even if it is not
the situation of the ancient period. But this way of talking of
things presupposes, implicitly if not explicitly, an unproblematic
demarcation between the natural world and the social world, and
hence between studies of the natural and studies of the social.[3]
Notice that naturalism, anti-naturalism and humanism all accept
that there are natural studies and there are human studies.
Whether one should ape the other, as naturalism and humanism
maintain, or they should go their separate ways—as anti-
naturalism maintains, it is acknowledged that they are separate
and distinct. This is an assumption in common that I shall
challenge. For the moment it is enough to notice it and to stress its
philosophical and historical importance. Its key component is
that although the study of nature is an endeavour undertaken by
human beings, it is not just another social activity. It has an
autonomy and separateness all its own.

When Copernicus, Kepler, Galileo and Newton worked on
celestial and terrestrial mechanics, they did not bother to suit their
findings to harmonize with such social factors as public opinion,
morality, taboo, status and power.[4] On the contrary, they urged
the autonomy of the scientific enterprise whatever offence it gave
to its sponsors or the authorities. The received views they opposed
usually meshed neatly into the existing social fabric, and they
could hardly fail to be aware of the repercussions their ideas might
have on that delicate material were they to be taken seriously.
Pious men, on the whole, by no means social outcasts, if they were
accused of upsetting the social order their ultimate defence was
that the social order was one thing and the order of nature (the
facts) was another thing.[5] The attempt to establish this demarcation was a cognitive break of the greatest magnitude: science and

the scientists were held to get their authority not from the powers that be in the society they inhabited, but in some way directly from nature itself.[6]

The result was an incredible success. As Bacon had forecast, if science made a radical break with the past and asserted its autonomy from all worldly authorities, and trusted only to every man's innate talent for inquiry, it would flourish.[7] Within a generation of Bacon's death, Newton had appeared with an achievement that dwarfs most others in the intellectual history of mankind.[8] This triumph for the mechanization of the world picture[9] even moved some philosophers to argue for the mechanization of man. My point, however, is to note that no Newton appeared to dominate the study of society, despite the greatness of those who dabbled in the social sciences such as Plato, Aristotle, St. Augustine, Hobbes, Locke, Mandeville, Smith, Comte, Tocqueville, Mill, Marx, etc.

II
The Demarcation Between Natural and Social

Ironically, the process I might call the secularization of cognition was reinforced by means of ingenious theological arguments to the effect that scientific investigation was legitimate because it was a carrying out of God's will. God has made the natural world and man as a part of that world, and he has endowed us with the God-like capacity to study and understand his creation. This study of creation should of course include man and his works, including his social life. But somewhere along the line this argument wouldn't quite go through; social life is intractably separate from the rest of creation. I don't know whether the reason for this is the introduction of the factor of free will, thus demarcating man and his works in some decisive way from the rest of natural creation, or whether it goes back to the distinction we find so clearly in Ancient Greece between nature, what is given, and convention, what man has wrought. Those thinkers who tried to assimilate man and social studies to the general study of God's creation were often not believers in God at all, such as La Mettrie, who wrote *L'Homme Machine*, and Comte, who saw sociology, the natural science of society, as the queen of the sciences, and moreover a queen who would give birth to a new nature-worshipping religion.

The distinction between nature and convention, on which I shall concentrate, seems roughly to be this. What is natural is what cannot be otherwise, what is ruled by natural law. All creation is subject to this rule. Natural law, however, does not prescribe for all situations. There is leeway, there are contingencies. In particular, men can manipulate certain things themselves. This is the realm of convention, things that are thus and so only because men have made them so, and, where they want them to be different, they can be.

If you like, then, I can trace back the notion of a social science as something distinct from a natural science to the view that the social or conventional is something metaphysically distinct from nature in general. I cannot today give a scholarly history of this distinction. Clearly, it is controversial. Some naturalists want to repudiate it and suggest that natural laws govern all phenomena, that there will one day be a social physics, that we are simply rather behindhand in developing it. This argument is hard to sustain, for it is almost certainly going to have to fall back on some special qualities of the social as opposed to the natural in order to explain the relative backwardness of social studies, yet that is the very distinction it seeks to overcome.

In his important recent book *Legitimation of Belief* Ernest Gellner has stressed the other side. He maintains that once upon a time all cognition was social, as it still is in many less developed societies, including less developed sub-societies within our society. His view is that as far as cognitive success is concerned most of these world views were much of a muchness: while some may have been marginally better than others at gaining power over nature, the gap between them and the scientific world picture is enormous. On these pre-scientific views everything is in our terms conventional: the world picture saturates all explanations of events which, if not the product of human volition and action, are then the product of animate forces like witchcraft and magic, or capricious spirits like gods. Withal, there are no iron laws of nature detached from the manipulations of the social world. The great breakthrough, or ditch as Gellner calls it, is between this antediluvian view, and the view that the natural world is rational, non-magical, non-enchanted, non-manipulable, is the way it is without reference to human social arrangements, wishes, values, religious beliefs and practices, power structures, hopes, or what have you. So long as man took himself and his miracles and magic as the measure for all things he did not get very far; indeed it was easy to lose ground. The Middle Ages might have had less knowledge than the Greeks. Social conditions immediately before the scientific and industrial revolutions may have been worse than in Neanderthal times. A major shift in cognitive outlook was needed. Instead of the meaningless proliferation of rival attempts at understanding by rival social systems, crossing the big ditch enables mankind to cooperate and make progress in his cognitive endeavours. Once the assimilation of nature to convention was broken, that made possible the scientific revolution, the industrial revolution it in turn made possible, and the immense progress in the growth of wealth, power, human longevity and so on which make us hesitate any longer to deny that we are better off than our Neanderthal ancestors.

Gellner's vision that it is our achievement of a concept of nature beyond our control, yet rationally intelligible, that makes possible the enormous improvement of cognition and of life, is one I fully accept. What, I now ask, are its consequences for the social sciences? They are, so far as I can see, innocuous enough. It follows from Gellner's view that the demarcation between what is under human control and what is not is of the greatest importance, and that studying the emergence and consequences of the great transition is a central problem.[10] The line between nature and convention is not a given.

Also of late there have been a number of writers called the socio-biologists who have presented other arguments for attacking the distinction between nature and convention. It is an obvious enough line of thought. Mankind is part of natural creation; has, for long, evolved under the control of natural forces; and may still be far more their creature than his delusions about free will, moral autonomy, God-given capacity to understand and control nature would allow. Great play is made with the fact that our final physiological form seems to have been fixed when our mode of livelihood was as roaming bands of hunters and gatherers. How far this argument is to be taken depends on the specific individual thinker you look at. For my purposes, all I need is to stress how the drift of the position is again to emphasize that far more of social life can be explained by reference to natural conditions than was thought by those inclined to separate nature and society sharply.[11]

Without associating myself with the socio-biologists' project in general, I do want to go along with them in their downplaying of the gap between the natural and the social. Yet I also want to accept Gellner's crucial point about the great difference the discovery of non-anthropomorphic nature made. Perhaps what I really want to quarrel with is the metaphysical separation of nature and convention. By this I mean a sharp demarcation between the two settled on before scientific inquiry begins: The idea that the phenomena of the world can be unproblematically classified into natural and social, natural or conventional. My general philosophical position is that the identification of phenomena is a product of our theories and that *a fortiori* the classification of the phenomena identified is also under the control of our theories. These issues are not prior to theory.

To signal what I shall be arguing for requires me to say this. There is indeed only one scientific enterprise: science is a unity.[12] However, the problems we face, and the theories we devise to solve them, from time to time lead us to make distinctions such as that between nature and convention. Our views on these distinctions change from time to time just as do our theories. Perhaps the line between the natural and the conventional is itself conventional, i.e. not laid down in advance, not itself natural, but a function of our intellectual and practical interests. As we pursue these, we from time to time find it convenient to note how some aspect of the natural world is not amenable to this or that theory or practice. We then assign it to some special category, social or whatever, and explore it separately. For a very long time now we have concentrated our theoretical endeavours on what we call the natural world, i.e. those aspects of nature we found most readily assimilable to abstract and general laws. Social, political and economic matters have been dealt with on a practical rather than a theoretical level. Yet all the laws of physics, chemistry and biology are of course obeyed by human beings, indeed some of what it has become possible for societies to accomplish has been possible only because of that understanding of the natural constraints on man which enables him to turn them to his advantage.

For example, it was once thought to be impossible for men to fly; or impossible for them to fly outside the atmosphere; or impossible to fly to the moon; or impossible to fly to the sun. Where the line of possibility would be drawn now is moot. Most likely we would say it is impossible to fly to the sun, but how near we can get, like how near to absolute zero, how near to the speed of light, how far we can shave away at the time it takes to run a mile, these are not absolute given values. The limits nature places on us are yet to be mapped.

III
Responses in Detail

I will put a little flesh on that sketch of my own view later in this paper. For now, I want to contrast it with the various other approaches to the problem of the feebleness of social science vis-à-vis natural science. Let me do this with an eye on the social science I know and appreciate most, anthropology. The three responses I mentioned earlier, naturalism, anti-naturalism, and radicalistic humanism, have all played over anthropology. Theoreticians as various as the structural-functionalist Radcliffe-Brown and the cultural materialist Leslie White have offered the naturalistic programme of 'a natural science of society.'[13] Their conception of natural science was a positivistic one, and hence they searched for a data base, for a method, and for fundamental categories of cognitive organization. The data base was to be empirical facts about human social and cultural life collected by direct contact in the field with the societies and cultures concerned, the method was to generalize these field findings in the inductive direction, and the fundamental categories were left in dispute. White wanted a holistic science of culture; Radcliffe-Brown wanted a holistic, structuralist science of society. An anti-naturalist backlash was to be expected.

Around 1950 the late great British anthropologist E. E. Evans-Pritchard, later to be dubbed Sir Edward by his Queen, rose up against this well-established scientism and argued that social studies, concerned as they were with the life of man, should take as their model the humanities, and especially history.[14] He poured scorn on the scientific pretensions of the positivists, especially Durkheim (presumably a stalking-horse for his then still-living predecessor Radcliffe-Brown) for seeking a science of society yet not being able to produce a single example of a law of anthropology.[15] He hinted that social studies dealt in meanings as much as fact, but he continued to endorse intense field study as the only method of coming to grips with the true meaning of social events. It was an irony to see one of the most gifted contributors to theoretical social anthropology arguing that his subject was not a science after all. Underlying his arguments seemed to lurk a deep respect for human autonomy; the idea that it was presumptuous for social scientists to reduce and explain human behaviour on the model of inanimate nature. From the provenance of a later lecture one could deduce that there were religious convictions underpinning these views.[16]

As to radicalist humanism, of late, some social scientists have turned the tables completely and argued that the human sciences have much to teach the natural sciences. Gellner has suggested that this is part of a general anti-scientific revolt, a rejection of the cold, mechanical and comfortless world picture offered by natural science, and an attempt to re-enchant the world and make it warm, cosy and human once again. This line of attack is not the exclusive property of one school or group, it is widely diffused. Although few go so far as to want to re-enchant physics and chemistry, to bring in gods, spirits, magic, ESP or human volition, there is an impulse of that kind at work. Strength is drawn from what can only be described as the de-bunking of science by social studies of science. From Robert Merton[17] to Thomas Kuhn,[18] all unwittingly at first, social studies of science have demystified it; have said scientists dazzle us with their tricks, but, like stage musicians, they are really no more than extremely skilled ordinary human beings, organized in understandable, even standard ways, with all the characteristics and foibles of any social group. The triumphs of science are to a considerable extent attributable to that organization. The most radical proponents of this view go so far as to suggest that what the social organization of science does is to construct reality, thus making the study and mastery of it something of a foregone conclusion. The reality it copes with is only *a* reality, not the reality; there is on this view, sometimes called 'the radical programme in the sociology of science,' no such thing as reality as such.[19]

What are the positions of the naturalists, anti-naturalists and radical humanists on the question of the demarcation between nature and convention? The radical humanists are close to assimilating everything to convention. This move is surprisingly simple. What man does is convention, what man knows is part of what man does, therefore what man knows is convention(al). A total cognitive relativism is inescapable, and often imperturbably embraced. The anti-naturalists want to preserve the soul of man and his works from assimilation to the rest of nature. Nature as portrayed in science they see as cold, deterministic, amoral, aspiritual, irreligious. But man groups himself into society for warmth and support, to gain control over hostile nature, and characteristically develops morality, spirituality and religion. Comforting as this view is, its consequences for social studies are rather grave. The project of man gaining a general understanding of himself and his works in order, among other things, to improve his life in society is set back. If history is to be the model of the social sciences, one can only gloomily recall Hegel's apothegm: the only thing we learn from history is that no one ever learns from history.[20]

In continuing to press the project of sciences of society, united with rather than hauntedly separate from natural sciences, I would offer as their aim that of learning from experience in a systematic, progressive and hence transmittable manner: quantitative where appropriate, qualitative where called for. What I would like to do is rehabilitate the naturalism of Radcliffe-Brown and White, while jettisoning its positivist and inductivist baggage. What I like about the approach is that it neither ends up in a relativism of unassessable conventions, nor does it have to rely on an uneasy metaphysical demarcation between cold, mechanical, push-pull nature and warm, organic, spiritual man. What it does, rather, is to investigate the limits of nature and map the extent of convention *as part of its scientific approach.* Bronislaw Malinowski, for example, tried to link basic human biological needs with diverse arrays of social conventions; the diversity, he argued, was simplified if one saw each variation as simply a grace-note on the themes of food, shelter, defence and reproduction.

In criticism of this, Radcliffe-Brown stressed its triviality, since, by definition, societies that did not satisfy the basic human biological needs of their members would not have any humans around with needs to satisfy, still less with social institutions to explain. In place of Malinowski's biological explanation of society Radcliffe-Brown argued for a subtler and more shaded picture. Of course, he did not deny that all social systems are devices for coping with the basic problems involved in human survival. Perhaps, however, man was not free to devise any old social conventions he pleased. Certainly, such social conventions as were observable by anthropologists and reported in historical documents revealed a very wide diversity; but closer scrutiny of the evidence revealed certain themes and patterns widely separated by time and place that might portend there were constraints on human social ingenuity, rules or even principles that had to be followed for social arrangements to work. Within the conventional, then, there might be inescapable patterns and connections. This subtle blending of nature understood as what could not be otherwise because ruled by law, with convention understood as what man can alter, but not to his heart's content, strikes me as a model for the human sciences. Man is, to be trite, part of nature. It can be argued that he is unique in having the capacity to grasp nature, to turn its inexorabilities to his own uses, and to discover within it degrees of freedom and of necessity, and to adapt his actions accordingly. Social scientists, then, in making a commitment to the metaphysics of determinism, or materialism, or relativism are preempting their own task and choices, they are even foreclosing issues that are part of their empirical work. If Radcliffe-Brown is right that there are limited degrees of freedom in the patterning of kinship systems, e.g., we learn something important about our own options and about other societies. His hypothesis already bore fruit in the form of enlightening studies of puzzling matters in Homer and the Old Testament.[21]

So much for anthropology. What of other social sciences? A few inconclusive words about some of the other social sciences is all I dare venture before an audience as distinguished as this one. A great economist like Keynes is great, one might argue, because he altered the lines between nature and convention, between what is given and what can be manipulated. In particular, he repudiated the view that the business cycle was an inevitability which just had to be let run its course. Psychologists and political scientists who adopt behaviourism as an article of faith avoid, I would have thought, the main task, namely offering theories about minds and politics respectively, theories which contain ideas about the line between nature and convention. In the end, the problem of drawing the line between nature and convention in the case of the human mind may be one of the deepest in human intellectual inquiry, so difficult that it provokes men to despair or to mysticism. In their recent book on the body-mind problem, one of the key interfaces of the control of nature and the limits of human autonomy, Eccles and Popper confess that the problem may be inherently insoluble.

> The problem of the relation between our bodies and our minds, and especially of the link between brain structures and processes on the one hand and mental dispositions and events on the other is an exceedingly difficult one. Without pretending to be able to foresee future developments, both the authors of this book think it improbable that the problem will ever be solved, in the sense that we shall really understand this relation. We think that no more can be expected than to make a little progress here or there.[22]

Progress will consist of chipping away at a block of ignorance so vast that we can no more expect to live to see it as a finished sculpture than we can expect to see a three-minute mile just because runners keep on trimming fractions of a second off the present record.

IV
Conclusion

To sum up, then, the notion of a social science that I have tried to formulate here is one which does not stand in awe of, or attempt to ape, the natural sciences. Rather it is one that accepts the methodological unity of science because of the metaphysical unity of the world. Science is simply critical inquiry, into whatever problems interest us, with empirical tests as its cutting edge. A fundamental problem that interests us is that of drawing the line between what cannot be otherwise (nature) and what can be otherwise (convention). What cannot be otherwise constrains what can be. Men believe that they straddle this line both as individuals and as social beings. As man tries to live in harmony with nature, so the social sciences need to live in harmony with, even symbiotically with, the natural sciences. This concludes the exorcism.

Notes

[1]See K. R. Popper, 'The Nature of Philosophical Problems and their Roots in Science,' *British Journal for the Philosophy of Science*, 3, 1952, 124-56; reprinted in *Conjectures and Refutations*, London 1963, chapter 2.

[2]There are even those who maintain that there is no social science at all, the whole thing is merely a pretentious redescription of the application of common sense to the affairs of man. See A. R. Louch, *Explanation and Human Action*, Berkeley and Los Angeles 1966. For a vigorous critique see Ernest Gellner, 'A Wittgensteinian Philosophy of (or Against) the Social Sciences,' *Philosophy of the Social Sciences*, 5, 1975, 173-99.

[3]See chapter 5, 'Nature and Convention,' of K. R. Popper, *The Open Society and Its Enemies*, London 1945 et seq. Also, G. H. Von Wright, 'What is Humanism?' The Lindley Lecture, University of Kansas 1977; and J. Agassi, *Towards a Rational Philosophical Anthropology*, The Hague 1977.

[4]This viewpoint is forcefully urged by Ernest Gellner in his pathbreaking *Legitimation of Belief* (Cambridge 1974):

> In a traditional belief-system, cognition, the discovery of endorsement of beliefs, is an event in the world, and this means the social and moral world. Hence they are subject to the same kinds of obligations and sanctions as are other kinds of conduct.... Man the knower is not alienated from the citizen and the moral being. At this point, it is...hard not to suppose that in one sense the traditional outlooks are correct: we do not believe that our cognitive activities are *really* extra-territorial, are qualitatively distinct from the rest of our lives. Nevertheless, as Kant pointed out, we assume (contrary to all consistency) that such extra-territoriality does in fact obtain, and our attributions of 'objective validity' to our own thinking hinges on this odd assumption. (P. 166)

[5]One thinks of the beautiful story, whether apocryphal or not, of Galileo under the greatest pressure to recant and admit error, murmuring of the earth, 'and yet it moves.'

[6]Cf. Ernest Gellner, 'The Pure Enquirer,' in *Spectacles and Predicaments*, Cambridge 1979; and P. K. Feyerabend, *Against Method*, London 1975, p. 46.

[7]Francis Bacon, *Novum Organum*, London 1620, Aph. CXI-XCIII, CXXII.

[8]Alexander Pope wrote:
Nature and Nature's laws lay hid in night:
God said, Let Newton be! and all was light.

[9]See E. J. Dijksterhuis, *The Mechanization of the World Picture*, Oxford 1961.

[10]See his *Thought and Change*, London 1964.

[11]E. O. Wilson, *Sociobiology*, Cambridge 1975; for criticism see Michael Ruse, *Sociology: Sense or Nonsense*, Boston 1979.

[12]J. Agassi, *Science in Flux*, Dordrecht 1975, chap. 18.

[13]A. R. Radcliffe-Brown, *A Natural Science of Society*, Glencoe 1957; Leslie A. White, *The Science of Culture*, New York 1949.

[14]E. E. Evans-Pritchard, 'Social Anthropology: Past and Present,' *Man*, 50, 118-24; also in his *Essays in Social Anthropology*, London 1962.

[15]Op. cit., p. 20 in *Essays*.

[16]E. E. Evans-Pritchard, 'Religion and the Anthropologists,' The Aquinas Lecture, 1959, *Essays in Social Anthropology*, London 1962.

[17]Robert K. Merton, 'The Sociology of Science: An Episodic Memoir,' in Robert K. Merton and Jerry Gaston, eds., *The Sociology of Science in Europe*, Carbondale 1977.

[18]Thomas Kuhn, *The Structure of Scientific Revolutions*, Chicago 1962.

[19]Especially those who might be called the Edinburgh Relativists, grouped around the journal *Social Studies of Science*. See John Law, 'Is Epistemology Redundant? A Sociological View,' *Philosophy of the Social Sciences*, 5, 1975, 317-37; John Dean, 'Empiricism and Relativism—A Re-Appraisal of Two Key Concepts in the Social Sciences,' *Philosophy of the Social Sciences*, 8, 1978, 281-88; Barry Barnes, *Scientific Knowledge and Sociological Theory*, London 1974; David Bloor, *Knowledge and Social Imagery*, London 1976. Some criticisms are offered by Roger Trigg in 'The Sociology of Knowledge,' *Philosophy of the Social Sciences*, 8, 1978, 289-98.

[20]G. W. F. Hegel, Introduction to *Philosophy of History*: 'What experience and history teach is this—that people and governments never have learned anything from history, or acted on principles deduced from it.'

[21]For Homer see M. I. Finley, *The World of Odysseus*, London 1956 and S. C. Humphreys, *Anthropology and the Greeks*, London 1978; for the Old Testament, see Isaac Schapera, 'The Sin of Cain,' *Journal of the Royal Anthropological Institute*, 85, 1955, 33-43.

[22]Sir John Eccles and Sir Karl Popper, *The Self and Its Brain*, New York 1977.

The Unity of Science:
A Few Observations
Prompted by Professor Jarvie's Paper*

Ken Reshaur, University of Manitoba

I should like to suggest that an adequate ontology must come to
terms with the view that man is a playful as well as reasoning
being. To deny or neglect the symbiotic relationship between
rational and playful human capacities is to relegate reason to an
instrumental role while transforming the creative, exploratory
aspect of playfulness into an addictive fascination with the
following of explicit rules. Now this view that one of the
inherent predispositions of mankind is to engage in play as a
medium of self-expression and self-presentation has been stated
in a variety of places. However, I want to consider an implication
of only one aspect of this complex concept. To conceptualize
certain aspects of human activity as prompted and permeated by
an urge and a capacity for play is to acknowledge the various
degrees of indeterminacy involved in the satisfaction of needs and
wants and the realization of purposes which may have a more or
less explicit gradient of definition. Expressed otherwise, the
notion that all action is rule-governed or that, in principle, all
activity is susceptible to description and explanation—after it
occurs if not before—in terms of rule-observing behaviour,
becomes untenable once certain hitherto unexamined presuppositions are made explicit. For example, the rule-following
postulate assumes that a viable equation can be drawn between
contextual regularity and tact or explicit rule-observance. But it
is, at best, problematic to conceptualize action in terms of an ideal
model, goal or purpose. As well, such an orientation assumes an
existential as well as analytic dichotomy between means and end
while presupposing that an explicit, precise and exhaustive
specification of the end is possible. To do this is to believe that we
experience external reality and then endow it with significance.
The more adequate view is, of course, to avoid the epistemological caricatures presented by both realism and idealism and see the

---

*This is a revised version of my oral comments delivered at the Second Annual
Symposium of the Faculty of Social Sciences, The University of Calgary, October, 1978. These comments are included in a more lengthy article, "Consciousness and the World", *Canadian Journal of Political and Social Theory*, Fall,
1979.

actor and his context as reciprocally and jointly involved in the project of definition.

Similarly, truth and meaning appear to be dichotomous, and articulate with science and social science respectively, if one assumes that human embodiment in respect of the physical environment is necessarily static, while *vis à vis* the cultural environment it is indefinitely malleable. However, to the extent that men cease to be creatures of the earth—subject to the invariant constraints of nature—and become creatures of the world, modifying their physical context by "acting into nature", the distinction between physical and social science becomes less viable. On the other hand, in as much as men lose the capacity to act and behave instead, with the concomitant homogenization of culture, so the universal possibilities of social science are enhanced.

The contention that science is characterized by unity rather than discontinuity can be supported by additional ontological and epistemological considerations. The ontology of the physical and social sciences, it is sometimes claimed, is asymmetrical with respect to the constitution of phenomena. The world of physical reality is autonomous: it exists irrespective of our wishes or actions; it is that with which it is necessary that we come to terms. The social world, by contrast, is generated through human activity; the specific contours and nuances of social phenomena are the result of human interaction. The question as to whether this distinction is viable, I shall consider shortly. For now, it is necessary to note that this difference should not obscure an important dimension of continuity between nature and society which consists in the fact that both are experienced as environments susceptible to use and modification in such ways as to facilitate the creation and realization of human needs, wants and purposes. That is to say that nature, and the regularities it exhibits, constrains human options while at the same time it makes possible the continuation of life as we know it. Men breathe unaided by artifice, it is necessary to reckon with the force of gravity, the sun provides light so that we may see. Examples of capacities made possible, and constraints which must be taken into account due to the structure of our natural environment, could be multiplied indefinitely; the coincidence of freedom with necessity in terms of natural parameters which define the human species is very evident. Not so apparent is the possibility that it could have been otherwise. For instance, we have no reason to believe that oxygen would not exist were our physiology radically different. Nor are there grounds for believing that the sun would leave the sky if we were not possessed of the capacity for vision. Or, to make the same point another way, the world of nature may possess indefinitely various structures and characteristics of which we are not aware and which we cannot even imagine simply because they do not articulate with the structure of our nature. For example, if we were beings not endowed with auditory and visual abilities, the fields of physical science which deal with light and sound would be absent—and meaningless. This very elementary but frequently unnoticed phenomenon seems to be indicated even by our linguistic habit of using synonymously or interchangeably the terms "physical" and "natural" when referring to science. So-called "hard" science deals with the physical world; but what is intended by this usage is the world which appears "natural" to us not because, in some basic sense, it is self-evident in itself but because it is the world with which our "nature", as a species, articulates. In short, the very being of the physical world—its bare existence—is testified to by our senses in a way that is logically prior to our being able to speak of it. But this being, of which we are aware at a non-cognitive level, may be ineluctably partial, dependent upon the structure of *our* being, which prohibits the possibility of making contact with the structure of nature as a whole. To speak of nature as a whole is to suggest that it enjoys an internal, comprehensive equilibrium and coherence. One implication of such a view is that aspects of physical reality—including any that may exist of which we are necessarily ignorant due to our psychophysical constitution—may be interrelated in unanticipated and unimaginable ways.

Assuming that the above is not, literally speaking, incredible, the same can be said to apply to society. The institutions, practices and "common meanings" characteristic of a society are indicative of human capacities and potentialities; they reflect the interests and abilities of the members of a society. While it is true that they are the result of human interaction—that they are created—it would be misleading to suppose that they have determinate authors. Every person is born into an intricate matrix of life-routines which may be more or less resistant to modification or ripe for change. For most individuals the impact of their lives on their society will be negligible; for the outstanding few, their creative or destructive acts make sense only if account is taken of the matrix they attempt to transcend. In the most basic sense, however, social phenomena, however variable, testify to universal propensities of the human species. Alternatively expressed, the social is no less "natural" than nature. Consider, for example, the fact that every society of which we have knowledge has generated a variety of self-interpretation, whether magic or myth, history or philosophy. Moreover, although there are significant emphases and differences, all societies exhibit the capacity for developing and appreciating works of art as well as for coping with the imperative to satisfy the less ambiguous needs such as sustenance and reproduction.

The conclusion to be drawn, then, is that selection of problems for study is not distinct from the constitution of problems, even though it may seem to be the case. For example, in the case of physical science there are phenomena which are as they are and could not be otherwise, at least insofar as human action affecting them are concerned. The earth, the physical world, is there for the scientist to explore and analyze; it is refractory, thereby providing a constant check on his imagination of the characteristics and structure peculiar to it. At the same time it may be readily acknowledged that the theories generated and laws derived from the study of nature have not provided complete and perfect knowledge of physical reality and the processes characteristic of it, since the fit between conceptualization and data do not enable error-free testing and application thereby leading to anomalies which precipitate scientific change. Could people constitute phenomena other than the ones they do? Could people select problems other than the ones they do? Is the difference in the medium(s) of self-expression that are constituted, significant? Or is it simply a matter of convenience—and on a continuum of sophistication defined in terms of simplicity, consistency, comprehensiveness—which in turn is dependent on a concept of rationality and effectiveness? If this is the case, then all media are a variety of response to *universal* issues and problems and in both natural and social science the degrees of freedom are bounded by constraints indicative of *both human and external givens*. The conclusion is, then, that natural science is not the model *nor* is social science. They face similar problems and are prompted and accounted for by formally similar relationships of people and phenomena.

In terms of epistemological considerations, the concepts employed by both physical and social science do not correspond in a direct, unmediated fashion to the reality they are designed to grasp. Phenomena are conceptually constituted in both cases, idealization takes place in both instances, and the strongest claim to be made is that the theories generated in each field have a bearing on the reality appropriate to that field. Another, and more fashionable, although frequently ambiguous way of making the same point, is to say that both sciences employ paradigms to relate observation to theory.

To acknowledge the presence and role of paradigms in scientific activity is to endorse a number of propositions which include but are by no means exhausted by the following. First, physical science does not deal with uninterpreted, unambiguous particles of matter. Aside from the consideration that "matter" is, itself, a problematic concept which requires a theoretical matrix to enable specification, the characteristics of any physical data bear a symbiotic relationship to the problem in terms of which conceptualization takes place. This activity on the part of the scientist both presupposes and makes possible the practice of his professional role. This role, in turn, is predicated on a prescientific, culture-dependent understanding of the physical environment as well as on his membership in a scientific community which supplies him with categories of discrimination which may be modified as a result of his action. Second, social science assumes and requires that the scientist be able to understand the awareness possessed by social actors of their environment. What is sometimes called the natural attitude or first-level conceptual orientation of social actors, cannot be reduced to a behavioristic account of meaning. Therefore, in order to secure the viability of concepts appropriate to social science, these concepts must, in principle, be explicable in terms meaningful to the actors themselves. Third, in both physical and social science, the concepts of truth and proof must be seen to have an intra-theoretic status: they are objective and have meaning and application only insofar as they are understood in the same way. In short, laws must be interpreted; rules require application; and the correct procedure to follow in either case is not self-evident. Data completely independent of the scientist-actor, which are discrete, determinate and unambiguous do not exist; or, if they do, they are that of which we cannot speak.

Jarvie's Reply to Reshaur

Professor Reshaur accepts my thesis that we should break down the distinction between the natural and the social, but he thinks my reasons for doing this profoundly mistaken. He notices that I rely heavily on a conception of nature as a given, what could not be otherwise. But he is tormented by two possibilities: that we may have at best only a partial access to the totality of nature; and, that what seem to us its necessities may stem simply from the particular sensory and intellectual equipment that we possess. If there is a fixed and immutable nature, perhaps it is an undifferentiated manifold to which we have at best partial access, at worst no access at all. All that we have to mediate between our observations and whatever is there are paradigms, and these at best can be said to have a 'bearing' on the reality appropriate to the field. There are no pure data, however; and science is itself a form of social organisation. Social science has to respect the natural attitude, has to be 'etic.' Truth and proof need interpretation.

This sort of move, attempting to break down the distinction between the natural and the social sciences in a direction that favours the social was criticised in section 3 as radical humanism. Perhaps I will just add a few remarks here. That all knowledge is human knowledge, that all putative knowledge is putative human knowledge, goes without saying. But is all knowledge simply knowledge of humans striving to create knowledge? It is difficult to accept this. We strive to gain knowledge that literally transcends men; knowledge that encompasses nature, the universe, or whatever else you want to call all there is; knowledge that is true of times when there were no men and will still be true when there are no longer any men; knowledge that gives true state-descriptions of space where men have never been; knowledge that itself explains men and their quest for knowledge. Moreover, we attempt to devise communication systems to capture this knowledge and store it for the use of men not yet in existence, even for the use of 'others', possibly not human, far away in the reaches of time and space.[1]

This then is the aspiration: our ideal of knowledge begins from the puny human being, a mid-sized object able to perceive some physical phenomena directly, but unable to perceive many more, and leaps to the exciting possibility that we can know anything and everything. Two issues arise: is the project in principle possible; is the project in practice possible? Clearly, my view is that it has in fact been done in practice and so *a fortiori* can be done in principle. This will not convince Professor Reshaur, who already knows that and clearly is not convinced. So the obvious move is to start at the other end and offer some in-principle arguments.

Professor Reshaur says that if we could not hear and see then sound and optics would not be fields of science, they would be meaningless. This confuses science with subjectivity: the colour-blind man cannot see colours, but he can do the physics of them regardless of the failure of his imagination. But it might be said he can do it only because others who could see colours have started off the inquiries. I am not sure. We can do the scientific exercise of reconstructing the world as it might seem through the eye of a fly, or a spider. None of us has ever been there.[2] Further, we do the physics of particles that are invisible, colourless, tasteless, smell-less, soundless, weightless, pressureless. When we do this work we operate exactly like the shadow-watchers in Plato's cave. He thought that his metaphor showed that the senses were no guide to certain knowledge. I think it dramatises the human cognitive condition, and warns us to be alert to our own fallibility. Indirect knowledge, by report, shadow or inference is to be judged by its success, not its origin. The phenomenologists' overvaluing of knowledge by direct acquaintance seems to me to avoid the intuition that we are far better able to turn back criticism of assertions such as $E=mc^2$ or $2 \times 2 = 4$, than we are able to turn back criticism of 'I am conscious of being in a world of intentional objects'.

Behind the resistance to this principle there often lurks a suspicion of hubris in the scientific enterprise. For one thing, it is highly esoteric and devalues much of the quasi-cognitive endeavours of mankind, i.e. all traditional thought-systems, including those of ordinary plain men of today. Ernest Gellner has given the best answer to this charge that I know of. He suggests that scientific-generalizing, transcendental thought comes about because traditional thought has broken down in the face of the Great Transition (the industrial revolution, modernisation, affluence). It is the loss of traditional anchors that sets men on the quest for non-traditional, free-floating, non-perspectival knowledge. Thus it is not hubris but desperation that underlies science, and it is fear and nostalgia that resists it.

Notes

[1]See H. Freudenthal, *Lincos: Design of a Language for Cosmic Intercourse*, Amsterdam 1960, and the review in *British Journal for the Philosophy of Science*, Vol. XII, 1961-1962, 332-338.

[2]Although Kafka tried to see what it would be like to be a cockroach in "The Metamorphosis".

Session Three

Structuralism
and Development

Developmental Structuralism: Without Self, Without History

John M. Broughton
Teachers College, Columbia University

> It is hard to overestimate the importance of method or technique
> everywhere, or the difficulty of destroying a false technique when
> it is entrenched in social or practical interests, and when there is no
> adequate procedure at hand to replace it. Rather than doing nothing
> to avert disaster or to assure the favour of fortune, men will con-
> tinue to do what they no longer believe in.
>
> (Baldwin, 1915, p. 146)

> All history is contemporary history: not in the ordinary sense of the
> word, where contemporary history means the history of the com-
> paratively recent past, but in the strict sense: the consciousness of
> one's own activity as one actually performs it. History is thus the
> self-knowledge of the living mind. For even when the events which
> the historian studies are events that happened in the distant past,
> the condition of their being historically known is that they should
> vibrate in the historian's mind.
>
> (Collingwood, 1946)

Romantic philosophy and nineteenth century thinking drew their inspiration from the root metaphor of the *organism*. The key notion of 'function' bound together the diachronic changes in the organism with its synchronic structure of interrelated organs. (Jameson 1972, p. vi). However, there is a too substantial quality to the biological metaphor, and it is in reaction to this that more relational metaphors have been sought. The basic model of *communication systems* is in its ascendancy (e.g., Wilden 1972). This could perhaps be understood as a reflection of the eclipse of nature in the abstraction of the labour process, with its resultant other-directed world and its intricate technocratic networks of information and messages. Or it could possibly be construed as an expression of despair at the loss of human relatedness these changes have occasioned. The surge of recent linguistic 'dis-coveries' has consolidated an expectation originally provoked by

Thanks to Adrienne Harris, Ellen Carni, Edmund Sullivan and Sara Zarem for critical suggestions. Special thanks to Katherine Sutton-Smith for her gener-ous and gracious assistance, and Stephanie Lafarge for kindly providing inter-view material and inspiration. Rocky Schwartz, Candice Leonard and Edward Mysak helped considerably in the preparation of the manuscript. Other mem-bers of the Teachers College interview research group contributed greatly to these ideas. For anyone interested, a much expanded version of the first half of this chapter is available upon request from the author.

information theory. This is the hope that there is still a way for the impoverished social sciences to capitalise upon the hoarded treasures of natural science—deductive rigour and mathematical precision. Modern structural linguistics looks like the way because it has these qualities while still dealing with those most social of phenomena: speaking and understanding. It is, therefore, not surprising that *language* has become the new root metaphor, and that the human sciences recovering from the short and incomplete reign of information theory should turn to *structuralism*.

The consensus of opinion (e.g., Caws 1968, Jameson 1972) used to be that French structuralism does not include the genetic epistemology of Jean Piaget, Lucien Goldmann or Lawrence Kohlberg since for these developmentalists it is 'structure' that is central, rather than language. In the wake of Piaget's book on structuralism, however, more recent analyses (e.g., Blasi 1976, Venn & Walkerdine 1978) have reversed this trend. My sympathies are largely with this second view, although it is true that Piaget's particular amalgam of psychology and epistemology, logic and biology departs in many respects from the French intellectual tradition. My purpose is to show how the benefits and deficits of structuralism are exemplified in Piaget's bio-psychology, and by so doing to bring developmental theory into the orbit of a critical historical psychology.

French Structuralism

In the 1920's there was an empiricist "structuralism" in psychology, spearheaded by Wundt's student Titchener (1929). Opposing itself to the functionalism of Dewey, Angell and Baldwin, this structuralism developed an architectonics of sensation. Its basic model was a three-dimensional image of a rigid synchronic scaffolding, a composite linear arrangement of parts. This image has re-emerged in the structural theory of mental traits proposed by Guilford (1959). Piagetian theory owes nothing to these approaches, and it is important to see that his structures are abstract systems of transformation, rather than static crystalline organisations of sensational elements or traits. In this, he comes closer to Continental structuralism.

The latter is often characterised rather generally as a "method" (e.g. McConnell, 1970, p. 268). However, we would be slipping back into positivism (against which structuralism has revolted), if we were not to point out that the method implies a theory. This is a theory of mind as the adequacy of language to meaning, a kind of linguistics originating in de Saussure (1965). What this implied for the human sciences was that they could be seen as primarily "semiotic", concerned with deciphering surface phenomena or 'signs', thereby revealing their 'signification' within a system of underlying meaning. The system is one of internal relations or differences, the units of which are defined only by their function in the system. This system is posited as an abstract synchronic "competence", a universal code which under-lies the generation of signs as well as their understanding. The code typically comprises a finite set of fixed and discrete elements, the archetypes of which are the binary phonological elements suggested by the early structural linguist Jakobson (Levi-Strauss 1963, Gardner 1972). In Levi-Strauss's case, the analogous ele-ments are the polar metaphysical dimensions in the mythical unconscious of the culture, while in Piaget's case, they are the binary propositions in the formal cognitive structures appearing at adolescence, and in Kohlberg they are the binary "issues" of moral discourse. What makes the "competence" competent is a quasi-algebraic combinatory capacity, an ideal set of rules which allows for the permutation of the elements of the code into a multiplicity of possibilities (Ricoeur, 1976). These finite systems of transformations are essentially "closed", and autonomous, in the sense that the relations between elements are immanent to the system, the latter being self-sufficient and having no intrinsic relations with external realities. Language as a system is viewed as complete and at any point contains all the possibilities of meaning. Thus the deep levels of grammar, logic and myth have a formal and epistemological priority and purity.

The code therefore involves a system of unconscious formal rules which governs the internal relations of elements consti-tuting meaning, and the combinations or transformations from "deep structural" logical possibilities into "surface structural" signs, and vice versa. The 'vice versa', i.e. understanding, is the translation or reduction of sign to signified—a kind of 'detective work.' In describing this process of mind, Levi-Strauss has talked of the binary elements as elaborating a

> system which plays the part of a synthesising operator between ideas and facts, thereby turning the latter into *signs*. The mind thus passes from empirical diversity to conceptual simplicity and then from conceptual simplicity to meaning-ful synthesis. (1966, p. 131)

While there is a risk of scientism in proposing a unitary scientific method as the basis of knowledge, Levi-Strauss argues in opposition to positivism, that the structuralist method tran-scends the segregation of the sensible from the intelligible. The deep structures *make observation possible*. They are inaccessible to "direct" observation; they are rules and not facts. Yet while these rules may give the same meaning to different embodiments, this does not imply that there is a disembodied apprehension of structure:

> Form defines itself by opposition to a content which is exterior to it; but structure has no content: it is itself the content, apprehended in a logical organisation conceived as a property of the real. (Levi-Strauss, quoted in Caws, 1968, p. 81)

In giving the mind interiority, and altering the traditional positivistic approach to observation, structuralism has claimed for itself a novel epistemological position. While it remains for this to be carefully spelt out, it is clear that the "structures" spoken of are neither substances nor mere theoretical fictions.

Piaget's Structuralism

Piaget's "biologism" has been used to differentiate him from Levi-Strauss, Chomsky and others. However, the fact that the notion of "code" is central to modern molecular biology and genetics makes the separation seem less significant. What most demarcates Piaget from other structuralists is his claim that all knowledge can be construed as a biological structuring process of *equilibration*, the principles of which are essentially the same in all biological systems, and can best be understood as a cybernetic process. Piaget does not postulate a static hierarchy of structural types, despite Chomsky's (1968) claim to the contrary. In his study with Inhelder of child and adolescent thought (Inhelder & Piaget, 1958), for example, the stress is on continuity between stages rather than discontinuity, the stages being only very temporary resting points. As suggested by Bourbaki mathematics and Gödel's theorem, a structure has to be transformed through inclusion in a higher order structure to safeguard its consistency.

Piaget's structuralism is a functional one, in some ways the mirror image of Parsons' structural functionalism in the sociological sphere. It owes this quality to its roots in the evolutionary functionalism of James Mark Baldwin, one of the original opponents of Titchener (Böhme 1973), and to the influence of that most modern form of functionalist thought, systems theory. Influenced directly and indirectly by the nineteenth century notion of "organic structure", Piagetian psychology claims six major properties for cognitive structure, listed in table 1. (Piaget 1966; Gabel 1975; Blasi 1976; Venn & Walkerdine 1978).

TABLE 1—PROPERTIES OF COGNITIVE STRUCTURE

1. *Totality* System is a consistent and irreducible whole. Elements obey holistic laws of system. Parts take their character from functional role in system.
2. *Closure* Structures bounded, i.e. closed and autonomous.
3. *Self-regulation* Structures tend to conserve themselves through systematically coordinated laws of internal equilibrium, which govern relationships between parts.
4. *Precariousness* Deformation or removal of a part entails disturbance of the functional totality, which reverberates throughout the whole, destructuring all its internal and external relationships.
5. *Hierarchy* Structures are nested as sub-systems within larger wholes.
6. *Equilibration* Structured wholes tend to transform in direction of greater consistency and precariousness, through inclusion in larger wholes.

Logic and psychology

The structures of thought are special kinds of structures only in that they are interiorised by reflecting upon the most general co-ordinations of actions, and that they tend towards a fully reversible logico-mathematical equilibrium which represents their ideal form. The highest level of biological evolution is the emergence of a system of fundamental necessary relationships in the operations of the mind, at the so-called stage of "formal operations" (Table 2). At this level, formal logic and scientific method represent the axiomatic and empirical aspects of the same mental operations.

Piaget can be faulted for conflating mathematics and logic, ignoring vast realms of mathematical discourse such as calculus and statistics, ignoring the fact of mathematical discourse as a social practice, and failing to link logic and biology in any convincing fashion. However, he does establish an interesting relationship between logic and psychology, not unlike that suggested by transformational grammarians between "competence" and "performance". Logic is seen as a normative question of foundations, of deductively discovering under what conditions reasoning can be accepted as formally valid. Psychology, on the other hand, is said to aim at causal explanation and deal with matters of fact concerning the actual mechanisms involved in reasoning (Beth & Piaget 1966). Thus Piaget's theory is not refuted by findings such as those of Wason and Johnson-Laird (1972) that adults fail to reason consistently in terms of ideal formal logic. Logic is an axiomatics of reason, it is not a set of principles to be "applied" in everyday thinking. Actions do not apply principles, but are organised according to a set of rules immanent to actions themselves (Broughton, 1979a). Intelligence is incapable of spontaneously applying axiomatic principles, since these in fact serve to codify theoretical patterns formulated *after* the construction of thought, and do not describe the continuously creative constructive process of thinking itself. Logic affects psychology insofar as the structuralist psychologist must ask "What must our thinking faculty be for its products to have such logical properties?"

TABLE 2—PIAGET'S ERAS AND STAGES OF LOGICAL
AND COGNITIVE DEVELOPMENT
(from Kohlberg and Gilligan, 1971)

Era I (age 0-2) The era of sensorimotor intelligence

Stage 1. Reflex action
Stage 2. Coordination of reflexes and sensorimotor repetition (primary circular reaction).
Stage 3. Activities to make interesting events in the environment reappear (secondary circular reaction).
Stage 4. Means/ends behavior and search for absent objects.
Stage 5. Experimental search for new means (tertiary circular reaction).
Stage 6. Use of imagery in insightful invention of new means and in recall of absent objects and events.

Era II (age 2-5) Symbolic, intuitive, or prelogical thought

Inference is carried on through images and symbols which do not maintain logical relations or invariances with one another. "Magical thinking" in the sense of (a) confusion of apparent or imagined events with real events and objects and (b) confusion of perceptual appearances of qualitative and quantitative change with actual change.

Era III (age 6-10) Concrete operational thought

Inferences carried on through system of classes, relations, and quantities maintaining logically invariant properties and which *refer to concrete objects.* These include such logical processes as (a) inclusion of lower-order classes in higher order classes; (b) transitive seriation (recognition that if $a > b$ and $b > c$, then $a > c$); (c) logical addition and multiplication of classes and quantities; (d) conservation of number, class membership, length, and mass under apparent change.

Substage 1. Formation of stable categorical classes.
Substage 2. Formation of quantitative and numerical relations of invariance.

Era IV (age 11 to adulthood) Formal-operational thought

Inferences through logical operations upon propositions or "operations upon operations." Reasoning about reasoning. Constuction of systems of all possible relations or implications. Hypothetico-deductive isolation of variables and testing of hypotheses.

Substage 1. Formation of the inverse of the reciprocal. Capacity to form negative classes (for example, the class of all non-crows) and to see relations as simultaneously reciprocal (for example, to understand that liquid in a U-shaped tube holds an equal level because of counterbalanced pressures).

Substage 2. Capacity to order triads of propositions or relations (for example, to understand that if Bob is taller than Joe and Joe is shorter than Dick, then Joe is the shortest of the three).

Substage 3. True formal thought. Construction of all possible combinations of relations, systematic isolation of variables, and deductive hypothesis-testing.

Structure and Function, Rational and Empirical, Theory and Practice

> Each element of the system returns to the whole but this whole is dead if every moment does not take it up and make it function. (Sartre, 1971, p. 111).

Since one can talk about thinking without seeing it as an instrument of adaptation, one can talk about function without being a functionalist. Logical structures form the grounds for action, but how is each thought constructed out of these conditions? For Piaget, this is a question of how the facts of psychological process, the causal relations involved in reasoning mechanisms, are related to the norms of rational competence. Here he introduces the biological metaphors of assimilation and accommodation.

However, comparing the mind to a stomach has several drawbacks. The life function of digestion does not allow an explanation of understanding (which is more than metabolic breakdown and absorption), or failure to understand (which is more than the rejection of indigestibles). It does not allow us to account for the production of meaning, or the reciprocal construction of the self. In short, there is no way to conjure out of the biological any of the significant epistemological questions.

At the formal operational stage, Piaget sees the assimilation/accommodation process as systematically guided by scientific methods for experimentally determining cause/effect relations. Yet, the world is more than cause/effect relations, as indeed is the psychological process of reasoning. The individual's practical relationship to the world cannot be reduced to a hypothetico-deductive one (Broughton 1979b). In addition, Piaget has only juxtaposed deduction and induction, logic and method, rational and empirical, without ever really explaining the connection. Since structuralist assumptions claim that meaning is internally self-defined within the code, it is hard to see how the construction of meaning relates to practical engagement with the world.

As with assimilation and accommodation, Piaget splits the epistemological problematic into two parts, balancing the rationalist's concept with the empiricist's counter-weight. He appears to hope that by then invoking the nebulous idea of an "interaction" between them, he will somehow explain the functioning of structures, the relation of judgment to action, and of justification to discovery, the construction of knowledge, and the progress of development.

The intention to dynamically integrate theory and practice is clearly present in the theory. The very fact that knowledge is to be derived from the interiorisation of action assures us of this. It is a mistake to simply brand Piaget as an "intellectualist". Unlike the French structuralists, his functionalist psychology leads him to a notion of rationality based upon instrumental, goal-directed problem-solving. This reflects the pragmatists' respect for biology as the propadeutic science, and for scientific method as the propadeutic subject/object relation: "the interrogation of nature by experiment", in the naive individual as in the professional scientist. Objectivity is thus united with adaptation, the criterion of truth being practical efficacy—the success of purposive-rational action.

However, when the language of control systems is applied to consciousness, it is only at a certain cost. Making judgment a kind of "virtual action" in the absence of its object, leads to the treatment of mental processes as though they were activity in themselves (Sève 1975, p. 16; Broughton 1978). By making all *experience* into a kind of action too, perception loses any autonomy from conception, and so there is no clear way for *evidence* to reach the level of structural organisation, much less to transform it. How, in Piaget's system, can the conception be distinguished from its object? How can the world really offer any *resistance* to assimilation, and how is the world really transformed by the individual's activity? Cognition in-forms action, but how can action in-form cognition? How can the part restructure the whole? The spontaneous philosophy of cybernetics is an "ideology of models" (D'Amico, 1973). The human subject is a mere constructor of plausible models, rather than a person in a relationship of mutual transformation with reality. We are left begging the two vital questions for a developmental structuralist: how do structures actually function, and how does structural functioning lead to developmental restructuring?

Self and Mind

The difficulty in comprehending the contact of the individual's actions or experience with the formal deep structures of his or her own code is paralleled by the problem of how the individual subject is related to the universal rule-system. Piaget claims that he is dealing with the development of the knowing subject. However, by this he means not the concrete individual self, but the 'epistemic subject', the transcendental subject which reflects "what there is in common with all subjects" (Beth & Piaget 1966, p. 254; cf Turner 1973). This subject is the "structurer of all structures", to be equated with assimilation and accommodation, the functional invariants of the knowing mechanism.

The individual is not simply absorbed in the mass, however. It is one of Piaget's great strengths that he has presented a way in which development can achieve the differentiation of self from other. It is more the case that Piaget, like other structuralists, tends to see the universals of Mind as comprising an anonymous corpus of knowledge that overwhelms and acts *through* the individual. The latter's own knowing and doing is incidental to the operation and maintenance of the systems of transformation. The self is thus truncated, reduced to a purely objective meaning. Much the same problem is raised by the notion of psychological development as "decentration" (Blasi, 1975; Kohlberg, in press). Structuralism is therefore what Paul Ricoeur calls "a Kantianism without a transcendental subject". The subjective unity of consciousness is pre-empted by the totalising dialectic of structure, which operates above and beyond consciousness and will. Piaget's formal operational individual becomes an unconscious instrument of Logic and Scientific Method, which are the real source of choice and decision, usurping the individual's own possibility of making intelligent judgments. In its haste to avoid a substantial self, structuralism has concocted a relational "self" that has no subjectivity (cf Broughton & Riegel, 1977 Broughton, in press). As in the case of modern art (Steinberg 1972), the mid-twentieth-century self is a vanishing self.

Structure and History

Piaget, like Levi-Strauss, has focussed on formal relationships whose "origin is drawn exclusively from the structures of the mind," and not from the "exigencies of the social life." (Levi-Strauss, 1970, p. 59). This is, in a sense, Piaget's naturalism, since the code, with its combinatory power, is the modern view of natural order, and of the generativity of life itself (Benoist 1973).

It would be incorrect to say that structuralism is purely synchronic in orientation; it can also embrace diachronic phenomena. But it does so in a quite mysterious way, failing to embrace any truly historical dimension (Riegel, 1975). Even though an admixture of organismic theory allows Piaget to make the diachronic aspects of structure even more salient, he still presupposes an abstract opposition between structure and history. In its ideal formal character, structure itself cannot be explained. It has its origin in the "structuring of all structures", the organic structure of the mind (D'Amico 1973, Bergmann 1978). Without a selecting self, the appearance of one sign or content rather than another can only be attributed to "exigencies" —socio-historical *accidents*. From the vantage-point of the priority of structure, history lacks form and can only appear as fragmentary. It is therefore capable of contributing only to the degeneration of formal systems, a view of history as irrational entropic tendency which Collingwood (1945, p. 26) has suggested is predominant among natural scientists.

For Piaget, where history should be, strands structure, and like cognitive operations, historical ones turn out to have no subject either. "History" is the dynamic but passive unfolding of *order*, and for Piaget, this order is the progress of scientific ideas, conceived as an internally generated history of the knowing subject parallel to the abstract intellectual biography of the child. The latter is a sub-system imbedded within the former. This so-called "history" analyses the internal economy of process and product in theories, tracing "the progress of discovery, the formulation of problems, and the clash of controversy" (Foucault 1970, p. xi). Any disorder, any destructuring or resistance, is externalised and attributed to the environment. If it were instead treated as essential to scientific discourse and a positive part of the process of discovery, even though its regularities lie outside the boundaries of specific theories, the validity and very scientific quality of science would seem to be called into question.

Merleau-Ponty (1964, Picciarelli 1978) has pointed out, that in Piaget structural progress seems too much determined by its telos. Similarly, the progress of science is subjected to a "Whig Interpretation", and "presentist" historiography (Buss 1977). Seeing the past only as a unilinear sequence leading up to the present state of knowledge is an abstraction which screens out the concrete nature of the historical process.

It is of course correct to take a totality of relations as the object of study if that whole is already constituted, at which point

> it is the moment of structure, where totality appears as the thing without man, a network of oppositions in which each element defines itself by another . . . But at the same time this thing without man is matter worked by man, bearing the traces of man. (Sartre 1971, p. 111)

Sartre argues that "the moment of structure", abstracted from its process of historical transformation, is a species of optical illusion. It is the illusion experienced by the outside observer seeing human behaviour not as praxis or action in course, but as an already constituted object (Jameson, 1971, p. 269). Illusions of course have ground in the real world, and are not total hallucinations (Merleau-Ponty 1962). Thus, Sartre is not aping the romantic Bergsonian criticism that all analytic organisations are a spurious geometrising of the stream of life. The perceived structure is not an invention, but rather it is the inert material structure that human beings and groups temporarily give to themselves so that they can "work on themselves."

Unger (1975) has suggested that this problem is encountered by structuralists as a direct result of the power and scope of their method. It can be applied at any level of analysis. Piaget (1968) for example, has been involved in research that attempts to locate in the patterns of neuro-physiological activity in the brain an INRC group parallel to the INRC group of formal operations. If formal models apply to any level of structural analysis, be it physiological, psychological, etc., then the particular totality chosen to be explained is relatively arbitrary. It is therefore hard to see how one can claim that for a whole which is merely postulated for methodological reasons, there can be any real historical process by which the parts have been incorporated and reshaped into the whole. Piaget's stages then take on the appearance of levels ordered hierarchically in terms of their progressively increasing logical adequacy. They do not have the kind of sequentiality and directionality that could only be accounted for *historically*. Whatever diachronic quality they have can only be borrowed through their formal congruence with the successive strata of order in a history of science.

As we have seen in our frustrated search for self, the impression left by structuralism is that structures make men. It should come as no surprise then that they cannot be modified by men, "Man is in some way developed by the development of structure," to quote Sartre (*ibid.*, p. 112) once more. Men cannot create new possibilities because what is possible is restricted to merely that which is not actual—the non-actualised combinations of the code. The possibility of transcending the code itself is denied to man inasmuch as the code itself never reaches conscious awareness, nor can it sensibly be allowed to do so if the human subject has vanished.

> The disappearance or . . . the "decentration" of the subject is needed just to discredit history. If there is no more praxis, there can no longer be a subject" (*ibid.*, p. 112)

Sartre goes on to sketch the relationship of praxis to structure:

> Man is the product of structure, but yet he goes beyond it. If
> you wish, there are moments of history that are structural.
> Man receives structures; and in a sense it can be said that they
> make him. But he receives them as he is engaged in history,
> engaged in such a way that he cannot fail to destroy them, to
> constitute anew that which in turn will condition him.
> (*ibid.*, p. 112)

The message here is that the code which at one moment appears to
be a natural matter, perhaps even innate, in another moment
reveals itself as "matter worked by man". Systems of internal
relations construct consistencies, maintain paradoxes, and resolve contradictions only because they were historically "constituted anew" by men to serve that purpose. They may become
"second nature", but this new universal of human nature that
comes to "condition" man does so also through the way man
works matter, knows that he does, and legitimates how he does it.

Cognition and Ideology

One response to the ahistorical theory and practice of developmental psychology and its failure to deal with society as anything
more than a concept has been to designate it as an outgrowth of
liberal ideology. Such a critique argues that not only does a
cognitive-developmental theory fail to distinguish true from false
consciousness in the psychology of individuals, but it fails to
distinguish them in its own constitution, thus becoming itself a
species of false consciousness. Such a critique has been mounted
almost simultaneously against Piaget, Kohlberg and other developmentalists by nine authors (Buss, Jacoby, Unger, Sullivan, B.
Bernstein, Lasch, Venn & Walkerdine, Reid and Yanarella, and
Buck-Morss). The last of these is perhaps the clearest prototype.

> With the advent of wage labour, production as well as
> exchange acquired abstract value, and the purely formal
> language of mathematics (the language of commercial
> transactions) became the expression of the social relations of
> production as well as those of the marketplace... Kantian
> dualism, the separation of mental operations from the
> perceptual objects which provided the content of thought,
> was the cognitive counterpart to the alienation of workers
> from the object of their production. (Buck-Morss 1978, 1975)

The nine analyses can perhaps be treated as a composite

picture—an ideal type of the ideology-critique of stage theories. The prototypical argument quoted from Buck-Morss suggests that the separation of form from content, and the idea of abstract cognition, are themselves historical consequences of capitalist modes of commodity production and division of labour in urban commercial cultures. The ideal-type critique also tends to undermine the whole notion of "development" as a reification of history deriving from the nineteenth century ideology of progress.

Such a critique appears to resist the structuralist's isolation of cultural super-structure from the politico-economic base, and to supplant the internal dynamic of cognitive development with the external or social dialectic of history. Formal thought arises as a by-product of the specific long-term transformations of western historical praxis. It does not simply emerge when unsuccessful or conflicted actions reveal the inadequacy of concrete operational thought. According to the ideology-critique, the universality of categories and stage sequences is reinterpreted as the reified product of the mechanism of cultural reproduction mediated by techniques of socialisation. Developmental theories are forms of legitimation which rationalise the socialisation process as a "natural" quasi-biological sequence. Both stage sequence and the theory of it would therefore represent purely *conventional* meaning systems, with no clear objectivity.

It comes as something of a shock to your average receptive developmental psychologist to be informed by erudite intellectual historians that formal thought and principled morality are forms of domination, and that stage theories explaining their natural development are mere legitimations. The emotional impact is roughly equivalent to finding out that 'How much is that doggy in the window, the one with the wagg-ely tail' is an old sailor's song about prostitutes.

There are admittedly certain problems with the critique. The careful historical work has yet to be done that reconstructs the discourse within which developmental theory was formulated, and adduces evidence for the connection of economic phenomena to the cognitive structures in children's minds. Also, the critics are not always scrupulous about which ideology is being attacked. Are developmental theories to be faulted for their bourgeois ideological commitment to civil liberties and free enterprise, or for their adherence to the very different ideological precepts of technological society and instrumental rationality?

What the ideology-critics of the 70's have succeeded in doing is to reconnect developmental theory to history, and to establish the legitimacy and even the necessity of some form of ideology-critique in a radical psychology. What is not yet established is what exactly ideology-critique is, the criteria for how it should be conducted, or what it implies for the future of structuralism.

Ideology critique and structural homologies

The ideal-typical trend in ideology-critique has been to demonstrate structural homologies between categorical stage structures and ideological systems. The latter in turn are revealed as reflexes of specific concrete historical transformations in the political economy, particularly associated with the rise of capitalism and its 'development' from free enterprise into monopoly capitalism.

It is by no means clear whether the homologies are meant to exist between all three levels (cognitive, ideological and economic), or just between the first two. It is not even clear sometimes whether the "homology" isn't just a surface similarity between the *theory* of ideology and the *theory* of cognition. This is the error of the idealist, who fails to clearly distinguish a theory from the objects of its explanation.

Assuming for the moment however that the homology claimed is one between cognition and ideology, the immediate danger is that this claim might do nothing more than set up an abstract *isomorphism* between two levels of reality. Such an endeavour threatens to result in just that static view of the inter-relationship of structural levels for which structuralism has been so roundly taken to task. The drawing of abstact parallels and equivalences is in fact one of the very ideological devices that Buck-Morss has demystified in tracing it to its origin in abstract exchange value. If on the other hand one falls back to the weaker position that the parallel is just an *analogy*, not a true homology, then one cannot go on to establish the claim that formal or principled thought serves the same function as ideology.

Ideology-critique *could* claim that it establishes between levels a relationship of *part-to-whole*, not just a parallel. Such would be the case if ideology-critique were itself a kind of structuralism, which took developmental theories as 'signs,' the political/ historical signification of which is a specific organisation of false consciousness. The false consciousness would presumably be demystified and revealed for what it is by virtue of a deciphering code, an analysis of the deep structure of liberal ideology for example. When Buck-Morss, Sullivan, Unger et al. point to liberal psychology's false dualisms between form and content, judgment and action, nature and culture etc., are they not formulating a system of binary oppositions that specify a deep-structural code in a fashion similar to that of Piaget, Jakobson or Levi-Strauss? That ideology-critique offers this kind of *meta*-structural analysis is suggested by Buck-Morss when she argues in opposition to a rigid form/content dualism that Piaget's structural forms are in turn the contents of ideological structures. This would make the relation between structural levels one of whole to part, rather than cause to effect. In that case, stage theories would have to be respected as non-reducible subsystems, the observation and analysis of which would be necessary to an understanding of ideology, the whole that included them.

However, if ideology critique is structuralist, it must fall prey to the problems of structuralism that have already been outlined. When attention is focused on cognition and ideology, the dialectic is confined to the superstructure, and the historical aspects of the politico-economic infrastructure of society are again bracketed. This reinstates a kind of mind/body separation. An ideology-critique confined within the superstructure would, like a developmental theory, fail to construe its object (in this case, the liberal psychology code) as a man-made moment of historical transformation. As a consequence, this superstructural ideology-critique would always be threatened with the possibility that the critique of liberal ideology would itself need to be imbedded in a more comprehensive system—a critique of the ideology-critique.

Mystification and the sociology of knowledge

As we move away from a structuralist type of ideology-critique, with its emphasis on "form," we gravitate towards *causal* explanations, with their tendency to reductionism. What Allan Buss has aptly called the "sociology of psychological knowledge" would explain both the structure and the propagation of developmental theories in terms of particular social conditions, thus undermining their claims to objectivity. A crude sociology of knowledge degenerates into a debunking—often via a search for hidden motives and class interests in the theorist's unconscious. A sophisticated sociology of knowledge, on the other hand, such as Mannheim's, realises that ideology cannot be reduced to the psychological level of subjective "values," but must be understood as a total structure of consciousness, a consciousness that is epistemologically false, rather than psychologically distorted. False consciousness cannot therefore be demystified by a facile appeal to causes external to theory, whether these be subjective motives or values, collective *Zeitgeists*, or objective advances in technology or industrialisation. False consciousness tends towards rational systematisation in its own right, as ideology.

While ideology is systematically rational, its constitutive false consciousness is not however remediable by a "genetic epistemology." The latter offers only a rational reconstruction of stages of knowledge showing how consciousness can be elevated to a new total structure, i.e., given a more adequate ground for the possibility of theoretical knowledge, through natural processes of equilibration. In contrast, false consciousness is a *mystification*, central to which is a suppressed self-consciousness. This reverberates throughout the self, so that not just intellect, but perceptual experience, understanding, communication and action, as well as self-understanding, are systematically falsified. When we have false consciousness, all that we take to be the case is systematically ungrounded. Rational reconstruction is no solution here, because it merely explicates correct know-how, through an increase in reflectivity, and has no necessary practical consequences (Habermas, 1973, p. 183). A greater truth cannot itself bring about the transformation of a false consciousness into a true consciousness. Only a *liberation of the dominated self* can do that.

Freedom of the person, as opposed to reflectivity of knowledge, depends upon a certain kind of interpretation that makes suppressed structures and contents conscious. What it is the task of therapy to do in interpreting individual biography, it is the job of ideology-critique to do in history. What is interpreted is not an effect simply attributable to a cause. A false structure of consciousness cannot be attributed solely to the agency of ideology, or to the political economic system which ideology protects. Even bourgeois psychology has given up such a primitive model of causality. In the same spirit, the interpretation is not *externally* given. The contribution of critical theory here is that it has identified the complicity of the self in a truncated awareness of both self and reality. Another way of saying this is that the entrenchment of ideology is as profound as it is by virtue of its "wisdom," its ability not only to constitute human needs but also to serve them (Gadlin, 1978). Self-liberation through interpretation of self and other therefore requires more than a theoretical exposée; it requires a practical self-transformation.

But what is the "pre-understanding" of true consciousness that therapist and ideology-critic alike must have in order to identify false consciousness? How can they or the subjects of their interpretation recognize "true consciousness" when it is attained, and know it to be in some way "truer" than the previous consciousness? Paradoxically, by calling into question the whole structure of consciousness, ideology-critique appears to remove all potential for truth from the grounds of such a consciousness. Ideology-critique resembles the sociology of knowledge in its record of concern with untruths. Its attitude strikes the psychologist as one of suspicion, its activity one of puncturing.

Unless it claims an epistemologically privileged position, how can it then avoid self-suspicion, and eventually self-puncture?

Restoration and truth

One way in which ideology-critique might be able to avoid self-contradiction is by resisting the tendency to reduce the object of its critique (e.g. developmental theory) to one dimension. If we view developmental theory as an example of symbolic material in general, then we can apply Paul Ricoeur's analysis of such material to good effect. Ricoeur (1973; 1970, pp. 26-36) has argued that the most prominent characteristic of symbolic material is its polysemy—the fact that it has more than one dimension, that it always stands at the intersection of a multiplicity of meanings. Ricoeur sees two major ways of interpreting such meanings (as Cooper's chapter in this volume describes). In the first place, any symbolic discourse is subject to a "hermeneutic of suspicion." In other words, every discourse conceals, disguises and mystifies, calling for a reading which demystifies. In the second place, every discourse has an expressive quality and function. Symbols not only cover up and dissemble, they also embody possibility and imagination, acting as a leading edge or act of faith. Thus discourse is subject to a second kind of interpretation, cast within a "hermeneutic of restoration." Such a hermeneutic restores to the symbol the synthetic integrity and intentional thrust which are endangered when demystification reduces the symbolic "envelope" in order to reveal the unconscious origin of its form. Ideology-critique has typically adopted a hermeneutic of suspicion, an attitude which, applied to developmental theory, would interpret it exclusively as a wolf in sheep's clothing. The critique "suspects" logical sequences of cognitive stages, and reveals them as mystifications of underlying political-ideological interests conditioned by particular forms of social-historical development. Yet, if Ricoeur's analysis is correct, and appropriate in this instance, a restoration of meaning to developmental theory is necessary to balance the potential reductionism of suspicion taken alone. In parallel, ideology-critique, itself viewed as symbolic material, requires some restorative moment, if it is not to devour itself in the hunger of its own criticism.

The restoration of developmental theory, the interpretation of its expressive truthfulness, is largely built into the notion of expanding rationality and logical adequacy. However, it is less clear where ideology-critique is to regain its "teleology." It has founded itself upon a methodical "archaeology" which digs down to origins and roots. It seems as ill-equipped to supply its own symbolic restoration as developmental theory is to supply its own demystification. Ideology-critique often appears to assume a position of epistemological privilege. It allows itself to hang suspended with no visible support while it conducts its *tour de force* of demystification, pointing with skill and penetration to the socio-historical, ideological conditions which shape the formative processes in development and developmental theorising alike. While those thinkers who articulate ideology-critique may have some justified claim to be cognitively privileged, for they often can see further and more clearly than their victims (psychologists, etc.), they cannot ground their attitude of *epistemological* privilege. Their work and inspiration and the discipline within which they operate are rooted in the social conditions just like anyone else's, the very conditions that they view critically. This is a fact of the historical, collective nature of subjectivity itself.

In the sociology of knowledge, a vision of escape from this vicious circle is afforded by the notion that truth can be attained if theory "appropriately reflects" the social reality. The idea here seems to be that theory grounds itself solidly if it finds a way to participate in a practical involvement with society and historical transformation, if it manages to gain a concrete "timeliness." Perhaps a good example in the sphere of developmental theory is Kohlberg's revision of his basic theoretical and meta-theoretical position in response to several years' extensive and intensive experience of working in prison and school interventions (Kohlberg, 1978). However, one cannot adopt a purely pragmatic criterion of truth. A theory cannot be said to be either true, or resistant to dismantling by a demystification, simply on the grounds that it participates effectively in social transformation. In the end, this boils down to saying that a theory is good, true and liberating if it works. Behaviour therapy "works," as we never cease to be told by its adherents. However, *how* does it work, for whom, and by what criteria can we judge this to be the *right kind* of working? Furthermore, the pragmatic criterion of truth is always open to the objection: what evidence is there that *it* works, as a criterion of truth? If the pragmatic criterion ceases to work at some point, should we then give it up? Indeed, how could we ever recognize that it had stopped working? The critics of instrumental rationality have already pointed out these kinds of difficulties, and others besides. Any position based upon the concepts of 'appropriateness,' 'involvement' or 'commitment' inevitably leads back to relativism in the end (Trigg, 1973), unless the theorist also supplies a positive critique of the current situation that prevents one from committing oneself to an ideologically distorted social "reality." But how can that critique be supplied without some conception of "true consciousness" to counterbalance the all too powerful and incisive critique of false consciousness?

No final solution to the conundrum will be presented here. However, it is possible to find in developmental theory itself a thrust towards rationality which ideology-critique may be able to capitalise upon (cf Flax, 1978). One restorative insight is the realisation that a critique of the origins of stage theories does not necessarily compromise their validity entirely. To demonstrate that Piagetian stages constitute a reification of knowledge, and that this reification originates in ideological structures, does not imply that the stage sequence is an epiphenomenal vacuity, which fails to convey any true understanding of the facts of human development. It may indeed be true that the assumptions of Piagetian theory reify socio-historical reality, and systematically remove from reality its dialectical quality. However, the inadequacy of assumptions does not imply the invalidity of theory, nor the invalidity of evidence garnered through the instrumentality of the theory. "Undialectical" does not mean "untrue" (Gabel, 1975). If things were otherwise, then there would be no need for any kind of critique besides ideology-critique. Ideology-critique of the kind we have been considering would pre-empt any psychologist's analysis of the facts, the procedures by which evidence was obtained, the criteria by which evidence was evaluated, and the theoretical framework of concepts, postulates and inferences guiding the whole undertaking. But ideology-critique cannot claim to have usurped the role of psychologists or metapsychologists. There is a legitimate endeavour called "theoretical critique," and another called "empirical critique," neither of which are reducible to or upstaged by ideology-critique (Broughton, 1978). There is both analysis of scientific adequacy and analysis of philosophic rationality apart from the analysis of false consciousness. It is the existence of these other forms of criticism that allows ideology-critique itelf to be criticised, without fear of an infinite regress. It is in that sense that this present essay attempts a critique of ideology-critique that does not itself appeal to ideology as its cornerstone.

In addition, Adorno (1969, pp. 247-9) has pointed out that, by a strange twist, the reified categories of bourgeois theory often lend it a peculiar capacity for unwittingly identifying and characterising types of alienated consciousness. Ironically, the best of cognitive-developmental theory, appropriately reinterpreted, may do a very good job of describing the facts of an alienated socialisation. It is true that in the process of reinterpreting stage theory, one might make all kinds of amendments. One might, for example, wish to add on 'higher' stages of anti-reificational consciousness. This was the purpose behind Klaus Riegel's (1973) argument for adding a fifth stage of "dialectical operations" to Piaget's four stages of cognitive development, an example more recently emulated by Basseches' (1978) theory of dialectical cognitive structures in early adulthood.

Nevertheless, critical theory must appropriate some such account of the development of normative thought structures if only to make possible the identification and interpretation of the progressive penetration of alienated reason into the individual psyche. Without some such account, ideology-critique will not only lose the potential for establishing some positive definition of true consciousness for itself, but it will be impotent to bring that definition to bear upon the vital task of educating or re-educating people in a development of consciousness that is compatible with the liberation of self. It is this realisation that is at the root of Habermas' recent attempts (Habermas, 1979) to integrate critical theory with the developmental theories of the genesis of normative structures. True, in certain respects, Habermas is too uncritical in his appropriation of developmental theory (see, for example, Broughton & Zahaykevich, 1979). One must retain one's critical perspective upon the very theories that one attempts to incorporate in a more comprehensive vision. This vision can maintain a dialectical balance if it is careful to differentiate from each other, and yet articulate reciprocally, the two important components of *interpretation and criticism*. Ideally, developmental theory explicates the implicit structural meanings of consciousness in its genesis. It yields a "textual meaning in and for itself" (Hirsch, 1967, p. 211). Criticism builds on the result of this interpretation, arriving at the *significance* of the text by relating it to the larger content of a critical theory of history.

It appears then that only a rather unexpected symbiosis between theories of normative structure and critical theories interpreting ideology would prevent the former from being ahistorical and the latter from presuming to hold an epistemologically privileged position. Each would thereby criticise and transform the other. Stage theories would have to a) change in theory and practice to embrace false as well as true consciousness and b) find a way of explaining movement between stages that is more than an internal intellectual equilibration. Ideology-critique on the other hand would have to a) give up the simplistic notion that cognition just *reflects* ideology, a variety of mechanistic learning theory already discredited by Piagetian psychology, and b) give up a purely pragmatic criterion of truth to generate a theory and practice that are critical of the current social conditions. Such a theory and practice would protect ideology-critique from a meta-critique and would prescribe those conditions which would afford the possibility of a true consciousness and a development of freedom. Under those conditions, or in actively moving towards them, ideology-critique could justify its practical reintegration with the social situation, for example in the tasks of education and socialisation, in a way that would not leave it as an isolated theoretical activity removed from institutions and academic disciplines that it denounces as alienated.

An Empirical Postscript: Development and Interpretation

Cognitive-developmental psychology has come to be identified with the establishing of a sequence of formalisable structures. However, Piaget's commitment since the 1940's to formal mathematisation is one of the least indispensable parts of his approach (Venn & Walkerdine, 1978). The cognitive-developmental approach is much broader. Sullivan (1977) and Taylor (1971b) point to this when they say that the prototype of truth need not be 'operative,' in Piaget's sense. Both correctly point to the possibility of a more comprehensive concept of rationality. Both draw us away from the beguilements of scientism. However, there is no need to throw out the baby with the bathwater. There is also "science" without scientism, and science that is *not* operative. One is not obliged to pass over the study of scientific reasoning just because operative knowledge is found too narrow a base for truth. Science is not exhausted by the logical empiricist's vision of it, much as natural science is not exhausted by hypothetico-deductive method (Broughton, 1977, 1979). There is science, both natural and otherwise, which cannot be accounted for in terms of construction and testing of hypotheses. There is science which is not mathematised, and never will be.

This is not a daring new idea. It is actually a rather old one. As Husserl (1978, pp. 1-3) points out:

> What we today call science...is not science in the historically oldest sense, that of a naively, straightforwardly effected work of theoretical reason...Science, in the form of special science, has become a sort of theoretical technique.

Even in Platonic science, which stressed the role of "logic," technique was not dominant. Logic guaranteed necessity, in the sense of logical insight into principles fit for any cognition. The evolution of Piaget's own thinking has paralleled the historical developments subsequent to Plato. Logic became differentiated as a special science, and was reappropriated as the formal core of a logical empiricism which wanted to develop science as a theoretical technique. Similarly, Piaget rejected his early interview studies of children's meaning systems or 'worldviews' (the child's "theoretical reason") and moved to the investigation of implicit logical rule-systems underlying problem-solving technique.

With the assistance of students at Teachers College, I have returned to Piaget's earlier style of work, and his earlier conception of children's science as worldview. Elsewhere (in preparation), I have summarised the research done in this style by previous investigators. It seems to us that normatively ordered structures in the domain of logic, mathematics and hypothetico-deductive method may be of more limited application than those in the realm of philosophy (including, for example, metaphysics, epistemology and social theory). None of us attempts to formalise the structures of thinking that we describe, and none even suspects that such a reduction to a formal matrix is either desirable or possible. In this sense, we are less concerned with the development of operative rationality in Piaget's or Kohlberg's sense than we are with the emergence of the kind of common sense wisdom that implies progressively more meaningful rational assumptions about the nature of living[1] (Arendt's [1977] distinction).

We have been looking at the qualitatively different views of *life, death, war, freedom, love, identity,* and *development* itself, as they emerge in conceptual systems from childhood to adulthood. I, myself (1978, in press) have concentrated on concepts of *knowledge* (naive epistemology) and *reality* (naive metaphysical views of self, soul, mind and matter). All of us are interested in the way these issues inter-connect to form a general belief-system or philosophical worldview. We are especially concerned with the developmental potential for philosophies that will *critically* conceptualise each major life issue. It seems to us that tracing developments in *concepts* of self, society, life, reality and knowledge—in other words, the individual's worldview—could be misused in an intellectualistic way to avoid dealing with *actual* selves, societies, living, etc. Nevertheless, it need not be used that way. The cognitive approach is not necessarily either intellectualist or idealist. Once it has posited the teleological end-point of development as a *critical* consciousness, it already holds the potential for integration into a critical understanding of man that embraces both thought and action, both ideal and material transformation (Habermas 1979).

Empirical Examples:
A) Clinical, Cognitive and Ideology Interpretation

In developing a methodological awareness of what we have

been doing, we find that we diverge from Piagetian psychology not only in our relative lack of interest in formalisable competences, but in our concern with the 'polysemy' of interview discourse.[2] Statements made and themes constructed in the communicative context of an interview tend to represent the intersection of several different types and levels of mental functioning. Statements and themes are overdetermined, and represent condensations of different concerns. The following excerpt is from one of many long interviews with a 23 year-old middle-class woman, Katherine Sutton-Smith. She is suffering from Hodgkins Disease, a form of cancer that she has had for six years. She is talking about her self vis-à-vis her body:

> It is not more real, it is longer lasting. There is more value in it than the body, I put the body on a lesser step of the ladder than the mind, or the spirit, or the self. Because it is just a vehicle, a tank to ride around in . . . My self is not involved with the body. It is totally separate . . . My sense of self right now is —— —. Well, I perceive reality as it is channelled through my senses. I've already established that as real, and given credence to it. Whether or not it's a fabrication, it's my premiss. It is the premiss to my whole philosophy of life . . . But when the self is released from the cage of the body, it has multitudinous ability to perceive, not just through the five senses.

How should this fragment be interpreted? Let us consider three possibilities: From a *clinical* perspective, we might point to a tense ambiguity in Katherine's sense of her body. On the one hand she seems frightened by its vulnerability. On the other hand, her body is felt as an iron shell or cage that protects the spirit perhaps more than it would like. This is reminiscent of what Reich called "character armour", and helps in the denial of a sensed vulnerability. There is a splitting of self from body, with the latter made distant and sensed as alien. The image of self as soldier, trundling around in a tank reflects a kind of aggressive isolation, a reaction formation that turns something cumbersome, limiting and inert into an instrument of death. The warlike imagery may represent counterphobic tendencies, turning a passive death into a brave, active risking of life. Similar defensive structures sometimes arise in other conditions of extreme stress and threat to life. The exiled Soviet dissident, Vladimir Bukovsky, for example, reports in his autobiography that a phantasy of constructing a castle sustained him through twelve years of imprisonment.

I lived for hundreds of years in that castle and shaped every stone with my hands. I built it between interrogations in Lefortovo, in the camp lock-up and in the Vladimir punishment cells. It saved me from apathy, from indifference to living. It saved my life... How were they to know that I was talking to them from my castle battlements?... What could they do against my thick walls, my crenellated towers and embrasures? Laughingly I returned to my guests, firmly closing the massive oak doors behind me. (Bukovsky, 1978, pp. 23-24)

Lacan reports encountering such phantasies in analysis, phantasies which he associates with a fragmented body-image, and which attempt to compensate for disintegration by the assumption of

the armour of an alienating identity, which will stamp with the rigidity of its structure the whole of the subject's mental development... This fragmented body... regularly manifests itself in dreams when the movement of the analysis encounters a certain level of aggressive disintegration of the individual... Correlatively, the formation of the "I" is symbolized in dreams by a fortress, or a stadium... where the subject founders in quest of the haughty and remote inner castle, which, in its shape, symbolizes the *id* in startling fashion. Similarly, on the mental plane, we find realized the structures of fortified works, the metaphor of which arises spontaneously, and as if issuing from the symptoms themselves, to describe the mechanisms of obsessional neurosis— inversion, isolation, reduplication, cancellation and displacement (Lacan 1949, p. 453).

In a later version of this paper, Lacan refers to modern industrial man's vehicular metaphors in the following manner:

The relations between this *Homo psychologicus* and the machines he uses are very striking, and this is especially so in the case of the motor-car. We get the impression that his relationship to this machine is so very intimate that it is almost as if the two were actually conjoined—its mechanical defects and breakdowns often parallel his neurotical symptoms. Its emotional significance for him comes from the fact that it exteriorizes the protective shell of his ego, as well as the failure of his virility. (Lacan 1953, p. 17).

During the interviews, Katherine herself communicated a vivid self-interpretation in which she grappled with her own defensiveness:

> Sometimes I wonder if that is a defense mechanism—to use Freud's term loosely—the fear of physical pain or physical loss. Having had operations, I might be physically marred in some way, and setting myself up in some way for that loss by saying it doesn't matter. Maybe that is why I have developed that notion of the body being a tank. I think a lot of physical pain does that to you. Also a sense of the fallibility of the physical being. It is subject to disaster at any moment. You can walk under a falling chunk of building, and that is it. Yet most people don't have a real feeling for that. They only have an intellectual perception that "Yes, I can lose my life." It has not been felt as personally as I have felt it. That I am subject to something external, that is not the "me". There is where the separation of the mind and body comes from— that great gulf that I do feel. That I have no control over this mad cell that wanders around my body and grows at odd times and mucks things up. To that extent my body is not me...I accept the lack of control and disassociate myself from that uncontrollable mechanism. Then it doesn't come as a blow when that lack of control manifests itself. It doesn't diminish 'myself' because 'myself' is not involved with the body. It's totally separate.

In addition to the clinical perspective, there is a second kind of interpretation that can be made of the "tank" imagery. This second perspective is the *cognitive-structural* one which we have been discussing at length in this chapter. From this point of view, the metaphorical forms employed are not unique, either to this subject or to people who have experienced serious illness, or to people who have suffered extreme physical and psychological stress. Clinical sense may indeed be validly made of the "tank" in terms of levels of aggressive disintegration and defence, precipitated by illness which effects gross ruptures of bodily integrity, and occasions losses in psychological vitality. Nevertheless, certain intellectual structures form and support a cognitive matrix in which dynamically loaded images can lodge, and by virtue of which the affective tone of experience can be communicated. The particular cognitive structures that are of relevance here are those which constitute conventional thinking about mind and body. Some evidence from my own longitudinal study of adolescent intellectual development (Broughton 1978, in press) indicates that in late adolescence and early adulthood, there is a tendency for our common sense understanding of the world to articulate itself in terms of a Cartesian dualism of substances. Such a psychophysical dualism does not appear to be a specific acquisition resulting from either formal or informal instruction in philosophy or psychology. Rather, it seems to be a "natural" cognitive stage in the development of western adolescent world-views, one which emerges gradually out of less differentiated, pre-Cartesian worldviews (Broughton, in preparation). A 22 year-old male undergraduate, studying Classics, illustrates this way of thinking about the person:

> To me, my mind is my soul is my psyche. It is me. I mean, the body for me is just the appearance, is just a shadow. It's the living force inside, you know, the ideas that emanate, that are the self...I always say the external thing doesn't matter... The body for me is just something to encase you.

This young man is a healthy, cheerful, well-balanced fellow. He is not downplaying the body because of illness, depression, or some passing stress. He compares the body to a shell (and elsewhere in the interview to a corpse) because his level of conceptualisation has reached the point where corporeal and spiritual substances can be conceived as mutually exclusive forms of existence, each with their own properties. As in Cartesian dualism, sensation, feeling, and action are part of that "external thing" we call the body, which has been segregated from the inner spiritual being and joined with the outside world of mechanistic, inanimate nature.

This level of "natural metaphysics" is typical of late adolescents, and many adults. Taken alone, the clinical interpretation is perhaps too powerful. Descartes himself, in a moment quite sane, was able to capture the philosophical problem in the following excerpt:

> If I chance to look out of a window on to men passing in the street, I do not fail to say, on seeing them, that I see men..., and yet what do I see from this window, other than hats and cloaks which can cover ghosts or dummies who move only by means of springs.
> (Quoted in Jones, 1975).

One bright, normal adolescent in my longitudinal study reported a phantasy which was quite similar to Descartes' thought experiment. While riding with his family in the car, he would often imagine that everyone but him was a robot, even his family members. They were disguised as human beings, and were testing him. Any clinician who failed to make something of this would not be worth his or her salt. Nevertheless, one of the reasons that the phantasy takes this particular structure is that the metaphysical reflections of the adolescent have reached a point of deliberation formally similar to the philosophic theorising of Descartes.

Following the cessation of chemotherapy, and in a state of remission,[3] Katherine responded to the above analysis of her interview, which was sent to her for comment. In a written reply, she said:

> My appreciation of my body has broadened somewhat since (the time of the interview, a year earlier). I decided to get into good physical condition. I began taking exercise classes at the YWCA. A remarkable thing happened after about 3 months of this process: I started to feel much more in touch with my body. It was no longer simply a receptacle for my self. I recognised that, after a time, my self actually felt more peaceful and happy after my morning exercise. In a sense I felt that my body and I were developing a more mutually agreeable relationship: if I were good to it, then it would respond in kind. I realised that my state of mind was very contingent on my state of body. Now I realise their inter-connectiveness. I used to be at odds with my body, to endure it passively, if not actually fight it. But now I realise that if I am to be as intellectually and emotionally effective as I am able to be, then I have to be good to my body. I recognise that we are in this game together.

Despite a movement from mind/body opposition to co-operation, however, Katherine's basic understanding of her metaphysical status as a person is still deeply divided. Her effectiveness is still split into intellectual and emotional halves. "I have to be good to my body", and "I recognise that we are in this game together", also suggest that the breach is far from healed. Katherine comes close to repeating Aristotle's metaphor of the soul as a pilot with the body its ship.

In addition to clinical and cognitive interpretations, the material from Katherine's interview can be seen from a third theoretical perspective, that of an *ideology-critique*. Ideology is implicit in the very mind/body dualism that we have just described. In particular, there is reason to suppose that the philosophic distinction between immutably separate mental and

physical substances reflects the historically conditioned segregation of the spheres of intellectual and manual labour (Sohn-
Rethel, 1978; Young, 1976; cf also Sennett & Cobb, 1975, and
Broughton, in press). To be "effective" a white collar elite must
"be good to" the blue collar workers upon whose simpler, bodily
labour the privileged mental workers depend, and whose labour
they must form, manage and direct in a constructive co-operation.
Katherine is no elitist, neither does her own work fit the model of
careerism, upward mobility and professional self-interest. However, her upbringing and interests have brought her into continuous contact with the professional spheres of academics and
health services. When it comes to articulating an understanding
of the existence of the person, it is not surprising that she is
constrained within the conventional bourgeois conception of
"mental" versus "physical" which is the historical outcome of
our modern mode of social organisation and productive activity,
and a distinction which the professions of mind and body have
actively served to maintain. For her, there is "more value" in mind
than body, the body being "on a lesser step of the ladder" (see
quotation above). Although she may not subscribe to the assumptions upon which such ideological thought is both philosophically and historically premised, she is in some sense a natural
heir to them, as they reside in the very structure of knowledge,
work and communication that provides the context for both her
life and her disease.

Other aspects of her thinking also reveal potential material for
interpretation as cognitive manifestations of the ideological
context. Katherine's dualistic approach to her person is part of the
larger dualistic worldview, in which the material world is a
Cartesian self-operating mechanism. It is this presumptive framework that makes it possible, under the stress of her illness, to
envision the "mad cell" that wanders around her body as part of
an "uncontrolled mechanism", and which encourages her to
defend herself from the reality by dissociating herself (her self)
from that self-operating machine. The separation is facilitated by
the Cartesian assumption that body and spirit (intellect) are
already metaphysically independent. Sohn-Rethel (1978, see p.
123, for example) has presented an analysis of this Cartesian
philosophy that makes it seem likely that in contemporary
society, such concepts are rooted in the perception of the
productive process as an external self-operating mechanism with
its own laws apart from the qualitatively distinct laws of the
human self. The only imaginable relation between man and
material nature (including the human body) is one of *control*.
Relationships less dominating, more affiliative and nurturant,

are not possible when the self is a substance absolutely opposed in quality to the material substance of body and world.

The separation of substances also forms the basis for a sense of the self as nothing other than the individual thinking ego or subject. This self is like the owner of the citadel, the driver of the car or tank. It is a disembodied, internally reflective mind. This disembodiment allows us to hand over "control" of our bodies to the technical expertise of medicine and its practitioners, much as we would take our cars to the garage (Ingleby 1972, in press). The disembodiment at the roots of the dualistic metaphysic also encourages in the ill the phantasy of being "released from the cage of the body". What Cartesianism and Kantianism commit us to is "logical individualism". Its analysis starts from the individual theoretical rationality, imbedded firmly in the intellect rather than in the practical life (Broughton, in press). Adorno (1978), Horkheimer (1978) and others have shown how this philosophy rose in close co-operation with the historical transformation of productive forces. To quote Sohn-Rethel (1978, p. 77):

> As it assumes representation as the *ego cogito* of Descartes or of the 'subject of cognition' of philosophical epistemology, the false consciousness of intellectual labour reaches its culmination: the formation of thinking which in every respect merits the term 'social' presents itself as the diametrical opposite to society, the EGO of which there cannot be another. Kant has the appropriate formula for this contradiction: "There is no ground in theoretical reason from which to infer to the existence of another being." Nothing could be wrapped in greater secrecy than the truth that the independence of the intellect is owed to its originally social character.

Logical individualism cuts us off from others at the most basic level—communication becomes at best a miracle, and at worst logically impossible. Kant's formula is illustrated nicely by another section of the letter that Katherine wrote in critical response to my earlier draft.

> I think your perception of my fear of being vulnerable is on target . . . I realise that this is the approach I have taken to my body throughout my illness. Detaching myself from the operations performed on my body, be they radiation treatments or bone marrow biopsies, has given me a sense of control over and superiority to my body. The body must submit to external manipulations, but my mind is free and

infinitely stronger. In this sense the body is a cage that entraps the self. It does isolate the self from others and from nature at large in that the self can only perceive and communicate with the world through the senses of the body. In this sense, the body is a limitation and prevents the self from achieving a total knowledge or complete understanding of the world at large. But I view this isolation as more regrettable than "aggressive". When I envision myself as a tank, trundling along in my metal sheath, that rectangular aperture on the front of the vehicle is essential to the image. Because I believe, as does the poet, that the eyes are the window of the soul. So I focus my energy and attention through that opening on other people and on nature as much as any tank driver would. And I seek out other people's eyes because that contact allows for the most effective communication between two selves.

Katherine captures elegantly the desperate difficulty of communication between self and other, when each is encased in armour and permitted access to the other only through a restricted aperture.

As Sohn-Rethel pointed out, the gradual social and historical formation of such a concept of isolated, self-contained individuals is rarely entertained. The "self" becomes a reification of the real social person. In an intensive empirical ideology-critique of common-sense, Adorno (1974) and Gabel (1975) have pointed to the predominance of the assumption of reified individuality in our everyday experience and thinking. In Katherine's case, no amount of interviewing revealed in her an understanding of the origin of types of cancer in the historical shaping of biology by particular kinds of societal organisation and forms of production. What was revealed was her courageous attempt to fight for her *individual* control over the disease, and the *individual* transcendence of its debilitating by-products. Our culture offers no other conceptual or practical framework for confronting dysfunction. One is increasingly held responsible for the occurrence and duration of one's own illness, especially in the case of cancer (Sontag, 1978).

The impression gained from working with such interviews, and attempting to interpret them, is that it is not a question of using whichever of these three perspectives (clinical, cognitive, ideological) is most useful, or of a crude eclecticism. Rather, the verbalised material is truly polysemic. In our work, we try to hold all three kinds of interpretation in an awkward embrace at the same time. Each viewed separately must be simultaneously understood as an abstraction, like length, breadth or height. We look for possible structural identities and inter-connections, and potential points in the subject's life out of which such a network might be said to have arisen, or into which it might insert itself in concrete practice. In doing this, we take care not to reify either subject or life-history. We are therefore moving away from the kind of structuralist inquiry which sees itself as discovering the "sole determining structures".

We find that it makes sense to distinguish within the modes of interpretation the two moments of discourse already described: the mystified and the restored, the structural and the transformational, the suppressing and the liberating. In Katherine, the dialectic of mystification and restoration is particularly poignant, accentuated by her extraordinary suffering and consequent strength. Suppression and liberation are made more visible by her canny self-interpretations. Table 3 summarises all these aspects of her interview material.

TABLE 3—CONCEALED AND REVELATORY MEANING,
AND SELF-CRITIQUE, IN THREE MODES OF INTERPRETATION

Types and Moments of Interpretation	Example in Katherine
Dynamic mechanisms	
Mystified: *Defence*	Sees self as riding around in tank (reaction formation)
Restorative: *Coping*	Has located pragmatic means for the possible transcendence of pain and the continuation of daily living.
Self-interpretation	Understands own defensiveness.
Cognitive structures	
Differentiation: *Structure*	Opposes spirit and matter in dualism
Integration: *Transformation*	Recognizes interconnection of mind and body and attempts to reconcile.
Self-interpretation	Admits possibility of one's premises being fabrications.
Ideological devices	
Mystified: *Reification*	Tacitly reflects bourgeois hierarchy and domination symbolically as transcendence of spirit, its higher value and its control, over "mere" body or sensation. Isolated theoretical subject.
Restorative: *Critique*	Realises isolation of conceptual subject. Notes that most people intellectualise death instead of feeling it.

Self-interpretation .... Recognises subordination of body
                                    and seeks greater mutuality. Own
                                    work becomes more practical,
                                    emerging from own concrete life
                                    experience.

Having "suspected" Katherine's thoughts, feelings and
actions, we can avoid reductionism only by noticing the restorative aspects of her symbolic discourse. She has coped with
physical insult and debilitation, she is moving toward some
rapprochement of mind and body, and regrets the isolation of the
subject sufficiently to try to conceptualise a possible form of inter-
subjectivity. In addition, there is a superimposed level of reflection on these meanings. She is aware of her own defensiveness,
admits the relativity of her conceptual assumptions, and questions the necessity of her own earlier subordination of material to
mental. All these parts of her consciousness would appear to form
the "leading edge" of her development as a thinking, feeling,
criticising person.

Empirical Examples: B) The Genetic Psychology of
Basic Categories of Critical Social Philosophy
In parallel with the two types of meaning in our subjects'
development, there are two moments in the advance of our theory.
On the one hand, ideology-critique 'suspects' developmental
structuralism, and rightly so. On the other hand, developmental
structuralism has a certain momentum that must be conserved. It
is momentum towards a reduction of illusion. The illusion is the
orthodox Marxist one of 'reflection theory', of automatic socialisation. What this "learning theory" conceals is the fact that the
complex of cognition and ideology represented in people's
mental structures has not only a history but also a genesis. To
confine ourselves to a consideration of man's ability to duplicate
himself intellectually is to ignore the primacy of the fact that
humanity duplicates itself practically. It is also to ignore the fact
that through such practical duplication, which is material rather
than intellectual, humanity makes it possible to contemplate
itself in a world that it has created (Meszaros, 1970). Nevertheless,
we cannot restrict our purview to historical praxis, or to its
restriction through alienation and mystification. That would be
to ignore the dialectical inter-relation of practical and intellectual reproduction, and to ignore the possibility of defining a
"true consciousness" as a potential developmental attainment.
A brief example from the work of Barbara Schecter (1979) on the
development of concepts of "life" may illustrate the role that

structural analysis of intellect has to play in the critical social understanding of praxis and history. Specifically, Schecter's work on children's animism and vitalism suggests the outline of a genetic understanding of basic Hegelian and Marxist categories. Schecter has recently shown that the attribution of "life" to things, in 6 year-olds, found to be based on anthropomorphic criteria, shifts by the age of 8 to functional criteria (Table 4). By this age, man-made things and natural objects like the sun are differentiated out as manifesting a "kind of life", since they "work" (serve a purpose). But these 8 year-olds say that man-made things work, or are "kind of alive" only until they break down. This broad "functional" attribution of life to sun and man-made things presents an internal paradox, since these children know that animals are alive in a different or more "real" way than a sun or watch. This paradox appears to be solved through the emergence of genetic criteria for life: something is living if it grows or is born. This more detailed distinction between living and non-living eliminates the possibility of the quasi-living category. Thus by age 10-12, life has become specified more narrowly as generative and irreversible, although the reproductive cycle is purely repetitious and produces exact copies of the original. In early adolescence, the criterion for life becomes narrower still, being the capacity for voluntary choice and conscious purpose. This permits a distinction to be made between generative living beings and the cyclically operating mechanisms of mechanical production.

Although Schecter's study is cast in a Piagetian mould, central to the developmental sequence in cognition that she describes are the differentiations and integrations between standard Hegelian and Marxist categories: man, nature, work, mental and material function, and reproduction. My own research suggests that such concepts emerge in close relation to an understanding of what is "artificial" and what is "real". I raise the example of Schecter's study in order to suggest that within Marxist philosophy, there is an inclination towards reifying basic philosophic categories by divorcing their formation from the ontogenesis and socialisation of the common man. One possible step toward a critical psychology might be to integrate past and ongoing developmental research[4] into the philosophic categories already employed. According to this model, philosophy would involve inquiry into how philosophic categories progressively emerge in developing cognitive structures. (Since psychology presupposes philosophy, these philosophic categories would also be the basic categories of psychology.) One would need to supplement this with an examination of how such structured categories reflect historically produced forms of socialisation. Understanding the way in which socialisation provides a concrete matrix for the sequentially emerging levels of consciousness could suggest ways in which a liberating educational praxis could intervene. Intervention is necessary because, despite Piaget's apparent assumption to the contrary, the study of the development of consciousness does not commit one to a presumption that it is not false consciousness. An instance of potential reification and alienation is the notion that life can be defined primarily in terms of mind. We have already examined the sense in which this subverts truth and freedom, in examining Katherine's concepts of mind, body and self. Identifying reified ideas of this kind suggests points at which educational resocialisation might be directed.

TABLE 4—SCHECTER'S LEVELS IN THE DEVELOPMENT OF LIFE/MIND CONCEPTS (EVOLUTION IN CRITERIA USED TO ATTRIBUTE ANIMACY/CONSCIOUSNESS)

LIFE	CONSCIOUSNESS
1. (Age 5-6) *Zoomorphic/anthropomorphic*. No clear categorical boundaries. Human (and animal) orders confounded with inanimate nature. Attribution of life derives from global similarities to living beings, based on accidental biological characteristics, e.g., "has eyes," "sleeps." Activity is especially favored, leading to animacy of natural objects like sun, river or wind. Alive and real confounded. Non-living and dead not distinguished.	1. (Age 6-8) *Sensorimotor*. Bodily consciousness reduced to *sentience* ("feeling it") as defined by zoomorphic/anthropomorphic criteria (having eyes, nose, talking, etc.). Consciousness and life confounded. Must be alive to know. *Action* and even *existence* automatically imply conscious knowledge, i.e., feeling (to do or be something is to know it).
2. (Age 6-8) *Quasi-animistic*. Level 1 criteria still apply, plus inner biological characteristics ("has brain," "thinks," "senses things"). *Borderline* category formed of man-made and natural things "alive in a different way." This type of thing is defined *functionally* by the fact that it works or does something useful. At the same time, real life may be denied to the mechanical and natural because they are not "things" (unitary objects). Non-living partially differentiated from dead. Alive and real distinguished.	2. (Age 8-12) *Quasi-mental*. Knowing and sensing. *Cephalic organ* (brain or mind) necessary for *knowing*. Partial differentiation of *knowledge* as contents of thought or memory, e.g., in puzzling things out (math-thinking). Yet most knowing still connected with sensorimotor activity (brain "uses senses," or "tells you how to swim"). Knowledge still automatic. Must be alive to know yet consciousness and life show initial differentiation.

3. (Age 10-12) *Genetic-organic.* Concern with origins, natural form and formation. Integration into a temporal or spatial order. Things that *grow* are *born* rather than made, and are natural or spontaneous *wholes* resisting decomposition. Life as generative and irreversible, yet still cyclical (replication, self-substitution).

3. (Age 12-14) *Empirical.* Phylogenetically different ways of *experiencing* or coming to know (process becoming differentiated from product), correlated with presence and size of brain, and lying along a physical-mental continuum. i) *Registering impact* (objects/plants): passive knowledge, physical feeling rather than mental, allowed to inanimate things; a non-sentient knowledge still like a "sixth sense." ii) *Instinct* (plants/animals): repetitive mechanical reaction; requires brain/nervous system. iii) *Reason or understanding* (humans): poorly defined global notion; subjectivism possible (i.e., uncertainty and opinion different).

4. (Age 12-14) *Volitional.* Voluntary and reflexive choice, control or self-determination. Notion of immaterial cause (formal and/or final), purpose, tendency, or potential; "has a mind of its own." (No clear distinction between conscious and unconscious volition.) Also autonomous biological functioning.

4. (Age 14+) *Functional-instrumental.* Mental activity of humans: higher conscious functions or processes of imagining, interpreting, inferring. Capacity for rational (instrumental) choice and decision. Mental further differentiated as novel, creative and unique; able to extrapolate beyond empirical experience. Thus mind is both conscious will and subjectivity, relative to individual. Non-conscious biological activity.

Conclusion: Method in Structural Analysis

There are six ways in which our general approach to people has departed somewhat from the Piagetian structuralist one. *First,* we are pursuing tentative models of mind, rather than claiming to tap the "sole determining structures" (d'Amico, 1973, p. 74). In harmony with this, we are quite open to the possibility of branching rather than unilinear sequences. We are also more inclined to see in the life of the mind concerns with *meaning* as well as truth, often expressed in terms of *metaphor* rather than fact (Arendt, 1977). In keeping with these characteristics, we favour what Pettit (1975) has termed "straight" as opposed to "systematic" structural analysis. Straight analysis requires an explicit construction of neither theory nor analytic scheme. It nevertheless seeks to show the significance of every choice made by the subject. It asks questions such as i) What is the structure by reference to which this part of the discourse can be understood?

ii) What elements in this part work to produce the meaning?
iii) What specific contrasts give each element its particular significance? Straight analysis identifies dominant themes or patterns which act as organising motifs in the subject's worldview.

Second, we are more inclined to treat the models of mental
structure as historically conditioned, and less inclined to see them
as exclusively reflecting organic structures of mind. It is certainly
possible that these structures are eventually sedimented at the
organic level. However this "natural" level of structure is not
primary; it is "second-nature" formed first and foremost by
historical processes. In this second characteristic, we take a
position diametrically opposed to Chomsky, for whom history
has absolutely no significant impact on cognitive structure or
functioning.[5]

Third, we have more of a "lifespan" orientation to development than the Piagetian tradition is comfortable with. "For our
purposes", announced Piaget (1970, cited in Looft and Svoboda,
1975), "studies of adults are completely worthless," on account of
the fact that adults do not give spontaneous answers in the way
that children do. Piaget continued,

> If one wishes to continue the study of stages beyond adoles-
> cence, the only method would be to use history, for example
> the history of scientific thought; however, history is always
> very incomplete.

Elsewhere, Piaget (1972, pp. 11-12) revealed another interesting
aspect of his rationale for not studying adults.

> Unfortunately, the study of young adults is much more
> difficult than the study of the young child as they are less
> creative, and already part of an organised society that not
> only limits them and slows them down, but sometimes even
> rouses them to revolt.

We strongly dispute this opposition of creative thought to non-
structural or anti-structural social forces. Piaget reveals in this
opposition the conceptual aggravation experienced by those
systems theorists whose primary concern is with psychology
rather than sociology. All systems theorists postulate the individual as a system whose particular autonomy is inexorably
compromised by the general tendency for systems to become
imbedded as parts of more inclusive wholes (see Table 1). Piaget is
a structural systems theorist whose goal is the psychological one
of explaining individual intelligence as an evolving phenom-

enon in its own right. From such a perspective, the larger social whole is alien, and threatens to absorb the object of study, much as a systems sociology always presses towards the absorption of a systems psychology (for example, see the work of Talcott Parsons). The Piagetian antipathy towards society can be interpreted as an irrationality spawned by his adherence to the assumptive framework of systems theory. While it is not entirely clear what he intends in the quotation just presented, it seems as though Piaget's anitpathy is projected into young adults, and his irrationality is projected into the society which almost inevitably "rouses them to revolt". In the organismic imagery of systems thinking, rationalisation is equated with hierarchical differentiation and integration. As a consequence, from this perspective it is only by counter-rational (non-structural) processes, such as "revolt", that an individual sub-system can maintain functional autonomy in resistance to the ravages of an incorporating and subordinating super-system. Small wonder then that a psychologist envisioning the passage into adult society as a combat between contraries would prefer to confine his research to the childhood and adolescent years in which, supposedly, the individual is protected from societal incursions, and preserved as an integral object of study for the psychologist.

Taking a very different perspective, perhaps more interdisciplinary, we see the becoming "part of an organised society" as integrally bound up with the development of consciousness. Consequently, we find adults equally creative, spontaneous, and interesting as children or adolescents. Understanding the process of socialisation and the development of a critical revolutionary spirit are seen by us as central to an explanation of cognitive and other aspects of the individual's development. This follows from our second point, that historical conditioning is primary to structures, and their quality as organic or "natural" is included within and derivative from their historical formation. Thus creativity and spontaneity are not to be understood apart from our historical inheritance from Enlightenment humanism and individualism. They cannot be accounted for as just natural biological properties of mental activity. This is the kind of thing Sohn-Rethel intended by the passage quoted above in saying that "the independence of the intellect is owed to its originally social character".

Fourth, and consonant with the third point, we take the idea of the unconscious rather more seriously than Piaget. Where he talks only of the "cognitive unconscious" (1976), a level of cognitive activity that is necessarily non-conscious, we look at the *dynamic and political unconscious* as well. That is to say, we attend to the implicit domination of internal nature on the one hand and of external nature and society on the other (Broughton & Zahaykevich, 1979). Unlike structuralists, but in common with neo-Piagetians like Russell (1979), we feel that both the nonconscious and unconscious may emerge into consciousness, contributing to development. This comes close to Marx's view that unconscious conditions must be made conscious, through a self-transformation. It can be contrasted with a purely cybernetic self-regulation which is bound to maintain unconscious conditions in a nonconscious state.

Fifth, we do not treat the interpreted meanings as beliefs to be attributed hypothetically to subjects. We take the structures discerned to be *meanings for them.* These meanings are not to be viewed as just individual, subjective, and internal to mind, but rather as a mode of social relation. We tend to use biographical reconstruction instead of, or in addition to, prepared questions. Through such reconstruction we look for how meanings might reflect or express collective practices, such as professional self-enhancement (cf Taylor, 1971a). We consider man's attempt to duplicate himself intellectually in the context of his practical self-duplication. Thus the analysis of material from Katherine's interviews presented above is much more formal and abstract than we would choose, were there no limitation on space.

In harmony with the fifth characteristic we pay as much attention to the interactive "style" of the subjects in the interview as to the content of what they say, and look for ways in which observed communicative behavior fits in with or conflicts with the views explicitly or implicitly espoused by the subjects. We have moved somewhat away from the structuralist metaphors towards the metaphor of 'textuality' (Taylor 1971a, Jameson 1975/6, Sullivan 1978). Instead of seeking an underlying formalism, we prefer to try to *make sense* of a whole interview, or preferably, series of interviews. This involves us in a broader data base than most structuralists. We open ourselves to various contextual features which involve relations of subject to object other than just the *knowing* kind. To borrow a phrase from my colleague Dwayne Huebner, we focus broadly on processes of "self/social formation", implying by this that theoretical activities can be treated synthetically without excluding practical and expressive dimensions, all three being integrally involved in the simultaneous construction of self and society (Habermas, 1979).

Sixth, and building on our third and fourth points of difference, we do not hold that the ability to interpret and demystify is the sole prerogative of the researcher. The subject may take responsibility herself for her own *self-interpretation,* as Katherine does at several points. A parallel process may be precipitated in the interviewers, who are encouraged to interpret the others' development through an understanding of their own. The ideal possibility created by such an attitude is that the process of the interview, the interpretive superstructure, and the very *form of research* may be made transparent to the subject, and so made vulnerable to a joint analysis and practical transformation. This happens rather rarely, and only after an extended relationship. However, when it does, it can lead to the discovery and transcendence of constraints in the forms of communication and personal relationship in the interview, and even in the study as a whole.

This sixth point of difference reflects a concern with the politics of the interview discourse, and of developmental research as a whole. Klaus Riegel (1975) brought our attention to this in his discussion of "subject/object alienation" in the testing situation. Foucault's analysis of the process of science states similar worries more broadly (Kurzweil, 1977). Scientific structuralism is a powerful framework, which has transformed our own self-understanding by making us at first "strange" (as child, as savage, as madman). Nevertheless, it has failed, except perhaps with Foucault, to give rise to a self-critique. It does not provide room for a critical point of view on structuralists themselves. There is an ideal of the function of the intellectual as a totally reflective man with *no* preconceptions, the pure analytic critic of orthodoxies (McConnell, 1970, p. 279). Casting himself in this image, the structuralist theorist seems to have receded and become inaccessible, a virtual transcendent point of pure cognitive activity. In this respect, the self of the structuralist theorist has suffered the same fate as befell the concept of self in structuralist theory. Consequently what remains appears to be a neutral and dispassionate method or attitude. By virtue of unexplained assumptions, this method serves in the understanding of other civilisations (children, savages, madmen), who cannot themselves become conscious of the structural planes intersecting with their individual minds. The structuralist position, commonly posing as nothing more than a method, has become an instrument for the construction of a world cosmology. It is an instrument at least partially imbedded in the same celebration of rational theory and technique that in our own civilisation has contributed to those constraints on communication and freedom which typify the problematic modern world situation (Habermas, 1974; Bernstein, 1976).

These grand problems are by no means short-circuited by any of the innovations in methodology just mentioned. At the moment, as research psychologists, I and the students I have been working with are in transition. We are not satisfied that we have eliminated alienation of discourse in our work. Nevertheless, we are rationally convinced that the life of the mind is historical, and we are confident that setting development in the context of socio-historical self-transformation dereifies its stages, and makes its form and course more comprehensible as a whole. However, as yet, we really have no clear idea of how history intersects with ideas at the psychological level. We do know that simple models of causation are unsatisfactory, but not much more than this. However, we have made a start by examining and making explicit some of the key assumptions of structuralist thought and practice. It is our aim to transform and deepen the traditional structuralist approach simultaneously at the empirical and theoretical levels. One way to do this seems to be to bring it into relation with the critical meta-theory generated by the combined efforts of intellectual historians, philosophers, sociologists and ideology-critics. Hopefully, there is a reciprocal benefit to these large-scale conceptualisations in coming to terms with the particular structures and transformations of individual consciousness.

Notes

[1] The distinction between operative stages of cognition and levels of common-sense rationality is spelled out in Broughton, in press.

[2] It should be noted that structuralism does not eliminate the possibility of polysemy. Within a structural analysis, each word may have multiple structural meanings. Synchronic and diachronic differences may exist as well (Ihde, 1971, p. 177). Nevertheless, where binary relations are reduced to *logical* relations, as in Piagetian theory, polysemic metaphor, synecdoche, etc. *are* eliminated.

[3] Katherine's history of chemotherapy treatment is recounted in an article by E. Larson (1979).

[4] Thus, for example, Furth's work on the emergence of concepts of social institutions, Turiel's stages of understanding social conventions, Perry's stages of relation to academic authority, and Kohlberg's studies of decision between property and other rights all offer intriguing possibilities for a critical reinterpretation.

[5] In a recent conversation with Chomsky, following his presentation of "M.I.T. Cartesianism" at the annual meeting of the New York Psychoanalytic Association (1979), I was surprised to learn that he considers history to have absolutely no role at all in the formation of cognitive structure. In addition, it should be noted, he totally rejects Piaget's claim for the existence of developmental stages of cognitive structure. He bases this rejection on the claim that psychologists such as Mehler and Bever have demonstrated the innateness of the so-called operational structures. However, in psychological circles, the work of Mehler and Bever has fallen into considerable disrepute.

Adorno, T. W. "Types and Syndromes," in T. W. Adorno et al. *The Authoritarian Personality*. New York: Norton & Co., 1969 (1950).

Adorno, T. W. "The Stars down to Earth," *Telos*, 1974, *19*, 13-90.

Adorno, T. W. "Subject and Object," in A. Arato & E. Gebhardt (Eds.), *The Essential Frankfurt School Reader*. New York: Urizen Press, 1978.

Arendt, H. *The Life of the Mind*. New York: Harcourt, Brace & Javanovich, 1977.

Baldwin, J. M. *Genetic Theory of Reality*. New York: G. P. Putnam, 1915.

Basseches, M. *The Growth of Dialectical Thinking in College Students*. Unpublished doctoral dissertation, Harvard University, 1978.

Benoist, J. M. "Classicism Revisited: Human Nature and Structure in Levi-Strauss and Chomsky," in J. Benthall (ed) *The Limits of Human Nature*. London: Allen Lane, 1973.

Bergmann, F. Review essay on M. Sahlins, "Culture and Practical Reason." *American Journal of Sociology*, 1978, *83*, 4, 1007-1011.

Bernstein, B. "Class and Pedagogies: Visible and Invisible," in B. Bernstein (ed.) *Class, Codes and Control, vol. 3*. London: Routledge and Kegan Paul, 1975.

Bernstein, R. J. *The Restructuring of Social and Political Theory*. Oxford: Blackwell, 1976.

Beth, W. E. & Piaget, J. *Mathematical Epistemology and Psychology*. Dordrecht, Holland: D. Reidel, 1966.

Blasi, A. "Role-taking and the Development of Social Cognition." Paper presented at the Annual Meeting of the American Psychological Association, Chicago, 1975.

Blasi, A. "The Concept of Development in Personality Theory," in J. Loevinger, *Ego Development*. San Francisco: Jossey-Bass, 1976.

Böhme, G. *Der Streit Zwischen Baldwin und Titchener über einfache Reaktionen*. Unpublished manuscript, Max Planck Institute, Starnberg, Germany, 1973.

Broughton, J. M. "Beyond Formal Operations," *Teachers College Record*, Sept. 1977.

Broughton, J. M. "The Development of Concepts of Self, Mind, Reality and Knowledge," in W. Damon (ed.) *New Directions in Psychology: Social Cognition*. San Francisco: Jossey-Bass, 1978a.

Broughton, J. M. "Dialectics and Moral Development Ideology," in P. Scharf (ed.) *Readings in Moral Education*. Minneapolis: Winston Press, 1978.

Broughton, J. M. *Structuralism and Developmental Psychology*. Unpublished manuscript, Teachers College, Columbia University, 1979a.

Broughton, J. M. "The Limits of Formal Thought," in R. Mosher (ed.) *Adolescent Education*. Berkeley: McCutcham, 1979b.

Broughton, J. M. "Psychology and the History of the Self: From Substance to Function," in R. W. Rieber & K. W. Salzinger (eds.), *The Roots of American Psychology*. New York: Academic Press, in press.

Broughton, J. M. "Genetic Metaphysics: The Developmental Psychology of Mind/Body Concepts," in R. W. Rieber (ed.), *Body and Mind*. New York: Academic Press, in press.

Broughton, J. M. "Self and Identity in Early and Late Adolescence," to appear in B. Lee (ed.), *New Approaches to the Self* (in preparation).

Broughton, J.M. and Riegel, K.F. "Developmental Psychology and the Self." *Annals of the New York Academy of Sciences*, 1977, *291*, 149-167.

Broughton, J. M. and Zahaykevich, M. K. "Personality and Ideology in Ego Development," in V. Trinh van Thao and J. Gabel (eds.), *La Dialectique dans les Sciences Sociales*. Paris: Anthropos, 1979.

Buck-Morss, S. "Socio-economic Bias in Piaget's Theory, and the Cross-culture Controversy," *Human Development*, 1975, *18*, 35-49.

Buck-Morss, S. "Piaget, Adorno, and the Possibility of Dialectical Operations," *Stonybrook Studies in Philosophy*, 1978, *4*, 1-26.
Bukovsky, V. *To Build a Castle*. London: Andre Deutsch, 1978.
Buss, A. R. "Piaget, Marx and Buck-Morss on Cognitive Development: A Critique and Reinterpretation," *Human Development*. 1977, *20*, 112-128(a).
Buss, A. R. "In Defence of a Critical-presentist Historiography," Journal of History of the Behavioral Sciences, 1977, *13*, 252-260(b).
Buss, A. R. "Humanistic Psychology as Liberal Ideology: The Socio-historical Roots of Maslow's Theory of Self-actualization," *Journal of Humanistic Psychology* (in press).
Caws, P. "What is Structuralism?" *Partisan Review*, 1968, *35*, 1, 75-91.
Chomsky, N. *Language and Mind*. New York: Harcourt, Brace and World, 1968.
Collingwood, R. G. *The Idea of History*, London: Clarendon Press, 1946.
Collingwood, R. *The Idea of Nature*. Oxford: Oxford University Press, 1945.
D'Amico, R. "The Contours and Coupures of Structuralist Theory," *Telos*, 1963, *16*, 70-97.
Flax, J. "Critical Theory as a Vocation," *Politics and Society*, 1978, *8*, 2, 201-23.
Foucault, M. *The Order of Things: An Archeology of the Human Sciences*. New York: Pantheon, 1970.
Gabel, J. *False Consciousness*. London: Blackwells, 1975.
Gadlin, H. "Scars and Emblems: Paradoxes of American Family Life." *Journal of Social History*, 1978, *11*, *31*, 305-327.
Gardner, H. *The Quest for Mind*. New York: Vintage, 1972.
Glick, J. "Functional and Structural Aspects of Rationality." Paper presented at annual meeting of the Jean Piaget Society, Philadelphia, May, 1977.
Guilford, J. P. "Three Faces of Intellect." *American Psychologist*, 1959, *14*, 469-479.
Habermas, J. "A Postscript to 'Knowledge and Human Interests'." *Philosophy of the Social Sciences*, 1973, *3*, 157-189.
Habermas, J. "On Social Identity," *Telos*, 1974, *19*, 91-103.
Habermas, J. *Legitimation Crisis*. Boston: Beacon, 1975.
Habermas, J. *Communication and the Evolution of Society*. Boston: Beacon, 1979.
Hirsch, E. D. *Validity in Interpretation*. New Haven: Yale University Press, 1967.
Horkheimer, M. "On Truth," in A. Arato & E. Gebhardt (eds.), *The Essential Frankfurt School Reader*. New York: Urizon Press, 1978.
Husserl, E. *Formal and Transcendental Logic*. The Hague: Martinus Nijhoff, 1978.
Ihde, D. *Hermeneutic Phenomenology*. Evanston: Northwestern University Press, 1971.
Ingleby, D. "Ideology and the Human Sciences: Some Comments on the Role of Reification in Psychology and Psychiatry," in T. Pateman (ed.) *Counter-Course*. Harmondsworth: Penguin Books, 1972.
Ingleby, D. (ed.) *Critical Psychiatry*. Harmondsworth: Penguin Books, in press.
Inhelder, B. and Piaget, P. *The Growth of Logical Thinking From Childhood to Adolescence*. New York: Basic Books, 1958.
Jacoby, R. *Social Amnesia*. Boston: Beacon Press, 1975.
Jameson, F. *Marxism and Form*. Princeton: Princeton University Press, 1971.
Jameson, F. *The Prison-House of Language*. Princeton: Princeton University Press, 1972.
Jameson, F. "The Ideology of the Text," *Salmagundi*, 1975-76, *31-32*, 204-246.

Jones, B. "Cartesian Preconceptions in the Shift from Behaviorism to Cognitive Psychology." Paper presented at Cheiron conference, Carleton College, Ottawa, June 1975.

Kohlberg, L. "Revisions in the Theory and Practice of Moral Development," in W. Damon (ed.), *Moral Development*. San Francisco: Jossey-Bass, 1978.

Kohlberg, L. "Baldwin's theory of moral development," in J. M. Broughton and D. J. Freeman-Moir (eds.), *The Foundations of Cognitive-Developmental Psychology*. Norwood, New Jersey: Ablex (in press).

Kohlberg, L., and Gilligan, C. "The Adolescent as Philosopher. The Discovery of the Self in a Post-conventional World," *Daedalus*, 1971, *100* (4), 1051-1086.

Kurzweil, E. "Michel Foucault—ending the Era of Man," *Theory and Society*, 1977, *4* (3), 395-420.

Lacan, J. "The Mirror-phase as Formative of the Function of the I," *New Left Review*, 1949, *3*, 71-77.

Lacan, J. "Some Reflections on the Ego," *International Journal of Psychoanalysis*, 1953, *34*, 11-17.

Larson, E. Chemotheraphy: The Reality and the Fiction. *Bucks-County Courier Times*, Jan. 21, 1979.

Lasch, C. "Planned Obsolescence: Review of G. Sheehy 'Passages'," *New York Review of Books*, October, 1976, 7-12.

Levi-Strauss, C. *Structural Anthropology*. New York: Basic Books, 1963.

Levi-Strauss, C. *The Savage Mind*. London: Weidenfeld & Nicolson Ltd., 1966.

Levi-Strauss, C. A confrontation: an interview. *New Left Review*, 1970, *61*, 59.

Looft, W. R. & Svoboda, C. P. "Structuralism in Cognitive Developmental Psychology: Past, Contemporary, and Future Perspectives," in K. F. Riegel & G. C. Rosenwald (eds.), *Structure and Transformation*. New York: Wiley-Interscience, 1975.

McConnell, F. D. "Noam Chomsky: The Linguist as Anti-hero," *Soundings*, 1970, *53*, 3, 266-280.

Merleau-Ponty, M. *Phenomenology of Perception*. London: Routledge & Kegan-Paul, 1962.

Merleau-Ponty, M. "Maurice Merleau-Ponty à la Sorbonne," *Bulletin de Psychologie*, 1964, *18*, 236, 109-301.

Meszaros, I. *Marx's Theory of Alienation*. New York: Harper, 1970.

Pettit, P. *The Concept of Structuralism: A Critical Analysis*. Berkeley: University of California Press, 1975.

Piaget, J. *The Psychology of Intelligence*. Totowa, New Jersey: Littlefield, Adams & Co., 1966.

Piaget, J. "Explanation in Psychology and Psycho-physiological Parallelism," in P. Fraisse & J. Piaget (eds.), *Experimental Psychology, its Scope and Method, vol. I: History and Method*. London: Routledge & Kegan-Paul, 1968.

Piaget, J. "Invited Seminar," Catholic University, Washington, June, 1970.

Piaget, J. "Intellectual Evolution from Adolescence to Adulthood." *Human Development*, 1972, *15*, 1-12.

Piaget, J. "The Affective Unconscious and the Cognitive Unconscious," in B. Inhelder & H. H. Chipman (eds.), *Piaget and His School*. New York: Springer Verlag, 1976.

Picciarelli, P. *Merleau-Ponty's Theory of Development*. Unpublished doctoral dissertation, Teachers College, Columbia University, 1978.

Reid, H. G. & Yanarella, E. J. "Critical Political Theory and Moral Development," *Theory and Society*, 1977, *4*, 505-541.

Ricoeur, P. *Freud and Philosophy: An Essay on Interpretation.* New Haven: Yale University Press, 1970.

Ricoeur, P. Special issue of *Philosophy Today*, 1973, *17*, 2/4.

Ricoeur, P. *Interpretation Theory: Discourse and the Surplus of Meaning.* Fort Worth, Texas: Christian University Press, 1976.

Riegel, K. F. "Dialectical Operations: The Final Period of Cognitive Development," *Human Development*, 1973, *16*, 346-70.

Riegel, K. F. "Structure and Transformation in Modern Intellectual History," in K. F. Riegel & G. C. Rosenwald (eds.), *Structure and Transformation.* New York: Wiley-Interscience, 1975.

Riegel, K. F. "Subject-object Alienation in Psychological Experiments and Testing," *Human Development*, 1975, *18*, 2, 181-193.

Russell, J. "The Status of Genetic Epistemology," *Journal of the Theory of Social Behaviour*, 1979, *9*, 1, 1-22.

Sartre, J.-P. "Replies to Structuralism: An Interview," *Telos*, 1971, 9, 110-115.

Saussure, F. de *Cours de Linguistique Générale.* Paris: Presses Universitaires de France, 1965.

Schecter, B. *Animism and Metaphoric Thinking in Children.* Unpublished doctoral dissertation, Teachers College, Columbia University, 1979.

Sève, L. *Marxism and the Theory of Human Personality.* London: Wishart, 1975.

Sohn-Rethel, A. *Intellectual and Manual Labour: A Critique of Epistemology.* London: Methuen, 1978.

Sontag, S. "Illness as Metaphor," *New York Review of Books*, Jan. 26 - Feb. 23, 1978, *24-25* (3 instalments).

Steinberg, L. *Other Criteria.* New York: Oxford University Press, 1972.

Sullivan, E. V. "Kohlberg's Structuralism," *Monographs of Ontario Institute for Studies in Education*, 1977, *15*.

Taylor, C. "Interpretation and the Sciences of Man," *Review of Metaphysics*, 1971a, *25*, 1, 1-51.

Taylor, C. "What is Involved in a Genetic Psychology?" in T. Mischel (ed.), *Cognitive Development and Genetic Epistemology.* New York: Academic Press, 1971b.

Titchener, E. B. *Systematic Psychology: Prolegomena.* New York: MacMillan Co., 1929.

Trigg, R. *Reason and Commitment.* Cambridge: Cambridge University Press, 1973.

Turner, T. "Piaget's Structuralism," *American Anthropologist*, 1973, *75*, 351-73.

Unger, R. M. *Knowledge and Politics.* New York: Free Press, 1975.

Venn, C. & Walkerdine, V. "The Acquisition and Production of Knowledge: Piaget's Theory Reconsidered," *Ideology and Consciousness*, 1978, *3*, 67-94.

Wason, P. C. & Johnson-Laird, P. N. *Psychology of Reasoning, Structure and Content.* London: Batsford, 1972.

Commentary on
"Developmental Structuralism:
Without Self - Without History"

Adrienne E. Harris
Rutgers University

Paper presented at the 2nd Conference on the Social Sciences at
the University of Calgary. Calgary, Canada, October, 1978.

Piagetian theory has within the last two decades become the
centerpiece of North American cognitive developmental psychology. As an inevitable measure of this centrality, Piaget's work
and thought is currently the target of some critical reassessment.

In the current critical consideration of Piagetian theory (Siegel
and Brainerd, 1978; Riegel, 1976; Buck-Morss, 1975) the
arguments center chiefly on the cumulative and dominant role for
abstract reasoning, the historical and cultural myopia of a theory
which masks bourgeois western intellectual formation as
universal and general laws of cognitive development, and the
asocial caste to development present throughout Piaget's work.
Anyone intending to mount a successful counter to these charges
would seem to have to rationalize the role of rational thought
both as a method and as a product of human cognizing and to cast
Piagetian theory as a materialist theory of development. In
particular, the latter task requires the rehabilitation of a rather
carefully selected view of Piaget's theory. By contrast, I wish to
present a reading of Piaget in which his unusually nonstruc-
turalist treatment of language precludes a totally satisfying
recasting as a materialist (and dialectical materialist) theory of
development.

I want to first comment on Broughton's treatment or defense of
Piaget for he has recuperated a particularly dynamic version of
the theory. Such an active reading requires a selection and
attention to the early Piaget manifested in the writing on sensory
motor-thinking and the origins of intelligence and a careful
screening of all the synchronic preoccupations of Piagetians in
North America. The theory of transformed cognitive stages tamed
by psychometricians and educators reduces dynamically conceived moving structures to global descriptions of behavior
cognitive action assimilating to the American psychologists'
preoccupation with traits (Riegel, 1976).

A crucial feature of Broughton's analysis is that structure is rule
not fact. Formal thought is "apprehended in a logical organization conceived as a property of the real". It is the reflective

interpretation of the outcome of experience which leads to awareness of logical categories, a rule book for reference and legitimation. This gives formal thought somewhat the same status as traffic signals in New York City. Not certainly guiding drivers' actions but available in the event of disaster or argument as procedures for assigning responsibility. This is a valiant effort to restore dynamism to the cognitive system Piaget developed. But the analysis still sticks and slips at the point of integrating such mental structures with the process of thinking. I would like to suggest the question Broughton poses and tries to answer— namely what is the relation in cognitive developmental theory of deep structures of thought and thinking—is and always will be unanswerable within the context of Piagetian theory by virtue of its particular treatment of language in mental processing. Only when language is seen not merely as a cognizing tool but as a social activity with constitutive force in our self-understanding and world experience, can one break that conceptual impasse.

Another focus of attention in this paper and a troubling one is the status of the individual in Piagetian theory. Piaget's concern has been with the epistemic individual, i.e., the qualities of minding and cognizing that are true for all. Subjective experience is thus only interesting in terms of what universal structures or procedures can be extracted from it. This is a view of human functioning as transcendent but without sociability. That Piaget's notion of individual development is not one of passive registration is of course an improvement on earlier psychological theories. But the theory is distinctly asocial. Individuals construct rules, extract meaning, synthesize new structural regularities, but in a quite solitary encounter with the environment. This notion of the individual is really out of phase with the continental structuralist tradition at least in its psychoanalytic vein. The self in Lacanian theory is interiorized through a complex reflection of other social beings to whom one is tied in an intimate and terrifying connection. An individuated self is always located within an interlocking imaginary and real social nexus. This seems to render the social individual in Piaget's theory a sort of epiphenomenon. In this regard, the theory has a rather similar impact to that of sociobiology. Codes, inaccessible to consciousness in their active workings, whether genetic as in sociobiology, or cognitive as in Piaget, operate through the individual. Skin boundaries become almost arbitrary. There is no collective sociability with impact on the individual and no individual transcendence is deemed possible.

Another area of concern in Piagetian criticism is the whole issue of stages. This critique has been made on formal grounds

(Brainerd, 1976) denying that there is empirical and formal
support for conceptually distinct stages. What is somewhat
unusual for a *synthetic* developmental theory is that Piaget
proposes a structural developmental model in which earlier levels
are embedded but then inoperative at higher levels. Thought is
transformed. The notion of a developing individual who manifests his or her whole history is really not envisioned even in
Piaget's use of the concept of vertical decalage. There has been
some interesting writing on the question of multi-level functioning. Sameroff (1975) has suggested that parents' view of their
children as literal or figurative projections or as independent
beings constitute levels of cognitive functioning in the interpersonal domain. Riegel (1975) in suggesting a fifth stage of
dialectical operations was trying to permit ambiguity and contradiction and true synthesis into the system. But this remains
problematic in Piaget's own work. In Broughton's paper, he has
claimed that the logical system Piaget committed himself to is not
fundamental to the theory, nor is the concept of stage nor equilibration. What is left however after such surgery is little more than
procedure, the structuralist method. I want to turn now to a more
detailed consideration first of the treatment of language in Piaget's
theory and secondly to the question of ideology-critique raised
in Broughton's paper.

Language Functions in Cognitive Theory
  In one crucial respect Piaget stands outside the tradition of
continental structuralism: his consideration of language.
Throughout his writing Piaget has treated some format of
cognitive structure as central to evolving intelligence and relegated speech and language to the status of static material to be
manipulated by the thinking and structuring child. Language is
emblematic of thought, now integrated and interdependent. It is
the medium for cognitive activity. Language as a capability is
possible in Piaget's system with shifts in representational structuring at the end of sensory motor development. Language does
no more than expand the computing space for cognitive activity.
More recently in the empirical work of Piagetians like Sinclair-
deZwart, although some impact of the transformational grammarians revolution in American linguistics is in evidence, language is still primarily a terrain for the display of cognitive
processes or levels. Linguistic process reflects cognitive stage.
Language is thus the mirror of cognition or its tool and the
Piagetian school seems never to have entertained the notion that
language is itself a set of rich structures, a network of significance
providing a deep and intricate web of meanings whereby people

in dialogue or self-reflection constitute and negotiate understanding. Language in Piagetian theory seems neither social nor significantly structural.

This perspective is remote from the structuralist treatment of language which traces genealogy from Saussure, through Jacobson and is currently manifested in the work of Lacan, Derrida or Barthes. Specifically we might note Lacan's (1973) marriage of psychoanalytic interpretation to Saussurean linguistics as an acknowledged influence on Gadamer (1976) connecting thus to the hermeneutic tradition. We may characterize this perspective as one which captures language in its syntagmatic, paradigmatic and interactive aspects. Signifiers are interpreted always in terms of other meanings or systems of reference. Signs are read in terms of the network of substitutable and related signs or in terms of the connected structures in which they are embedded, the twin systems of metaphor and metonymy, to remind us of Jacobson's characterization. Language is, above all, not a tool to be picked up and used in the service of thought. It is the ongoing changing crucible of received tradition. An initiate in some language community does not simply pick up a linguistic apparatus through which to express thought but enters an arranged, linguistically constituted, social reality which encloses and places the speaker.

In Lacan's treatment of this process, when the child learns to speak, the signifier slips over the inchoate pre-reflexive experience with which it exists in a relationship of dialectical non-identity, and the child speaks—is spoken—in the name of the father. Need is thus transformed into desire and language enters, alters and interacts with emerging thought. So awareness and cognizing actualizes as language unfolds and becomes the mode for inter-subjective understanding. As Gadamer (1976) epigrammatically notes, "Being that can be understood is language. Societal reality brings itself into representation in a consciousness that is linguistically articulated." Language is essentially an act of self-forgetfulness, inherently social, profoundly I-less.

It is probably at this point important to snatch this particular viewpoint from the jaws of any of the variants of linguistic relativism. Language initiates us into a cultural and social system but the language user, in that act, connects pre-existent tradition and his own reflective appropriation of it. Language allows a 'venture into the alien' an expanding consciousness by virtue of its structure, its access to rich networks of significance, its rules of substitution, and combination. The underlying deep structure of language, its syntax, can be apprehended and analyzed, but these 'giant abstractions' are inaccessible to the speaker in the act of

producing the stream of speech either as inner dialogue or inter-
subjective negotiation.

What then are the implications of this perspective on language
for a cognitive developmental theory such as Piaget's? A cognitive
theory which does not conceptualize a knower both individual
and social, bound in a cognizing process where subject and object
are interconnected, cannot adequately describe the cognitive
process of a historical subject. The lacunae in Piaget's theory with
regard to language structure and its integrating functions in
thought denies his theory that possibility and furthers the schism
between structure and process. The frozen separation of thought
and language in Piaget is a fatal reification.

The process of knowing is actualized in language and particularly in dialogue. Knowing is negotiated intersubjectively,
interpretations are achieved socially with joint recourse to shared
assumptions (which may be entailed in structural or logical
premises of thought) as well as bewildered retreats to subjective
experience. These, I believe, are the key insights of continental
structuralists with regard to language. Alternatively Piaget has
generated a theory and an accompanying research program in
which experiment, interview or dialogue produces speech
samples which are then drained of their dialogic and constitutive
elements to reveal the skeletal frame of logical structure. This
strategy, which seems so deeply out of phase with his writing on
equilibration has been present in Piaget as early as the consideration of private and egocentric speech, in *The Language and
Thought of the Child* (Piaget, 1928), for which Vygotsky's (1962)
response still stands as an important alternative.

Ideology Critique

In the critical reassessment of Piaget's work, there has been one
strain identifiable essentially as ideology-critique. Broughton
counters these types of critique on important grounds. Thus far,
efforts to make an ideology critique of Piaget's work have
incorporated rather than overthrown the method of analysis they
criticize or have fallen into the trap of idealism through the
articulation of disembodied analogies between various levels of
social and cognitive functioning. The critical analysis of mediation remains to be undertaken.

Whatever the merits of Broughton's counter-arguments, it is
both acceptable and necessary to point out those moments in
theory writing where special interests are trotted out as universal.
The presentation of scientific methods and technological rationality as the cynosure of mature thought and the consequent claims

for universality are an appropriate focus of ideology critique. It is also important to stress that only a quite bankrupt and outdated form of Marxism would insist on the crude cleavages of base and superstructure which Broughton fears. Joseph Kockelmans has suggested that hermeneutics study the 'miracle of mediation of traditions' and to pursue this a hermeneutic psychology must take on (not historical or socioeconomic description) but an examination of precisely how social forces, tradition and historical conditions are mediated and internalized in individual life. For example, within the framework Habermas provides in *Legitimation Crisis* (1973) a variety of institutions exercise motivating and legitimating functions in the service of systems maintenance through various fissures and crises in post-liberal capitalism. However it remains for a critical psychology to establish how psychological theory and practice might come to serve legitimating functions. Habermas noted that the successful function of a legitimating apparatus was premised on its independence from the state and from political life in general. Any critique which begins to map out those relationships can potentially break out of the abstract idealist hold of ideology critique. The delegitimation of theory through the analysis of its interdependence with state and economic functions is a theoretical act with practical consequences.

Above all, in response to Broughton's analysis of ideology critique, I think it is important to set ideology critique in psychology in a historical context. This would argue, amongst other things, for an exercise of patience and supportive tolerance for this tendency. Unlike most other social sciences, at least in North America, psychology has been remarkably efficient in keeping discourse in the discipline free of these concerns. Educating its practitioners with *no* sense of genealogical depth, *no* exposure to the philosophical and social issues that are its underpinnings, and *no* tools to analyze the conflation of truth and method, psychology has successfully induced in student and professor alike a sort of 'social amnesia', to take Jacoby's (1976) perspective, divorcing its initiates from the grounded interests and values that lead them into psychology and producing instead an understanding of social and individual experience redolently 'psychological'. The two important questions to ask are why psychology is the dominant social science in North America and why its critical tradition has been so insistently underdeveloped.

Broughton's critique of ideology-critique stresses the continued reliance on structuralism. I suspect a more serious problem is the continued reliance on positivism. The project for ideology-critique in psychology is to ground the analysis in a political and

social practice. What is entailed in this is to locate the interests of
the critique and the involvement and investment of such work in
the production of human science and social meaning. Thus far,
critique in psychology has practised the same methodological
alienation from the phenomena studied as the standard empirically based science. But the grounded critique Broughton points
to requires a fundamentally different dialogue between scholar
and object of study. An example of an approach to problems in
human development which alters methodologically the project of
studying, is Buckholdt and Gubrium's (1977) look at classification systems in so-called pathological children in a treatment
centre. Their perspective owes much to Berger and Gouldner and
assumes that people in some sense talk themselves into cycles and
stages. They negotiate and construct their sense of their lives to
meet the structure or staged nature which they and others expect.
"Human development is generated out of people's lifework." So
they undertake to study human development as a problem in
practical knowledge—how typification of self and others occur.
But the data they examine are quite novel for developmental
psychology. In order to penetrate the finished product, i.e., the
classification and treatment recommendation for a 'disturbed
child' they recorded the process of staff negotiation and discussion
of a child. What they record is a fascinating process of negotiation in which experts and field workers, through dialogue, test
and develop rhetorical justifications for decisions. In the running
interview, one sees projected diagnoses set against behavior, staff
meeting the proposed categorization of the expert psychologist,
in order to come to decisions about whether the child in question
is really manipulative or really developmentally damaged. The
presentation of the reality of the child's performance in the
treatment centre literally changes in the course of the meeting.
Nowhere in the deliberations is there any awareness by staff that
this politicized, negotiated meeting plays a role as a constitutive
feature of that child's development. There is selection of pertinent
evidence which is designed both to feed into the power dynamics
of the centre, reinforce expertise, and match target classification
schemes. Making psychology dialogic in this manner has the
potential of reconnecting us with our own contributions to the
data and processes of human development and could make psychology more radically reflexive.

     In suggesting the appropriate mode of analysis and interpreta-
tion as the dialogue we make a different recourse to authority, we
speak not of received word or speech performed *ex cathedra*, but of
negotiated clarifying social exchange in language. Hermeneutics
has been referred to as a sort of philosophical psychoanalysis in

which the prejudgements, the interests of participants need to be critically evaluated and understood in the process of understanding the social meaning of phenomena under examination. I think that this is at the heart of Habermas' concern with communicative competence and a model for doing social science which entails essentially undistorted communication, i.e. shared, intersubjectively agreed upon interpretations, reference to common understanding. It is a view of social communication which is paradoxically a mutual understanding and an interrupted discourse. What will be of interest to psychologists who can follow this path are the surprises, the difficulty, the radical reflexive transformation that will be entailed as they enter the social life they study, or rather as they accept and make explicit their constitutive role in the social phenomena they work with. And, if ideology-critique begins to declare its interests, ground itself in a social praxis as well as a world-view, the possibility of antagonistic interests (long buried within the experimental or observational dialogue) will have to be faced and worked on.

Ricoeur's account of the hermeneutic method may serve as an instructive guideline. Activity in the human sciences must be circuitous and dialogic, trying to gain experience of the concrete phenomenon of interest in many modes and on many levels. In this activity, structuralist and semiotic analysis (theoretical hermeneutics) intertwines with the reading of context (interpretive hermeneutics). Both are enveloped in a context of radically reflexive critique exposing the interests and alliances of the investigators.

Bibliography

Brainerd, C. "Stage, structure and developmental theory," in G. Steiner (ed.), *The Psychology of the Twentieth Century.* Kindler, 1976.
Buck-Morss, S. "Socio-economic bias in Piaget's theory: Its implications for cross-cultural studies," in K. Riegel (ed.), *The Development of Dialectical Operations.* Karger, 1975.
Buckholdt, D. and Gubrium, J. "The Politics of Human Development." Unpublished manuscript, 1977.
Gadamer, H.G. *Philosophical Hermeneutics.* University of California Press, 1976.
Habermas, J. *Legitimation Crisis.* Beacon Press, 1973.
Jacoby, R. *Social Amnesia.* Beacon Press, 1976.
Lacan, J. *The Four Fundamental Concepts of Psycho-analysis.* Norton, 1973.
Piaget, J. *The Language and Thought of the Child.* Harcourt Brace, 1926.
Riegel, K. "Toward a Dialectic Theory of Development," in K.F. Riegel (ed.), *The Development of Dialectical Operations.* Karger, 1975.
Riegel, K. "From traits and equilibrium towards developmental dialectics," in W.J. Arnold and J.K. Cole (eds.), *Nebraska Symposium on Motivation, 1974-1975.* University of Nebraska Press, 1976.

Sameroff, A. "Transactional Models in Early Social Relations," in K. Riegel
(ed.), *The Development of Dialectical Operations*. Karger, 1975.

Siegel, L. and Brainerd, C. (eds.), *Alternatives to Piaget: Critical Essays on the Theory*. Academic Press, 1978.

Vygotsky, L. *Thought and Language*. MIT Press, 1962.

Structuralism in a Psychological Context

Edmund V. Sullivan,
The Ontario Institute for Studies in Education,
University of Toronto

...Structuralism is a method, not a doctrine, whose doctrinal consequences have been quite various. Because it is a method, its applicability is limited; that is precisely on account of its fruitfulness, it has become connected with other methods, it admits the legitimacy of these other methods.... Structuralism is as willing to get as to give; only, being a recent arrival and still full of unexpected riches, the exchange between it and the more established methods have been somewhat uneven. (Piaget, 1971; pp. 142-3).

The cognitivist fallacy—that culture consists ... of mental phenomena which can be analyzed by formal methods similar to those of mathematics and logic—is as destructive of an effective use of the concept as are the behaviorist and idealist fallacies to which it is a misdrawn correction. Perhaps, as its distortions subtler, it is even more so (Geertz, 1973, p. 12).

Introduction

In the late 1950's and early 1960's there appeared a rather interesting transitional period in American psychology. There was a crack in the wall of logical empiricism in its attempts to develop mechanical metaphors. Behaviorism was becoming much more complicated and there was a movement toward a "behavior theory" which could deal with the complexities of the "human organism" (e.g. Osgood, et. al. 1958). For the first time we see an attempt to address complex linguistic processes by incorporating the term "meaning" (Osgood, Tannenbaum & Suci 1958). The logical empiricism formerly presented by "behaviorism" was being stretched to its limits. New theoretical shifts were taking place at this time which would eventually lead to the decade of "structuralism" in American psychology. "Structuralism" as specifically presented to the psychological scene was to be an essential challenge to the prevalent "mechanistic" theories. When the Swiss genetic epistemologist Piaget entered the American psychological scene in the 1960's, there had already been a movement toward "centralist" or "mediated" behaviorist formulations. The psycho-linguist, Charles Osgood, was suggesting complex "mediational processes" to explain linguistic meaning. Behaviorism at this time, was now attempting to come to terms with complex mental processes and we also see at this time "information processing" models spinning off from computer simulation research (Hilgard & Bower, 1966). Behaviorists (e.g. Berlyne, 1966, and Gagne, 1968) and computer-simulation theorists attempted a rapprochement with Piaget's and Chomsky's structuralism, but for the most part these attempted marriages had ill fated results (e.g. Newell and Simon, 1961, Mc V. Hunt 1961). The reason for this is that at a fundamental level "structuralism" deviates radically from atomism, even in its complex guises, because there is a "synthetic" rather than an "analytic" conception of knowledge. Our focus on "structuralism" ultimately in this paper will dwell mostly on the contribution that the "interpretive horizon" has made to American psychology. We will therefore limit our discussion to the work of Chomsky, Kohlberg and Piaget. In order to place structuralism in an historical context it will be necessary to trace schematically some of its historical roots.

The Cartesian Legacy and the Place of Structuralism Within its Walls

Interpretation is an activity or process which attempts to make clear or give the sense of an object of study (Taylor, 1971). Normally it is considered a process which clarifies or renders the meaning of a text; but it can be extended to "text analogues" (e.g. a human person or community) which in some way, at first sight appears unclear, perplexing, confused, incomplete, cloudy, seemingly contradictory in one way or another. Interpretation aims to bring to light an underlying coherence or sense (Taylor, 1971). At times of radical cultural upheaval, the necessity of *interpretation* is evident. Usually some person or group attempts to give a reading or interpretation of the situation where there is no longer a clear coherent cultural formulation of what is good or true. Descartes faced the problem of a cultural breakdown of a medieval world synthesis and in one sense, his method of dealing with it may be said to be an "interpretation" to bring a new coherence where old meanings were being challenged. His method was an attempt to achieve certainty where a situation of uncertainty prevailed. It might be said that his interpretive method was, paradoxically, the first attempt to eliminate the need for interpretation. Descartes' "methodic doubt" was to lead to a demand for certainty by only accepting as true those expressions or ideas which could be said to have achieved clarity and distinction. Ultimately Descartes, the mathematician, found clarity and certainty in mathematical expressions. Clear and distinct ideas had no need for interpretation; their coherence or meaning would be self-evident. Descartes wanted assurance and a

firm footing for knowledge and the problems presented by the
interpretation of expressions ran against the grain of what was
ultimately to be called *rationalism*. Clearly, the demand for
certainty has been the legacy of the Cartesian methodological
synthesis. In this methodological world outlook, the method that
leads to truth and certainty was the one that was allied to
propositions or events which were "clear and distinct". As this
method has developed over the centuries in all of its guises, it is
usually allied with all methodological outlooks which eschew
ambiguity of *expressions* and attempts to relieve the embarrassment of conflict of interpretations by supplying a method which
believes that it can achieve certainty (truth) over interpretation
(Gadamer, 1975 a, b). In the context of our present discussion this
demand for *certainty* demands that the "hermeneutical circle"
must be broken out of because it is a vicious circle (Taylor, 1973).

Rationalism and Empiricism

Empiricism and rationalism are two historical ways of attempting to break out of the "hermeneutical or interpretative cycle"
(Taylor, 1973). Both of these methods issue from the Cartesian
mind-body dualism: rationalism issuing from concerns of our
understanding of the mind and mechanistic empiricism from our
understanding of the body. Thus, Western thought may be said to
be limited to a fund of basic schemes of explanations, and
ultimately they can, with all their variations, be boiled down to
two ideal types, logical analysis (i.e. Rationalism) and causal
explanation (i.e. Empiricism) (Unger, 1971). Both schemes provide an interpretation of what it means to account for something
both in the sense of telling what a phenomenon or event is like,
which is description, and in the sense of establishing why it had to
follow from something else, which is *explanation* in the strict
sense (Unger, 1976). Both of these schemes appear historically in
order to deal with the *interpretation* of physical and social events
(Taylor, 1971). Rationalism is essentially the use of deduction. In
deduction, certainty is achieved by grasping the inner certainty of
propositions. The method of deduction is "logical analysis"
which is a linear development of arguments (Unger, 1976).
Objectivity or certainty is gained by retreating to a "truth" which
is formal and abstracted from concrete historical events. The
conclusion in a deductive sequence is therefore a formal truth.
The methodological thrust of rationalism is to bring *understanding* (i.e. clear and true interpretation) to an inner clarity
which is absolute (i.e. logical argument). Rationalism provides
an ordering principle which is at the level of ideas (Unger, 1976).

It is essentially a historical method of arriving at certainty. Rationalism, as given to our time, issues from the philosophical systems of Descartes, Spinoza, and Leibnitz (Robinson, 1976). Persuaded by the proofs of mathematics that *certain* knowledge exists, it has eskewed its dialectical counterpart empiricism in its suspiciousness of the "imprecise and ephemeral *truths* of the sense" (Robinson, 1976). In its modern garb, it assumes that the very act of perception has a categorical framework, thus incorporating the concept of *a priori* cognitive capacity without which meaningful experience would be impossible (Robinson, 1976). In short rationalism is an

> ... epistemological system that asserts that all knowledge is the result of rationalism of the evidence of sense and this very evidence cannot be gathered except by a rationally directing principle. Accordingly, the primary "datum" of which our knowledge is comprised is that innate disposition called the laws of thought (Robinson, 1976, p. 199).

Empiricism by contrast, is a method for arriving at truth at the level of *events* in history. In contrast to strict rationalism, its truths are time-bound and concrete (Unger, 1976). It argues linearly at the level of cause and effect; the cause in a time sequence being antecedent to the effect. Empiricism attempts to break out of the circle of interpretation by attempting to move beyond the problem presented by human subjectivity (Taylor, 1971). Empiricism as a method is a systematic method to reconstruct knowledge in such a way that there is no need to appeal to readings or judgments. It is for this reason that the basic building block of empiricism is the sensory impression or sense datum which psychologists have come to know as the stimulus. As an epistemological system it asserts that:

> The evidence of sense constitutes the primary data of all knowledge; that knowledge cannot exist unless this evidence has first been gathered; and that all subsequent intellectual processes must use this evidence and only this evidence in framing valid propositions about the real world (Robinson, 1976, p. 198).

At the level of perception the stimulus is a unit of information which is supposedly not mediated by judgment (Ausubel and Sullivan, 1970). Subjectivity is played down within this formulation by alluding to the organism as a *tabula rasa*. Assuming to be working at the sensory level of *brute datum*, it is therefore perceived to be unnecessary to utilize subjective interpretation or judgement. Empiricism as a methodological ideal wants certainty anchored beyond subjective intuition. In this, it shares with rationalism a suspicion of subjective consciousness.

In the twentieth century the easy distinction between "rationalism" and "empiricism" has become blurred. Empiricism has become *"logical empiricism"* and any form of *rationalism*, if it is to have "scientific" respectively must be based on some form of empirical pursuits. Our contention is that "structuralism" at least in its psychological manifestations, constitutes a movement with its impulses embedded in historical rationalism while at the same time having an empirical program (e.g. Piaget). It is because of its roots in rationalism that it is seen as a methodological alternative to "logical empiricism". With this brief historical context completed, I would now like to turn to the method of "structuralism" *per se* to make some finer distinctions.

Structuralism

Structuralism has been described as a method, a movement, an intellectual fad, and an ideology. Each of these characterizations is in part valid. For structuralism is a loose, amorphous, many faceted phenomenon with no clear lines of democration, no tightly knit group spearheading it, no specific set of doctrines held by all those whom one usually thinks of as being associated with it (De George and De George, 1972 p. XI).

Althusser, Foucault, Lacan, Levi-Strauss, Piaget, Chomsky, Marx and Freud to name the more prominent ones have been labelled structuralists. They all share in the argument that surface events and phenomena are to be explained by structures, data and phenomena below the surface (De George and De George, 1972). A second point of similarity between these theorists is their position on self-consciousness which is, in effect, that individual self-consciousness has no privileged status within their theoretical formulation. In fact many theorists who go under the structuralist label explicitly reject self-consciousness as an important dimension for understanding human phenomena (Petit, 1975). It is in this sense that many structuralists see themselves as anti-phenomenological (Piaget, 1971a, 1971b, Petit, 1972). From our definitions it follows that structuralism cannot be considered a consciously formed school nor a united movement (De George and De George, 1972, Gardner, 1972, Piaget, 1971b). For this reason, our approach to the discussion of structuralism will be as follows: first of all we are limiting our discussion to three major theorists who have made a recent impact on the discipline of psychology (i.e. Piaget, Kohlberg and Chomsky), and who are seen as "structuralists" within the context of this discipline. The second major limiting condition is that we are restricting ourselves to theorists who, at least, attempt to formulate their theoretical constructions with a developmental perspective. In other words, we are discussing "structuralists" who systematically incorporate a concept of development into their theoretical and empirical formulations. We are therefore situating a body of theoretical work historically, at the same time suggesting certain structural coordinates which define a certain unity between the theorists to be discussed. These coordinates, or what one might call an "interpretive matrix", essentially show, despite internal divergencies and oppositions, a common theoretical tradition. They are (1) The Controlling Metaphor or Paradigm of a Structuralist Perspective, (2) The Epistemological Principle, (3) The Mode of Observation, (4) Interpretation and the Problem of Language, (5) Meaning and the Problem of Subjectivity, and finally; (6) The Nature of Social Relations.

1) The Controlling Metaphor or Paradigm of Structuralism

"Structuralism" is a form of systems theory. As such, systems theories began as an organicist revolt against "mechanistic" philosophy (Von Bertalanffy, 1971). Hence the appropriate interpretive metaphor is that of an "organism" rather than a "mechanism". The shift is therefore away from physics and toward metaphors of organism developed in the biological sciences. A metaphor is said to be organic when its symbol system employs terms which describe or explain individual human development in organic terms. In the present discussion, theories which employ analogs to biological organisms can be classified as "organic metaphors". As an example let me briefly quote a passage from Piaget's Structuralism under the topic heading "Organic Structures".

> The living organism is both a physiochemical system among other systems and a source of a subject's activities. If, then, as we have maintained throughout, a structure is a systematic whole of self-regulating transformations, the organism is, in a way, the paradigm structure. If we knew our own organism through and through it would, on

account of its double role of complex physical object and originator of behavior give us a key to a general theory of structure. But after centuries of simplistic reductionism on the one hand and of a vitalism more verbal than explanatory on the other, biological structuralism is as yet only in its beginnings (Piaget, 1971, pp. 44-45).

The use of organic metaphorical terms is employed by a wide variety of psychological and social theories, ranging from perspectives developed out of "structuralist" and "functionalist" models. We are focusing on a structuralist model for purposes of our present discussion, but it should be made clear from the outset that the use of "organic" analysis is not restricted to structuralism. For example, Donald Campbell's (1975) recent Presidential address to the American Psychological Association speaks from a "functionalist" position in proposing a systems theory of individual and societal development based on concepts drawn on the social and biological theory.

The use of "biological metaphors" was quite prevalent at the turn of the century, but with the advent of mechanistic behaviorism they receded to the background of American Psychology. With the renaissance of "structuralism" during the 1960's, we see the advent of "organic metaphors" in conflict with the previously dominant mechanistic explanatory systems. Just why structuralism should gain such power is a matter for some complex historical speculation; but it is clear that it is not just the result of the explanatory power of the theories proposed. It was surprising in its nascent stages that within a few short years, Piaget's study of cognitive development, Chomsky's conceptions about language development and Kohlberg's study of moral development were to become the most powerful and popular psychological metaphors on the American psychological scene. Wilden (1975) has characterized structuralism, information theory and general systems theory as a veritable epistemological shift in the way of conceiving living and social systems. He links this to a progressive transformation of the larger socio-economic structure surrounding psychological speculation:

The increasing size and complexity of business corporations, as well as their organization in tiers, trees, pyramids, and more intricate topological structures would naturally lead to the systematization of a body of theory designed to explain and control organization. Similarly one has only to consider the relatively sudden discovery by the industrialized nations that the pursuit of individual economic independ-

ence leads ultimately to increasing degrees of collective interdependence to realize that we would necessarily come to live
in an era when some form of systems ecology would be
applied to any and all complexities of system-environment
relations. The shift is both a mirror of contemporary socio-
economic reality and an illumination of it. (p. 91).

There has gradually been a shift away from mechanical metaphors and references to biological and human relations in
terms of aggregates, entities, atoms, individuals, closed systems,
linear causality etc. (Wilden, 1975). The new vocabulary employs
such terminology as wholes, interdependent structures, open
systems, feedback, information and communication (Wilden,
1975). Although this shift in epistemology is a contemporary
phenomena, it has its historical roots which go back to the 17th
century (Chomsky, 1968; Taylor, 1973). Even as early as Descartes,
there was a belief that mechanical metaphors in their nascent state
could not explain the complexities of the mind in terms of
quantity, but rather that a qualitative dimension was necessary in
any adequate form of explanation. It has taken well over two centuries to move away from a traditional and quantitative epistemology to be replaced by a multidimensional viewpoint of levels and
complexity which necessarily involves a comprehension of qualitative considerations as a prerequisite for any quantitative
analysis (Wilden, 1975). Dagenais (1972) notes that "structuralism" rose out of the amalgam of psychology, anthropology and
sociology, passed through the science of linguistics and has
passed back into psychology, psychoanalysis, anthropology and
sociology. In our present discussion it is being discussed as a water
shed (based on "organic metaphors") between a mechanistic
metaphor and a more self-consciously appropriated "hermeneutical paradigm". Charles Taylor (1973), sees "structuralism" in
exactly the same light. He outlines two major epistemologies; the
classical and the hermeneutical model:

> The classical one in its natural place in the first domain; that
> of psycho-physical or infrastructural studies; the hermeneu-
> tic model as the natural approach to the explanation of fully
> motivated performance. The third domain, that of compe-
> tence, is intermediate between the two others. It can admit of
> a high degree of formalization (e.g. Chomsky and Piaget),
> but the application of these structural concepts require an
> interpretation which cannot be reduced to brute criteria (p.
> 74).

Our contention is that "structuralism" substantially deviates from mechanism on the dimension of the epistemological principles. It is to this we now turn.

2) *Epistemological Principle of Structuralism*

Structuralism is one of several attempts to go beyond some of the dilemmas presented by the methods of logical empiricism (Unger, 1976). The interpretation of structure assumes that a structure (in whatever form it takes) is a *totality*, that is, the whole (i.e. structure) is greater than the sum of its parts. In contrast to "mechanistic explanation" which is fundamentally an "analytic" process, all forms of structuralism are based on a principle of "syntheses" (Unger, 1975). The "structure" called "stages" in the work of Piaget is a holistic entity in which the "whole is greater than the sum of its parts". As already mentioned, structure as a "synthetic principle" is diametrically opposed to analytic "atomism" exemplified by even the most complex behavior theories (e.g. Berlyne, 1966). A "structure" is a holistic entity characterized by *internal* dependencies. This is explicated by Piaget, for example, in his definition of a structure as a system of transformations which, as system, implies a lawfulness of organization independent of the elements which compose it (Dagenais, 1972). This system is characterized as a *totality*. In other words, whatever the "composing elements" in the system, they are subordinated to the laws which define the system. In addition, a system is characterized by multiple interdependent "transformations" which are also dependent on the structure itself. Finally, a "structure" is self-regulating, working for the conservation and enhancement of the system as well as a closeness toward all other systems (Dagenais, 1972). Similarly, in linguistics, Chomsky and his followers deny that linguistics can be built on the analysis of elementary particles of meaning. Transformational grammarians share the fact that the speakers of every language are able to construct an infinite number of formally correct and meaningful sentences. Linguistic structuralism has therefore been highly critical of "behaviorist" interpretations on how language is acquired. Consider Chomsky's observation:

> I believe that the study of human psychology has been diverted into side channels by unwillingness to pass the problem of how experience is related to knowledge and belief, a problem which of course presupposes a logically though not necessarily temporally prior investigation of the

structure of systems of knowledge and belief. No matter how successfully the study of stimulus—response connections, habit structures, and so on is pursued, it will always fail to touch these central questions. The systems of knowledge and belief that underlie normal human behavior simply cannot be described in terms of networks of association fabrics of dispositions to respond, habit structures, and the like. At least this seems to be true in the case of language and other known examples of human "cognitive processes" (Chomsky, 1971, pp. 47-48).

When "structuralism" is considered within a psychological framework the analysis of structural components represents a "genetic psychology". This form of analysis of holistic "structures" is said to be "organic" as a metaphor because there is always employed, as part of its explanatory rationale, a systematic link between intelligence, language and biological functions in general. For example, in Piaget intelligence is a fundamental biological activity. Structuralism à la Piaget or Chomsky substantially deviates from all types of neo-behaviorism on the genesis of structures. Both theorists, when talking about the development of cognition or language, see it as a "transformational" rather than an additive incremental process.

3) *The Mode of Observation and Communication*

The mode of observation within structuralist perspectives substantially deviates from a tightly knit controlled "experiment". If "behaviorism's" parental roots are weighted toward "empiricism"; "structuralism" traces itself in a more direct line to classical "rationalism". Structuralism, as we will be showing within a more psychological context, attempts to get at certainty in interpretation by grasping the inner certainty. This is done by the articulating "structures" or "formal" characteristics of phenomena (i.e. content). Structures are articulated through an "abstracting" process at the level of events (phenomena). Although this rationalism is combined with empiricism, the final resolution for "certainty" is at the level of ideas (forms) rather than events (content). This is the exact opposite from Skinner's "behaviorism" which partially accounts for the controversy between Skinner and Chomsky on the issue of language acquisition. Since the issue of "certainty" is attempted at the level of the order of ideas (i.e. articulation of an abstract structure) rather than at the order of events (i.e. the attribution of a causal sequence), the concept of "causality" as part of the "explanatory" system recedes in importance where "structuralism" is concerned.[1] The main theoretical and methodological thrust of "structuralism" is in the articulation of universal, abstract, formal structures (i.e. ideas) which are said to be underlying generative structures for the order of events. Certainty is therefore the articulation of a structure (e.g. a "stage"). For example, Piaget attempts the formulation of coherent "stages" which are generative principles for cognitive development. The term "stage" is a structural term to account for the qualitative changes in children's cognitive development and its changes with time. This type of structuralism is called "dia-chronic" because it deals with "structural" transformations over time. Note that the term "transformational" is used to mean that stage change is not incremental and additive over time but rather a qualitative shift of a "structure in totality". (i.e. syntheses) The "structures" of intelligence (i.e. stages) are formu-lated as biological (or organic) metaphors. Intelligence is defined as a fundamental "biological" activity, it being a process of adaptation and organization. The definition of "structural trans-formations" is the work of a discipline of "genetic epistemology". Piaget is essentially interested in how mature intellectual struc-tures came to be in the process of development. The mode of observation in attempting to depict these processes by articu-lating abstract structures (i.e. stages) has varied over time in Piaget's work. Although his earlier work was a type of free-wheeling interview format, increasingly in his later work he moved to a more formalized procedure called a "quasi experi-ment". Although substantially departing from the classical "experiment" outlined under our discussion of mechanism, this procedure shares many things with the "classical" experiment when one considers the nature of social relations that are operating in both procedures. Piaget ultimately couches all his *observations* within a "logico-mathematical framework". A *fact* is established by a process of "decentering". To "decenter" is to distance one's inquiries in relation to the self. The movement of "decentering" is essentially the same as attempting "detached observation" in that the ideal is to create a certain distancing between the *subject* and *object* of the observation. The most mature form of "decentering" is an operative knowledge called "formal operations". Piaget labels all stages prior to this stage as being more "centered" or "egocentric" and therefore, less ra-tional. In Piaget's own words:

> From the positive point of view this attitude consists in the ego being absorbed in things and in the social group but this absorption is such that the subject, while thinking that he

has knowledge of people and things as they are in reality attributes to them not only their objective characteristics but also qualities which come from his own ego or from the particular aspect of things of which he is aware at the time (Piaget, 1959).

Piaget has one thing in mind when he is conducting one of his "quasi-experiments" and that is to abstract certain general features of reasoning (i.e. "structures" or "stages"). Ultimately, Piaget shows his debt to Cartesian rationalism since by his definition *truth* is made accessible by elaborating "structures" which are essentially "mathematical" in nature. His most mature stage of development which constitutes the ideal end-point is a species of logical mathematical structure which he labels "formal operation" (Piaget, 1971).

The work of Kohlberg (1969) on the development of morality follows the Piagetian tradition. He, like Piaget claims that logic and morality develop through stages and that each stage is a structure that, formally considered, is a better and qualitatively distinct transformation from the preceding stage. Since "development" is considered a "total process" (i.e. a principle of syntheses) it is assumed that each new stage includes elements of earlier structures (stages) but transforms them in such a way that a more integrated, a higher order structure emerges, when the new stage is fully articulated. Morality, like intelligence in Piaget's work, is defined in terms of its end point (i.e. the most mature moral stage). For Kohlberg there are six stages of moral judgment, and the end point, stage six, is a universal-ethical moral principle which is formal and abstract in nature. All previous stages are viewed through this final stage when interpreting the adequacy of the lower stages. The "hermeneutical" key for both Piaget and Kohlberg is a mature moral and intellectual structure. Therefore, intelligence and morality are ultimately defined by their purported end points. The end points are formal, abstract, ideal, and universal by definition. Kohlberg (1969) uncovers this formal sequence of moral stages through a process of interviewing people of different ages who are asked to resolve hypothetical moral dilemmas. The dilemmas are not made or generated by the people interviewed but are structured by Kohlberg in advance. The specific dilemmas given by Kohlberg, or the quasi-experiments given to children by Piaget are designed in order to sample and tap latent "processes" which the subject brings to the situation. The assumption of "structuralism", be it in Chomsky, Kohlberg or Piaget, is that the "organism" has active organizing powers (i.e. structures) which are generative in nature. Further, the organism brings to experience active organizing power which generates different types of problem solution or linguistic output. The researcher, as structuralist, perceives him/herself as trying to capture and articulate these "active organism processes" in stable and changing states. In contrast to "behaviorism" and its method the "experiment", these active processes are uncovered rather than manipulated. The content of the interview, language sample or "quasi-experiment", becomes less important in and of itself; but rather serves as a vehicle for unveiling underlying cognitive, linguistic and moral structures. Chomsky (1968) puts it succinctly:

> It seems to me that the most hopeful approach today is to describe the phenomena of language and of mental activity as accurately as possible, to try to develop an abstract theoretical apparatus that will as far as possible account for these phenomena and reveal the principles of their organization and functioning and without attempting, for the present, to relate the postulated mental structures and processes to any physiological mechanism or to interpret mental function in terms of physical causes (p. 12).

Structuralism therefore seeks to resolve the problem of interpretation more at the level of ideas (rationalism) than at the level of events (empiricism). It assumes that the organism has active and organizing powers which when clearly articulated are called structures of whatever kind. Although structuralism has an empirical thrust and an interest in data or samples, it is not in the sentiment of the empiricism of Locke and Hume who are the parents of logical-empiricism. Rather, its lineage is in the tradition of Cartesian "rationalism" (Chomsky, 1968) and Kantian categoricism. It therefore demands the same "clarity and distinction" when linguistic terms are being utilized but it achieves its lucidity at the level of ideas (structures) rather than at the level of events (i.e. brute facts). We will now look at this process in greater detail.

4) Interpretation and the Problem of Language

The interpretive framework of "structuralism" in its psychological manifestation treats "ordinary language" as problematic. The initial content of linguistic statements are always transformed in the process of interpretation to a more formal language. "Ordinary language" is therefore not the language of structuralism. The "generative grammar" of Chomsky, the stage articulations of Piaget and Kohlberg are "formal languages" which are one step removed from the discourse of the subjects studied. Structuralist perspectives in psychology and linguistics are formal language systems. For example, Piaget's conception of "truth" allows him to treat all linguistic statements outside a logical framework as not having attained truth status. Metaphor, myth, and religious symbols, at best, attain the status of "wisdom" in Piaget's system but fall short of "truth" status since they cannot be assimilated to "formal logic". Although non-positivist in form, Piaget's system nevertheless assimilates all "truth" to a "scientific world perspective" with biology as the central organizing metaphor. When truth is assimilated to "formal logic" there is a corresponding narrowing of the field of symbolic adequacy. Piaget's framework is unsympathetic to all systems that do not meet the canons of "formal logic". Interest in the complex symbolism offered by human cultures demands a more exhaustive conception of "truth" which goes beyond "formal logic". The parameters of a logic beyond formal logic are far from clear, but nevertheless, intimated by the demands of the complexity of human language and communication. Ricoeur (1970) makes some substantial objections to all formal systems which attempt to reduce symbolism to some form of "symbolic logic". He points out quite clearly that logicians have invented symbolic logic with the express aim of eliminating equivocation from our language. In other words, the problems of interpreting events and symbols is resolved by moving from the level of events (i.e. content) to the level of ideas (i.e. formal, ideal systems). At the very least, it is reasonable to be cautious about this movement to eliminate the *ambiguity* of symbols. Ricoeur (1970) making the case for a wider interpretive system than "formal logic" says this about the interpretive episode:

> For the logician, the word "symbol" means precisely the contrary of what it means to us ... the only radical way to justify hermeneutics is to seek in the nature of reflective thought the principle of a logic of double-meaning, a logic that is complex but not arbitrary, rigorous in its articulations but irreducible to the linearity of symbolic logic, (p. 48).

We would contend that this opens the door to a much wider conception of "objectivity" which would incorporate the symbolic languages of art and religion (e.g. myth, magic, poetry etc.). Turner (1973) calls this form of symbolic activity "figurative symbolism". Figurative symbolism in Piaget's perspective is always relegated to a less mature stage of structuring experience. Turner (1973) sees a crucial missing element which the progressive "decentration" model fails to capture. Figurative symbolism (e.g. myth and poetry and religious language) is always "less scientific" and therefore less truthful. Turner (1971) suggests a more positive place for this type of symbolic activity and identifies it with a "re-centering" process rather than a "decentering" process as in Piaget:

> In other words, figurative symbolism can assert a determinate paradigm of relationships as a dominant principle ordering a series of contrast, in a way that expresses at the same time, a particular "sensibility" or subjective relationship to the phenomena it represents. Such forms might therefore be said, in Piaget's terms to effect a kind of "re-centering" of the subject-object relation. This "recentering" is in many ways the opposite of the "decentering" process which constitutes the leitmotiv of Piaget's model of mental development, but it should not be confused with the primitive egocentricity of childhood (p. 353).

The fact that Piaget relegates this process to a more primitive form of intelligence may be a reflection of the inadequacy of his system to deal with double-meaning "symbolism". This is probably the task of a more complete "hermeneutical psychology". As Taylor (1971) points out, Piaget's genetic psychology is a restricted "hermeneutic" based on a "scientific" world view and it suffers the corresponding limitations in exactitude and certainty by reducing all truth to "formal logic". Kohlberg's (1969) work on moral judgment is very much in line with the structuralism of Piaget, to which he acknowledges a considerable debt. His stages of moral judgment are a sophisticated extension of Piaget's (1932) earlier inquiry into the understanding (i.e. interpretation) of moral judgment or practical reasoning. In the work of both men in the area of moral judgment, there is a preoccupation with epistemological categories (Sullivan, 1977, 1978). For Kohlberg, the most mature stage of morality is the "ethical ideal" to which all morality strives. Because of the universality that he attributes to his stages of moral judgment, his most mature stage becomes the mode of the "true" moral person. Moral truth is expressed linguistically as a "formal structure". The "true" in the moral area for Kohlberg is "true form". Kohlberg (1969) makes the claim that his stages demonstrate that there is (a) an ontogenetic trend toward the development of morality as it has been conceived by Western moral philosophers (i.e. read Kant) and (b) that the development of such "rational" or "mature morality" is a process different from the learning of "irrational" or "arbitrary" cultural rules or values. Here Kohlberg follows Piaget and therefore shares his inherent "formalism".

Finally and briefly, Chomsky (1971) develops his linguistic perspective along similar structural lines as Piaget and Kohlberg when he states that:

> Intrinsic principles of mental organization permit the construction of rich systems of knowledge and belief on the basis of scattered evidence. Such principles which constitute an essential part of human nature, also determine which systems will be more accessible to the inquiring mind, and may indeed, impose absolute limits on what can be known (p. 49).

Thus structuralism draws heavily from the "rationalist" tradition going back to the Cartesian conception of the mind (Chomsky, 1968). Within this sytematic viewpoint certainty is said to be achieved at the level of ideas (i.e. formal structures) rather than at the level of events (i.e. content, performance etc.).

5) *Meaning and the Problem of Subjectivity*

We are assuming here that meaning is intersubjective meaning. In other words meaning is not within an actor (i.e. an I) but between actors (i.e. I-thou). Meaning is a way of experiencing actions in society which are expressed in the language and descriptions constitutive of institutions and practices (Taylor, 1973). Meaning is therefore an historical event. There is a tendency within the "structuralist" positions to disregard or distort the historical character of social phenomena and to lose oneself in a logic of supra-historical categories and capacities of the mind (Unger, 1975). In comparison to "behaviorism", "structuralist" perspectives are clearly more sensitive to the *objective* and *subjective* meanings of events; at least at the level of method. As a method, structuralism tries to unite the subjective and objective approaches to meaning by referring to universal tendencies or underlying patterns. (Unger, 1976). By postulating the existence of *"a priori* categories" (i.e. structures) which are *active* organizing principles for knowledge acquisition etc., this method at least concedes something to the notion that meaning is constituted by actors. This is achieved unfortunately by severing the *link between the idea of subjectivity and of consciousness.* In fact,

around the issue of the importance of the subjectivity and conscious intentions of the agents, structuralists are anti-phenomenological (Petit, 1975, Piaget, 1971). Structuralists by and large
reject the standpoint of subjective consciousness (Petit, 1975). The
articulation of the structures is a *scientific consciousness* which
is privy to the structuralist and not to those whom he studies. It is
not necessary for the agents being studied to be *conscious* of the
structures in which they are operating, be it language, cognition
or morality. Chomsky, Kohlberg and Piaget introduce structures
that are not generally part of the self-understanding of the agents
being studied. The universal meaning (i.e. structure) is in the
consciousness of the theorist but not part of the self-understanding of agents studied. The conscious meaning given to events, in
their particularity, is eschewed and side-stepped by structuralists
in their quest for meaningful universal forms or structures. This
raises the serious question of what these methods are teaching us
about people and how this fits in with the way people view themselves in the context of historical circumstances. This is essentially the problem between theoretical explanation and reflective
self understanding. For example, in Kohlberg's work, the concrete self understanding of a specific moral dilemma and the
choices involved are relegated to secondary status, since the
universal structures he defines are not contingent on the choice
or decision that a subject makes in a moral choice situation.
Choices are considered *content* issues and his theoretical perspective is developed around *formal* aspects (Kohlberg, 1969). With all
his sensitivities toward children, it may nevertheless be ventured
that Piaget's theoretical pre-occupations lend him to disparage
the child's own self-understanding of events. Silvers (1975) in
commenting on Piaget's study of "Language and Thought"
would concur with what I am saying here:

> When the child's accounts of why things happen in the way
> they do—for example, how a shadow is cast—departs from
> Piaget's common sense or scientific explanations, he does
> not try to pursue how the world could be understood their
> way. When the child informs him that the shadow emanates
> from the object, he does not pursue the poetic and practical
> understanding, but instead he uses the account to note its
> differences to a later stage which he titles, "The Correct
> Explanation is Found" (Silvers, 1975, p. 48).

Piaget's "interpretive scheme" places maximum emphasis on his
own "theoretical" preoccupations and this is probably his genius.

As with all great efforts it has its "shadow side". Silvers (1975) in reflecting on Piaget's own comments on "egocentricism" argues:

> For he does not take into account a notion of the differences in focusing upon himself as differentiated from the child in scientific analysis when he interprets the account of children; after beginning with an idea of separation between adults and children, he proceeds to interpret the child's talk without the necessity of addressing his own scientific reasoning in order to discover the child's view. In this egocentricism, the child's ways of organizing and making sense of the world are forever answerable to that of the adult researcher. In uncritical and unreflective scientific reasoning, Piaget creates an order of seeing that forever finds a world falling short of his standards, of his version of logic (p. 49).

Finally, in the case of Chomsky's work, the issue of the role of "inter-subjective meaning" would presumably show up in that part of his "structuralism" which would deal with the "semantic" components of structure. The main developments in Chomsky's work have been in the "structural" aspects of syntax; semantics having developed little within this theoretical perspective. The fact that linguistic structuralism à la Chomsky developed along those lines and not in others (e.g. semantics) is not surprising however, since structuralism as a method appears ultimately to play down the role of the conscious self-understanding of the agents it attempts to study.

6) *The Nature of Social Relations*

We have, to a certain extent, covered the nature of social relations within structuralist methods. A few points demand amplification however. First of all, it is clear that compared to behaviorism, structuralist methods are not systematically manipulative and controlling. Secondly, "structuralist" methods allow for much freer linguistic expressions on the part of the subjects studied. Finally, although the method is less controlling of linguistic expression, it nevertheless is quite restrictive at the level of "theoretical interpretation" of linguistic events that have taken place. As we have already stated, theoretical explanation (i.e. discerning structures) assumes much greater importance than the specific self-understandings of those studied under the method. It is in this sense that we would still have to label this method as *monological* in nature. First, insofar as "structuralism" assumes a synthetic ordering principle (i.e. the abstract structures) it brings to the analysis of the situation a more "holistic" and integrated viewpoint or horizon of interpretation when compared to a mechanistic explanation. Second, it resolves the issue of the meaning of events at the level of theoretical abstraction (i.e. structure). The event proper assumes secondary importance. It is referred to as *"performance"* by Chomsky while his emphasis is on the underlying "competence" or structure. In Kohlberg and Piaget it is considered *"content"* whereas their major emphasis is to demonstrate the "formal" aspects of cognitive and moral development. It is only after these "structures" or "wholes" or "totalities" have been recognized that particular elements within them acquire meaning. Third, "structuralism" attempts its interpretive activity of events by a dynamic interplay between theory and facts. Finally, at the level of historical events, "structuralism" drifts toward an *apolitical conservatism*.[2] By viewing social phenomena such as language, cognition and morality as if they were universal categories of mind, the structuralist produces the same political effect as "mechanistic" systems which dissolves all wholes into infinitesimal particulars.

> In the latter case, the infinitude of interactions among speakers or traders makes it seem that language is evolved by the force of human control, as parts of nature. In the former case, the universality of the categories they express leads to linguistic or economic organization the appearance of standing above history and therefore beyond politics. The structuralist view of totality illustrates the alluding alliance of skepticism and conservatism in political thought (Unger, 1975, p. 129).[3]

This may appear surprising if one considers Chomsky's radical political involvements. In retrospect, it would appear that he completely separates his political praxis from his theory of language. There is in his thought a rather thorough split between attempts at *interpreting* the world and movements to *change* it (see Chomsky, 1971).

Conclusion

Structuralism, in its psychological and linguistic manifestations, represents a substantial change in orientation from classical logical-empiricism. In contrast to the methods of logical-empiricism, it does not attempt to order phenomena at the level of events with the objective of demonstrating "causality" between events. Instead, the method of "structuralism" seeks through a process of "interpretive abstraction" to tease out the underlying "structure" of phenomena. Its controlling metaphor is "organism" rather than "physical" systems. It therefore draws its interpretive language from *biology* rather than *physics*; utilizing freely evolutionary concepts as part of its interpretive system. Structuralism deviates markedly from mechanism at the level of "epistemology". The "structures" that are articulated by structuralists are "wholes" or "totalities". A structure is therefore more than the sum of its parts. Historically, it is an offshoot of Cartesian rationalism and Kantian *"a priorism"*, where philosophy is concerned and draws heavily from 19th and 20th century biology where science is concerned. Structuralism has dealt with the problem of interpretation, by fostering a-historical categories which are beyond the vicissitudes of events (i.e. History). In eschewing human consciousness and subjective interpretation, it is therefore not overly interested in the "conscious intentions" of the actors that it studies. What then is the attraction of "structuralism" for contemporary consciousness? At the level of psychological interpretation, at least, one can say that it appeals to a longing for *"universality"*. This is probably very attractive to modern consciousness because of its constant dealings with "conflicts of interpretations" of social realities. It presents a synthetic viewpoint by ordering at the level of ideas (i.e. structures) quite discrepant social events (i.e. contents). It does this by abstracting from the contexts where dissimilarity reigns. It therefore clearly appeals to our need for order and clarity. Succumbing to this desire in its entirety, however, conceals some hidden dangers. In the case of "structuralism" it does so at the risk of destroying *contexts*:

> No sooner does the evisceration of particulars begin than a complementary process sets in, the evisceration of universals. The abstract qualities take on a life of their own because they are the sole possible objects of thought and language... From the evisceration of particulars there ensues a spectacle that would be strange if it were not too familiar to be noticeable. Though it is the particulars that are supposed to have concrete reality, it is to the universals that thought and action are addressed. The ghosts sing and dance on the stage while the real persons sit dumbly in the pit below. The observer may be forgiven for wondering who is alive and who is dead (Unger, 1975, pp. 136-137).

Notes

[1]This is not to say however that structuralists eskew the concept of causality. See for example Piaget's book on Structuralism.

[2]In spite of Chomsky's political radicalism, I would nevertheless hold that his linguistic formulation has an apolitical drift.

[3]Gardner (1974) noted the fact that one of the slogans for the student uprisings in France in 1968 was "Down with Structuralism".

Reference

Ausubel, D. P. and Sullivan, E. V. *Theory and Problems of Child Development.* Grune and Stratton, New York (2nd edition), 1970.

Berlyne, D. E. *Structure and Direction in Thinking.* John Wiley & Sons, New York, 1965.

Chomsky, N. *Language and Mind.* Harcourt, Brace & Weild Inc., New York, 1968.

Chomsky, N. *Problems of Knowledge and Freedom.* Vintage Books, New York, 1971.

Dagenais, J. *Models of Man: A Phenomenological Critique of Some Paradigms in the Human Sciences.* Martinus Nijhoff, The Hague, 1972.

De George, R. and De George, F. *The Structuralists from Marx to Levi-Strauss.* Doubleday Anchor Paperback, New York, 1972.

Descartes, R. *Discourse on Method.* Penguin Classic, Great Britain, 1960.

Gadamer, H. G. Hermeneutics and social science. *Cultural Hermeneutics 2,* 1975a, pp. 307-316.

Gagne, R. M. "Contributions of learning to human development," *Psychological Review,* Vol. 75, pp. 177-191, 1968.

Gardner, H. *The Quest for Mind.* Vintage Books, New York, 1972.

Hilgard, E. R and Bower, G. H. *Theories of Learning.* Appleton-Century-Crofts, (3rd edition), New York, 1966.

Hunt Mc V. *Intelligence and Experience.* Ronald Press, New York, 1961.

Kohlberg, L. *Stage and Sequence: The Cognitive-Developmental Approach to Socialization.* In D. Goslin (edition) Handbook of socialization theory and research. Chicago: Rand McNally, 1969.

Osgood, C. E.; Suci, G.; and Tannenbaum, T. H. *The Measurement of Meaning.* University of Illinois Press, Urbana, 1957.

Petit, P. *The Concept of Structuralism: A Critical Analysis.* University of California Press, 1975, Berkeley.

Piaget, J. *Insights and Illusions of Philosophy.* The World Publishing Company, New York, 1971a.

Piaget, J. *Structuralism.* Harper Torchbooks, New York, 1971.

Ricoeur, P. *Freud and Philosophy: An essay on interpretation.* Yale University Press, New Haven, 1976.

Robinson, D. *An Intellectual History of Psychology.* Collier MacMillan Toronto, Canada, Ltd., 1976.

Sullivan, E. V. "A Study of Kohlberg's Structural Theory of Moral Development: A Critique of Liberal Social Science Ideology." *Human Development* Vol. 20, (1977), pp. 352-376.

Sullivan, E. V. *Kohlberg's Structuralism: A Critical Appraisal.* Monograph Series 15, Ontario Institute for Studies in Education, Toronto, Canada, 1977.

Taylor, C. "Interpretation and the Sciences of Man." *Review of Metaphysics.* 1973, pp. 3-51.

Taylor, C. "What is Involved in Genetic Psychology?" T. Mischel (ed.) *Cognitive Development and Epistemology.* Academic Press, New York, 1971, pp. 3-416.

Turner, T. "Piaget's Structuralism." *American Anthropologist,* Vol. 75, 2, 1973, pp. 351-373.

Unger, R. M. *Law in Modern Society: Toward a Criticism of Social Theory.* Free Press, New York, 1976.

Unger, R. M. *Knowledge and Politics.* Free Press, New York, 1975.

Commentary

Michael Chandler

The task of discussing a paper which one does not like or would not want to have written is easy and filled with opportunities for small cruelties. Professor Sullivan's scholarly paper, however, is one which I very much liked and would like to have the skill to have written, and so I am filled with a much less productive sense of envy and of embarrassment at having so little to add. The feeling that I am left with reminds me of one of my favorite Peanuts cartoons in which Schroeder and Charlie Brown are on their backs on a grassy hill, looking up at clouds. Schroeder announces that he sees a cloud which reminds him of the drama of a Dvorak Symphony, another that looks like a bust of Otto Wiebel, and finally, a scattered patch reminiscent of three valkyrie riding through a nibelungenlied. Charlie responds somewhat sheepishly that he was going to say that he saw a ducky and a horsey, but changed his mind. Having been flown to Calgary at great expense I suppose I am not so free to change my mind and so I will try to say what I found especially helpful and also not so helpful about Professor Sullivan's fine paper.

What the paper seems to me to accomplish best is to first provide a clear and compact overview of the salient features of structuralist formulations in Psychology, and second, to pull together and extend a scattered series of radical critiques of such views. What I found understandable, in this interdisciplinary context, but still somewhat ill-fated or ill-advised was his decision to bracket together, and to treat as functionally interchangeable, the structuralisms of Piaget, Kohlberg, and Chomsky. My purpose is not to imply that Professor Sullivan is unaware of these in-house distinctions—I know that not to be the case—, but to suggest that his decision to lump these disparate theorists together for expository purposes has the unfortunate and I think unwarranted consequence of suggesting that his various criticisms of structuralist views fall with equal weight upon each of these psychological theories. It is my own view that this is not the case and that, instead, action based, diachronic brands of structuralism, such as that advocated by Piaget, may very well offer answers to, rather than provide examples of, the shortcomings he finds in structural models more generally.

In order to defend this claim I would like to first review the various criticisms which Professor Sullivan has levelled against structuralisms in general, to then expand upon what I intend by the distinction between diachronic and synchronic structuralisms, and finally to suggest how it is that the first, or more diachronic, of these structuralist modes avoids and perhaps answers many of these criticisms.

Structuralisms, according to Professor Sullivan, have the assets of sometimes being concerned with wholes rather than parts, with qualitative rather than quantitative distinctions, and with meaning rather than the meaningless. Despite these and other "approved" features, however, structuralists' models are also said to contain commonly a list of liabilities which includes the claims that they 1) are rooted in critical-idealistic philosophic traditions, Cartesian rationalism, Kantian categoricism, and practically everybody's innateism and apriorism and preformism; 2) that they trade in inherent formalisms, are abstract, alienated, decontextualized, other worldly, and lacking in a proper appreciation of concrete historical events—as such they are regarded as universalized forms, standing above history and politics; and 3) that by retreating from the level of concrete experience they disparage or ignore individual self-consciousness, treat ordinary language as problematic, and are at base anti-phenomenological.

The question, or rather my question, is whether this list of features and criticisms apply universally to all forms of structuralism, or whether some or all of them apply to some brands of structuralism and not to others.

Several brands of structuralism are, of course, available (open versus closed structural systems; elementaristic versus holistic structuralisms). The particular distinction upon which I want to focus at the moment, however, is that between what have been called *diachronic* as opposed to *synchronic* structuralisms. As Overton (1972) has pointed out, "the adoption of a structuralist position leaves upon the question of whether one posits a single general structure or system that is assumed to remain invariant across time, or whether to represent the event in question as a series of ordered structures." Many modern theorists of information processing, Chomsky's linguistic theory, Gestalt theory, and Levi-Strauss, choose the former (synchronic) alternative while Piaget maintains the latter (diachronic view). (Overton, 1972, p. 12) In his paper Professor Sullivan notes this diachronic-synchronic distinction, but does not attach to it the weight which I will argue it deserves.

The most salient, distinguishing feature of diachronic structuralisms, such as that of Piaget and perhaps Kohlberg, is that the several progressive or intermediate categories or structures which they pose demand that becoming take precedence over being, and that activity is primary while form is only derivative. In this vein Piaget defines structures as "the organizational forms of mental activity" (Piaget, 1971, p. 67), and states that "the being of structures consists in their coming to be, that is, their being under construction.... There is (accordingly) no structure apart from construction" (Piaget, 1971, p. 140). Unlike the passive templates or filters of more classical relationistic and categoristic views, structures as organized systems of *activity* are not apart from concrete reality and do not impassively gate or strain such experience. Within this dynamic, unfolding, diachronic structuralism there is assumed to be a constant interplay between the child's current self-regulatory system of transformations (commonly reified as his or her cognitive structure) and the particular concrete phenomenological experience of material events which must be partially assimilated and partially accommodated to. This dialectic interplay between the abstract and the particular, between form and content, between theory and praxis, if you will, is assumed by Piaget to constitute the essence of ongoing experience, as well as the description and explanation of ontogenetic development.

I can, without too much difficulty, see how the synchronic structuralism of someone like Chomsky, which assumes a single unchanging structure across development, can be properly characterized as rationalistic, performistic, ahistoric, abstractly alienated and desubjectivised. I find it difficult, however, to see the appropriateness of such characterizations for a dynamic, diachronic model such as Piaget's. Let me take as a single example the event of a pre-operational child, confronted with the task of interpreting Piagetic classic conservation of liquids problem. For those of you who may not be familiar within this paradigm, Piaget presents a young child (4-6) with 2 identical beakers containing identical quantities of a colored liquid. The contents of one of these is then poured into a taller, but thinner container. The child at this stage is said by Piaget to lack a system of transformations which allows him or her to appreciate that this pouring operation could be reversed without impact upon the quantity of available liquid. In the absence of a system for dealing with this transformation the child's judgement is controlled by the immediate phenomenological experience of seeing the water level as higher, leading to a judgement that there is more water, or seeing the water column as narrower, leading to an assumption that there is now less water than before. The child's understanding is consequently controlled by his or her immediate sensory experience. Such perceptual inputs often contradict one another, however. The taller but thinner container may look like more, but it is unlikely to taste like more, or give one a sense of being fuller. Discrepancies of this kind are assumed by Piaget to produce the unsettling dynamic tension which sponsors a new synthesis and new growth.

Where in all of this is the justification for Professor Sullivan's claim that, "Piaget's theoretical pre-occupation led him to de-emphasize or disparage the child's own self-understanding of events"? Where is the assumed pre-occupation with the formal at the expense of the particular, or the abstract at the expense of the concrete? How is this process not imbedded in the subjective context of some particular historical event and how is it a bid for rationalism and a rejection of phenomenology?

What I would like to maintain and to persuade you to maintain with me, is that there is, in emphasis upon the primacy of activity, a close analogy to Marx's emphasis on Praxis, and that in both instances action is to be understood as the mechanism for repairing the false dichotomy between the plane of the concrete particular and the plane of formal abstraction.

As Gramsci had argued, it was Marx's commitment to praxis which permitted him to transcend the classical dichotomies of subject versus object, and idealism versus materialism. I would argue as much for Piaget, and see in his commitment to an active, diachronic structuralism a means of escaping or transcending many of the so-called radical critiques levelled against structuralism in general, his own work included.

My larger purpose here is not so much to try to champion a particular theory such as Piaget's—he does that very nicely without my help—but to offer a caution against any casual or premature jettisoning of all structural models because some are less historic or phenomenological or context laden than we might hope.

As Carl Boggs (Boggs, 1976) has pointed out, one of the hallmarks of the English-speaking left has been an endemic hostility to theory. My concern is that in our fervor to champion the subjectivised, context laden and historical particulars of experience we not be stampeded into the anti-intellectual assumption that interest in these matters precludes a simultaneous commitment to theory.

Professor Sullivan recognizes this point in labelling Piaget's structuralism as a "partial hermeneutic system." On the assumption that being partial is a defining feature of any hermeneutic analysis, I take it we are not in sharp disagreement.

References

Boggs, C., *Gramsci's Marxism*. Pluto Press, London, 1976.

Overton, W., "General Systems, Structure and Development," unpublished manuscript, 1972.

Piaget, J., *Structuralism*. Harper Torchbooks, New York, 1971.

Session Four

Social Sciences, the "Real World" and the "Appropriate Methodology"

Appropriate Methodologies for Human Learning

Kenneth E. Boulding, University of Colorado

The human brain is capable of forming immensely complex structures, the exact nature of which we have hardly begun to understand, but which clearly constitute in some way a "map" of the universe in which we are placed in both time and space. Oddly enough, there seems to be no well recognized generic name for these structures. I have called them "images." Images begin with the first formation of the brain in the womb, for some of the patterns which it contains are genetic, that is, formed as the genes weave their structure of the interconnected neurons of the brain. From the very beginning these images are of two kinds—images of fact and images of value. Even in the womb and the faint pre-dawn of consciousness there must be some kind of image of the environment when the baby makes its first kick. At the moment of birth there are clearly genetically produced images of value—the preference for milk, for certain textures, for being held, for warmth; a dislike of cold and a sense of insecurity and hunger. These undoubtedly predate all experience or at least they stand ready to be triggered by the first experience.

All through our life the complexity and overall size of our structure of images increases, except perhaps at the very end, in senility. It is this increase in the size and complexity of the image structure which constitutes learning or the growth of human knowledge. There is something more, however, than mere increase in size and complexity. The image structure also has a property which we can call "truth." The image, as we have seen, is a map of the universe, including ourselves, including both what is outside us and what is inside us. The question is whether the map is a good one, that is, whether there is what the mathematicians call a "one-to-one relationship" between the structures inside us and the universe which contains us. The better the mapping, the closer the image is to truth. This, of course, is the famous "correspondence" theory of truth and this certainly seems to correspond very closely to the ordinary meaning of the word. "Error" is the failure of correspondence between the structure of the inner image and the structure of the universe which it is supposed to map.

We can distinguish three properties of correspondence between the structure of images and the universe: truth, error, and ignorance. These are capable of degree; these are "more or less" rather than "either or," just as a map can have various degrees of accuracy in representing the structure of a landscape. Truth is having a good map; error, a bad map; ignorance, having no map at all. Learning consists of improving the "mix" of the content of the structure of images, increasing the proportion of truth and diminishing the proportion of error. The quantity of knowledge is a function of both truth, ignorance, and error, with truth having a positive coefficient; error, a negative coefficient; and ignorance, a zero coefficient. Thus, movement from error into ignorance increases knowledge; so does the movement from ignorance into truth.

The processes by which in the course of our life experiences our image structure is changed are extremely complex and still very little understood. The critical question is to understand the processes by which knowledge increases, that is, by which the truth-ignorance-error mix becomes enriched. One thing is clear— at least from modern work on perception—that the human brain is engaged in the constant internal formation of images at all times, both when awake and when asleep. It is the scene of literally inconceivable activity. It is not in any sense a *tabula rasa*, waiting impassively to receive the imprints from information transmitted through the senses. It is constantly engaged in "imagination," that is, in the formation of new images without regard very often as to whether these correspond to the real world. Whether images are formed directly by imprinting from outside information coming through the senses is a matter of some uncertainty. The interaction between the internal information and image generating functions of the brain and the external information received through the senses is undoubtedly very complex.

Crucial to the learning process, however, is the experience of "testing." This is the process by which an image produces another image of expectation, that is, a prediction of some image to be formed in the future. As I am dictating this paper, I have an expectation that in a few days the paper will be transcribed, I will read it and correct it, eventually deliver it, and still later perhaps see it in published form. This expectation is an image of the future to which I attach a certain probability of being fulfilled (in the above case rather high). As time proceeds, however, what is now the future becomes the past, of which I will then have an image. I will then be able to compare my expectation which I have now with the image of the past I will have, when what is now the future becomes the past. If this comparison has one-to-one correspondence, I will say the expectation has been fulfilled. If it does not, then the expectation has been disappointed in some degree. If the expectation is fulfilled, the image of the world which produced it is presented with no challenge. If the expectation is disappointed, the image which produced it is challenged and is likely to be revised in some way. The disappointment of expectation, that is, turns error into ignorance. Expectation is derived from an image which is believed to be true. If it is disappointed, this image can no longer be sustained. The detection of error, however, does not lead immediately into an increase in truth but only ignorance. A much more difficult further step is needed if ignorance is to be replaced by truth.

A process of testing, therefore, consists in the formation of expectations and their fulfillment or disappointment. This is quite fundamental to the learning process in all organisms which are capable of learning, perhaps from the planaria up. To the behaviorists, of course, the image structure is a black box that should not be opened. We have not really opened it very much, except by the x-ray of conjecture, but from what goes in and what comes out we are pretty sure that something goes on inside.

Testing goes on at all levels of learning, from the rat into what we might call "folk learning," to the most elegant and advanced scientific learning processes. The rat, the ordinary citizen, and the scientist learn by being disappointed. We never learn much from success, that is, from the fulfillment of expectations, except to confirm what we thought we knew already, and if the success is a result of accident or random processes, as it sometimes is, success may even confirm us in error. Failure opens up the possibility of learning but does not guarantee it. It reveals error but does not necessarily increase truth. Even pigeons exposed to a random psychologist develop superstition, which may be defined as the perception of order where there is none, and human beings frequently do the same.

In ordinary life, in the development of "folk knowledge," the testing operates with considerable success. All of us, for instance, have a map of our own community in our mind which may by no means be wholly accurate, but which serves in getting us around town. If we go to where our cognitive map tells us the bus station is and it is no longer there, we will have a failure of expectations; what was previously error is changed into ignorance. In this case it is usually fairly easy to replace ignorance by truth. We simply ask somebody to find out where the bus station has moved, go there, our expectation is fulfilled by finding it, our cognitive map is moved towards reality, and our knowledge is increased. Because of the relative ease of testing and feedback, "folk knowledge" is often quite accurate, though once it gets into complex systems it can easily fall into superstition, where testing is difficult and where, therefore, error survives. When expectations are disappointed we draw the conclusions that prevent a readjustment of the image. We may conclude that there was an error in deduction from our weak image to the expectation. Or we may conclude that our image of disappointment was in some sense false and should be revised to an image of fulfillment. Human beings are so complex that the images we have of each other are almost certain to contain large amounts of error and these errors are often very hard to test, and we easily therefore fall into superstition in regard to our images of each other.

In the course of its "noogenetic" evolution, as I have called it, the human race has almost continually increased its knowledge structure and improved its methods of acquiring knowledge.[1] Biogenetics, that is, DNA and the genes presumably produced the human brain by a process which is still very mysterious. Once produced, the very earliest human brains had the potential and capacity for Einstein's theory of relativity, for Shakespeare's plays, Beethoven's symphonies, and Picasso's pictures, but it took fifty or a hundred thousand years of noogenetic evolution, in the development of images which were then transmitted from one generation to the next and continually expanded by mutation and selection, before this potential could be realized. Just as evolution itself evolves, that is, the process of evolution itself continually changes and becomes more complex, so in noogenetic evolution the processes of human learning also change and, we hope, become more efficient.

The universe is very large and extremely complex. It clearly operates at many different levels of complexity and organization. We should expect, therefore, a variety of epistemological methods and processes corresponding to the variety of structures and patterns that exist in the universe. Looking at human learning as a total process, therefore, we see that there is a problem of appropriate methodologies, that is, of discovering that process of learning (and particularly the processes of image formation and testing) which is appropriate for each of the different levels and structures of the universe. Methods which are appropriate in one field may be quite inappropriate in another. The problem of discovering the appropriate epistemological methodology has been somewhat neglected in the scientific community. There has often been an implicit assumption that there is only one scientific method and that all other methods are suspect and are incapable of producing truth. This is a gross oversimplification. There are many scientific methods and indeed many methods for increasing human knowledge outside what is narrowly conceived as the field of science. These all involve devices for reducing error through testing, and perhaps also for increasing error through the development of new images to test. There are situations indeed in which increasing truth is paid for by increasing error as well, and the more complex the system, the more likely are these patterns to be found.

The very fertility of the human imagination is likely to produce error as it deals with complex systems. Thus, the human imagination, in every culture known, has created enormous imaginary universes, such as the Hindu cosmologies, the Japanese and the Greek pantheons, Dante's *Inferno,* and so on. If a culture did not produce any myths it would almost by that reason be suspected of not being really human. All myths contain elements of truth, particularly insofar as they consist of metaphor, but they also consist of very large quantities of error, especially when they are taken literally. Science itself is in no way exempt from myth, even when it takes the form of mathematical theories. Truth indeed is a myth that passes the examination of testing. Thus, both alchemy and astrology were splendid myths but do not pass the examination very well; chemistry and astronomy have passed it much better, though here too the larger and more complex a system, the more elaborate the myth, the harder it is to test. The hypothesis of the origin of the universe in a "big bang" leaves as many questions as any other creation myth.

The problem of appropriate methodology in human learning manifests itself at two major levels—the level of theory, that is, the formation of abstract images of the world; and the level of testing by which these theoretical images are evaluated. In each area of human knowledge, the method should be appropriate to the nature of what we are trying to find out, that is, of the epistemological field, and methods which are suitable to one field are often not suitable to another. A good deal of trouble has been caused in science by the attempt to apply methods which are successful in one field to other fields where they are not appropriate. This is a problem where we still have to do a great deal of work.

In the last five hundred years the knowledge structure of the human race has been dominated by the rise of a specialized sub-culture of science, specializing in the advance of knowledge. The origins of science, of course, go back much further than this to folk wisdom and witch doctors, to Greek, Babylonian, Egyptian and Indian mathematics, the experimental methods of the alchemists and the observations of the astrologers. But there were many bypaths and dead ends, like Aristotle's physics and the alchemists' elements, and as an ongoing irreversible cumulative movement of the increase of human knowledge it is at least convenient to begin science with Copernicus. Celestial mechanics, therefore, was the first of the sciences that had a substantial and unquestionable success. The prediction of the movement of the heavenly bodies, which goes back, of course, before Copernicus, was the first example of successful prediction into a fairly long-run future. These predictions, furthermore, were capable of continuous refinement as the theory improved, from Ptolemy to Copernicus to Kepler to Newton to Laplace. The success of celestial mechanics in prediction, however, may have had a bad effect on many of the other sciences, simply because what was an appropriate methodology in celestial mechanics was not appropriate in systems of a different kind.

Celestial mechanics was successful because the solar system is essentially an equilibrium system in space-time, its evolution having largely ceased, though it is presumably still proceeding very slowly and has of course now been speeded up by human intervention. No one can now predict the number of satellites the earth will have in the year 2000, for this has become a matter not of celestial mechanics but of political astronomy. The solar system, furthermore, again because it is an equilibrium system, could be almost completely described in terms of numbers which could be fairly easily observed and calculated. The numbers themselves are essentially arbitrary constructs of the human mind. Nowhere outside the human mind is a circle divided into 360 degrees, or is the distance between bodies of the solar system measured in miles or even in kilometers. The numerical fiction, however, turned out to be a very useful one because it could be used to describe the essentially topological relations of the objects of the solar system in space and time, something that would be very hard to do with ordinary language.

Celestial mechanics pioneered in at least two of the great scientific methods. The first was the improvement of the image of the topology of a system as it moved from the folk image of the bowl of the sky to the Ptolemaic image of the earth surrounded by spheres, to the Copernican images of the heliocentric system, to Kepler's image of the planets moving in elipses, to Einstein's image of a four-dimension space-time continuum. This permitted very accurate prediction once the pattern could be described, for identifying a position in the future of such a pattern is essentially no more difficult than the problem of identifying points in a three-dimensional space.

The second great pioneering methodology of celestial mechanics was careful observation of the position of the bodies of the solar system relative to the position of the earth, from which of course could be calculated their position relative to each other. This observation began with the early astrologers and the work of Tycho Brahe, even before the invention of the telescope, which led to the great generalizations of Kepler and Newton. The telescope was perhaps the first major example of an essential method of science, the improvement of human perception by means of instrumentation, which led to a great increase in the accuracy of observation.

Celestial mechanics did not contribute much to the third great method of science—the experimental method. Careful and continuous observation on the one hand and experiment on the other constitute the major contribution of science to the testing of images of the world. Experiment consists essentially of creating a small artificial world as a subset of the universe, artificially simplified, in which observations can be made with an accuracy that may not be attainable in the world of simple observation, and in which also predictions can be made and expectations derived which are uniquely related to the testing of some theoretical structure. This is done largely by reducing the number of variables that are significant to the experimental situation. In the world of simple continuous observation the number of variables is often so large that it is hard to detect the patterns and relationships among them. In an experimental situation we literally reduce the number of variables in the hope of being able to detect a testing process, by creating expectations and seeing if they are or are not fulfilled. A failure of expectations then suggests error in theory, that is, in the postulates regarding the relations of these variables.

The experimental method was pioneered perhaps by the alchemists, who were so hampered, however, by a false taxonomy of elements that they fell easily into superstition and did not produce any very substantial concrete results. Physics and chemistry were the first successful experimental sciences, successful again because of the appropriateness of the method to the epistemological field. In physics and chemistry it is relatively easy to construct systems in which the number of variables is small, and in which the components of the small system are essentially the same as the components of the larger systems in the "real world." This is a field where what I have called "Reagan's Law" applies. Former Governor Reagan of California is reported to have said, "When you have seen one redwood, you have seen them all." This is not true of redwoods, but it is true of hydrogen atoms, of protons, of electrons, and of all the basic taxonomic elements of physics and chemistry. It is this character of the epistemological field which has led to the success of the experimental method. If individual hydrogen atoms had as much personality as individual human beings, the experimental method in physics and chemistry would produce some very odd results, as in the case of human beings it does.

As we move into more complex systems, for instance into the biological and social sciences, we move into epistemological fields where the great simplicities of celestial mechanics and of physics and chemistry no longer apply. The very success of physics and chemistry and of celestial mechanics have not infrequently led to an attempt to apply their methods in an area where they are inappropriate to the epistemological field. This is not to say that many of the methods of one epistemological field cannot be carried over to others, but they should not be carried over wholesale or without serious and detailed inquiry.

The biological sciences began like astronomy, with careful and detailed observation, in this case of living species. Here it was not so much the time patterns that were observed, as in astronomy, though there are some time patterns, for instance, in the growth of an individual animal from the egg to the adult, which have been observed though not perhaps studied very carefully from very early times. The science of biology, however, may well be dated from Linnaeus, a contemporary of Adam Smith, who made exhaustive catalogs of living creatures and developed an orderly taxonomy. With the development of paleontology, the identification of fossils, observations in space extended back to observations through time and indeed in space-time, leading to Darwin and the theory of natural selection. Experimental biology began in the area of folk and practical knowledge very early, with animal and plant breeding. It hardly existed in the scientific community, however, before Mendel, and only became important as a branch of biology in the twentieth century. The greatest triumph undoubtedly of experimental biology was the discovery of DNA, which has at least disclosed the structure of the language in which the instructions of life are written, even if we cannot yet write it.

The theoretical structure of biology, however, is very different from that of celestial mechanics. Evolution is not a system of simultaneous differential equations. It is a system with profound indeterminacies and in which, therefore, the power of prediction is extremely limited. I have defined evolution as ecological interaction under conditions of constantly changing parameters. Ecological interaction is selection; the change in parameters is mutation. Selection takes place through the interaction of populations of different species on each other affecting the birth and death rates of each. If for any species in an ecosystem there is some population at which birth and death rates are equal, and its population in equilibrium, this constitutes its "niche." If the population is below the niche level, it will expand to fill it; if it is above, it will shrink to fill it.

Any ecosystem will have empty niches, that is, populations which would have an equilibrium population in it if they existed. Where there is an empty niche, there is some chance it will be filled before changes in other populations close the niche, as will always eventually happen. If a niche is not filled before it closes, then the whole future history of the system is different. The system, therefore, has irreducible randomness. As long as it is not completely random, probabilistic propositions about the future can be made, but exact predictions in the style of celestial mechanics are impossible. Furthermore, over long periods the importance of improbable changes that happened cannot be neglected. The evolution of the human race may well have been through a series of quite improbable changes which came off. This takes us even further from celestial mechanics.

As we move into the study of human beings and social systems, the complexity increases even further, and we have to go beyond biological models. An individual human being is an organization of extreme complexity. We do not even know what the limits of our noogenetic evolution may be, or even how far along we are towards those limits. The ten billion neurons[2] of the human brain is a very large piece of apparatus. Its capacity, measured by the possible states it might assume, could be as large as $2^{10,000,000}$, a number that would take ninety years to write down. It is not surprising, therefore, that a structure parallel to that of the universe can be found within it in the form of images. It is a system, moreover, with strong, complex, value structures, preferences, and images of the future. Its behavior is not a matter of stimulus and response, or even of cause and effect, but the reaction of a total very large system built out of all previous inputs and outputs, as well as internally generated inputs.

The human mind is itself an evolutionary system in the sense that images themselves form an ecosystem, one probably far more complex than we find in the woods or the fields, for each image is unique in a way that not even a member of a population of field mice is unique. The ecological interaction is among individuals and clusters of related individual images. It is not surprising that the system lacks predictability even to itself. The random elements in decision, for instance, may be quite large. We throw dice and toss pennies all the time. The non-random elements are significant also and permit us at least probabilistic predictions.

Teleology becomes highly significant in the human being, teleology being defined as events which fulfill a plan or some image of the future. This does not exist in celestial mechanics or any equilibrium system. All biological systems are teleological in the sense that the genetic information in the fertilized egg is a "plan" for very complex chains of events which will build up the phenotype. The chicken is a centrally-planned economy, its growth (and decline) planned by its genetic structure from the egg. An ecosystem, and still more the evolutionary process as a whole, is strictly free private enterprise. It has no central plan and no government as far as we know. The directionality of evolution on this planet towards complexity culminating at the present time in the human race is rather puzzling, and suggests that even if there was not a plan at the beginning, there was certainly a bias in the evolutionary process, which is almost as good, though our ignorance of the past is so profound that we cannot be sure of this.

The human and social sciences, therefore, are a very long way from celestial mechanics. Systems similar to celestial mechanics which use models based on constant parameters, like the cruder models of econometrics, should be treated with the greatest reserve. They are not useless, for sometimes the parameters of a system are stable for a while, so these models may be valuable in short-range prediction. The longer the range we take, however, the more likely are the parameters to change and to change unpredictably. In the human and social sciences, therefore, models lead only to projections, whether this is population projections, economic projections, projections of the international system, or of political systems, and so on, and projections should never be mistaken for predictions. It is only predictions, however, that can be securely used for testing. When a projection fails it is hard to tell whether the parameters have changed or whether the basic model is an inadequate description of the real relations of the system.

In the human and social sciences quantification can be misleading. It has its uses, but it always produces evidence rather than truth. Even in celestial mechanics, as we have seen, quantification is the crutch of the human mind, to enable us to describe relationships which are essentially topological. In human and social systems, the topological character of the essential systems is even more pronounced. Under these circumstances, quantification and mathematization of the theory can easily introduce properties in the model which the "real world" system does not possess, and can also fail to take account of structures and properties which the system does possess, simply because these cannot be easily mathematized or quantified. Thus, there is a strong tendency for model builders to use linear relation-ships simply because they are easy for mathematicians to handle. One is pretty sure, however, that linear relationships are virtually unknown in the real world except over very small spans.

It is, of course, a very convenient property of numbers that they can be added, subtracted, multiplied, and divided. Thus, we can calculate a single number like the gross national product, which represents, however, a reality with a great multidimensionality in structure. A number like the GNP represents a single abstract property of a complex structure involving millions of prices and quantities. If some property of the structure is what is significant, the aggregate number may be very misleading. We might, for instance, have a constant GNP, with a rapidly changing structure in the proportions of things within the total. The aggregate total numbers may then be very misleading and give us an illusion of stability or of growth when the reality is quite different.

The other great danger of quantification is that it diverts attention towards those things which are easily quantifiable, which are not necessarily the most important features of a system. In economics, for instance, prices and incomes, things measured in dollar terms, are fairly easily quantified. Relations of reci-procity, which may easily determine satisfaction with the system or even its stability are neglected because they are hard to quantify. As we move into sociology and political science, the nonquantifiable factors can become even more important. This does not mean, of course, that it is impossible to have a mathematics of the orderly description of complex systems. But this would go far beyond the Cartesian-Newtonian type of mathematics which tends to dominate the social sciences today. It may well be that the appropriate mathematics for the social sciences has simply not been written yet.

The principle that the larger the system, the more difficult it is to test, applies with great force to the social sciences and reflects itself in apparently unresolvable controversies. We see this, for instance, in the Marxist controversy. The difficulty of testing and evaluating systems of centrally-planned economies versus free-market economies is so great that the appeal to evidence is discarded and we fall back on the appeal to threat, a certain sign that the scientific process has broken down. Such difficulties are by no means confined to the social sciences. In cosmology, for instance, controversy seems to be endless. Even when we look at the earth as a total physical system we find that meteorology has even less predictive power than economics, and that many problems of social policy, for instance in the energy field, fail in solution not because of our ignorance of social systems but because of our ignroance of the physical system of the earth. We do not know, for instance, what will be the effect of releasing CO_2 from burning fossil fuel into the atmosphere, and we understand very little about the long-range impact on the ecosystems of the world of tropical deforestation. The cases could be multiplied.

I have argued, indeed, that the distinction between the "hard" and "soft" sciences is a false one, that the real distinction is between the secure sciences, which are not likely to exhibit much change in their images of the world, and the insecure sciences, which will change. All the historical sciences are very insecure, whether geology, paleontology, evolutionary history, human history, and even cosmology, because all we know of the past is the record of it and this record is enormously biased by durability. There is no principle that says that what is most durable is necessarily the most important. The secure sciences are those which deal with a large part of their field, mainly in the present. This would include, for instance, chemistry, where the periodic table is not going to change much. It includes such things as anatomy, geography, and some aspects of the social sciences.

A critical question for all the sciences goes beyond testing and its difficulties, to what might be called "search," a process still very mysterious, by which new images are formed. New theories, for instance, are clearly not formed at random, but are related to older images. Once formed, new images are then subject to testing, but where do they come from in the first place? If we think of the "noosphere," as de Chardin calls it, as an evolutionary system, that is, the sphere of all human knowledge in all human minds, past, present, and future, together perhaps with its prosthetic devices in the way of libraries and computers, we see the search process as mutation and the testing process as selection. Even though selection may ultimately be more important, nevertheless, a mutant that does not take place cannot be selected and the process of mutation remains mysterious. Whether in the epistemological process these processes of search can be better organized we do not really know. Up to now they have often been the result of mysterious processes of the mind which we call intuition, insight, and belong as much to the poetical and mystical element in human experience as to the rational. We may be moving indeed towards something of a union of the sciences and the humanities, a recognition that the evolution of the structure of the human brain is essentially a single process, even though it has great varieties within it. Mutation and selection go on in the arts, in literature and in poetry, in philosophy, in religion, in all the activities of the human mind, not only in science. As we come to recognize the essential unity of this process in science, the humanities, and the arts, we may all be benefited.

Within this unity, however, we must also recognize a great diversity of epistemological methods, and the search for the appropriate method, both in the formulation of theory and abstract images and in the testing of these cognitive structures is crucial to the truth-enrichment of the cognitive mix. Unfortunately the rules and methods of this search itself are by no means clear, and a second order search for the methods of search would seem to be an important priority. Up to now this question has not been a high priority in the minds of the scientific and knowledge-seeking community. We have assumed far too easily that "Science" meant experiment, or mathematizing and quantification, or statistical tests of significance, or the recording or data, of the collection of time series. A critical examination of these easy assumptions is now very much in order. It is a frighteningly large task from which we may well shrink. We could, indeed, easily be paralyzed by the reflection that we cannot discuss appropriate methodology until we have the appropriate methodology to study appropriate methodology, and so in an infinite regress. It is never inappropriate, however, to cast our eyes beyond the present horizons which confine us, and we can comfort ourselves with the reflection that the fear of failure is the greatest obstacle to human learning.

Note

[1] K. E. Boulding, *Ecodynamics: A New Theory of Societal Evolution* (Beverly Hills, Calif.: Sage Publications, 1978), p. 14.

[2] The latest information suggests that the number of neurons in the human brain is closer to 100 billion and the number of synapses much larger than this so the total system may have a much larger capacity than the text suggests.